The Nonhuman Turn

Center for 21st Century Studies

Richard Grusin, Series Editor

The
Nonhuman
Turn

Richard Grusin, Editor

Center for 21st Century Studies

University of Minnesota Press
Minneapolis • London

An earlier version of chapter 6 was published as Wendy Hui Kyong Chun, "Crisis, Crisis, Crisis, or Sovereignty and Networks," *Theory, Culture, and Society* 28, no. 6 (2011): 91–112; reprinted by permission of SAGE Publications, Ltd., London, Los Angeles, New Delhi, Singapore, and Washington, D.C.; copyright 2011 *Theory, Culture, and Society,* SAGE Publications. An earlier version of chapter 9 was published as Jane Bennett, "Systems and Things: A Response to Graham Harman and Timothy Morton," *New Literary History* 43, no. 2 (Spring 2012): 225–33; copyright 2012 *New Literary History,* University of Virginia; reprinted with permission of the Johns Hopkins University Press.

Published by the University of Minnesota Press
111 Third Avenue South, Suite 290
Minneapolis, MN 55401-2520
http://www.upress.umn.edu

Library of Congress Cataloging-in-Publication Data

The nonhuman turn / Richard Grusin, editor, Center for 21st Century Studies. (21st century studies)
    Includes bibliographical references and index.
    ISBN 978-0-8166-9466-2 (hc : alk. paper)
    ISBN 978-0-8166-9467-9 (pb : alk. paper)
1. Panpsychism—Congresses. 2. Consciousness—Congresses. I. Grusin, Richard A., editor.
    BD560.N66 2015 141—dc23

                                        2014019922

Printed in the United States of America on acid-free paper

The University of Minnesota is an equal-opportunity educator and employer.

21 20 19 18 17 16   10 9 8 7 6 5 4 3 2

Contents

Introduction

RICHARD GRUSIN

THIS BOOK SEEKS TO NAME, characterize, and therefore to consolidate a wide variety of recent and current critical, theoretical, and philosophical approaches to the humanities and social sciences. Each of these approaches, and the nonhuman turn more generally, is engaged in decentering the human in favor of a turn toward and concern for the nonhuman, understood variously in terms of animals, affectivity, bodies, organic and geophysical systems, materiality, or technologies. The conference from which this book emerged, hosted by the Center for 21st Century Studies (C21) at the University of Wisconsin-Milwaukee, was organized to explore how the nonhuman turn might provide a way forward for the arts, humanities, and social sciences in light of the difficult challenges of the twenty-first century. To address the nonhuman turn, a group of scholars were brought in to help lay out some of the research emphases and methodologies that are key to the emerging interdisciplinary field of twenty-first century studies. Given that almost every problem of note that we face in the twenty-first century entails engagement with nonhumans—from climate change, drought, and famine; to biotechnology, intellectual property, and privacy; to genocide, terrorism, and war—there seems no time like the present to turn our future attention, resources, and energy toward the nonhuman broadly understood. Even the new paradigm of the Anthropocene, which names the human as the dominant influence on climate since industrialism, participates in the nonhuman turn in its recognition that humans must now be understood as climatological or geological forces on the planet that operate just as nonhumans would, independent of human will, belief, or desires.

The ubiquity of nonhuman matters of concern in the twenty-first century should not obscure the fact that concern for the nonhuman has a long Western genealogy, with examples at least as far back as Lucretius's *De Rerum Naturae* and its subsequent uptake in the early modern period.[1] The concern with nonhumans is not new in Anglo-American thought. In American literature, for example, we can trace this concern back at least to Emerson, Thoreau, Melville, Dickinson, and Whitman. The nonhuman turn gained even more powerful impetus in the nineteenth century from Charles Darwin's insistence on seeing human and nonhuman species as operating according to the same laws of natural selection and William James's radical contention in *The Principles of Psychology* that human thought, emotion, habit, and will were all inseparable from, and often consequent upon, nonhuman, bodily material processes.[2] The nonhuman turn in twenty-first century studies can be traced to a variety of different intellectual and theoretical developments from the last decades of the twentieth century:

- *Actor-network theory*, particularly Bruno Latour's career-long project to articulate technical mediation, nonhuman agency, and the politics of things
- *Affect theory*, both in its philosophical and psychological manifestations and as it has been mobilized by queer theory
- *Animal studies*, as developed in the work of Donna Haraway and others, projects for animal rights, and a more general critique of speciesism
- The *assemblage theory* of Gilles Deleuze, Manuel De Landa, Latour, and others
- New *brain sciences* like neuroscience, cognitive science, and artificial intelligence
- The *new materialism* in feminism, philosophy, and Marxism
- *New media theory*, especially as it has paid close attention to technical networks, material interfaces, and computational analysis
- Varieties of *speculative realism* including object-oriented philosophy, neovitalism, and panpsychism

- *Systems theory,* in its social, technical, and ecological manifestations

Such varied analytical and theoretical formations obviously diverge and disagree in many of their assumptions, objects, and methodologies. But they are all of a piece in taking up aspects of the nonhuman as critical to the future of twenty-first century studies in the arts, humanities, and social sciences.

To put forth the concept of the nonhuman turn to name the diverse and baggy set of interrelated critical and theoretical methodologies that have coalesced at the beginning of the twenty-first century is to invite the expression of what can only be called "turn fatigue": the weariness (and wariness) of describing every new development in the humanities and social sciences as a turn. Organizing a conference called "The Nonhuman Turn" ran the risk of placing it as just the latest in a series of well-known academic turns that have already been named and discussed for decades. This complaint is not without its merits; indeed I return to it at the end of the introduction, where I reclaim the idea of a turn as itself nonhuman.

Singling out the nonhuman turn among other recent turns, however, also runs the risk of inviting confusion with the posthuman turn, despite the very different stakes in these two relatively recent theoretical developments. Unlike the posthuman turn with which it is often confused, the nonhuman turn does not make a claim about teleology or progress in which we begin with the human and see a transformation from the human to the posthuman, after or beyond the human. Although the best work on the posthuman seeks to avoid such teleology, even these works oscillate between seeing the posthuman as a new stage in human development and seeing it as calling attention to the inseparability of human and nonhuman. Nonetheless, the very idea of the posthuman entails a historical development from human to something after the human, even as it invokes the imbrication of human and nonhuman in making up the posthuman turn.[3] The nonhuman turn, on the other hand, insists (to paraphrase Latour) that "we have never been human" but that the human has always coevolved, coexisted, or collaborated with the nonhuman—and that the human is characterized precisely by this indistinction from the nonhuman. Brian Massumi offers a "Simondian ethics of becoming" as a counter to the assertion that the human is entering "a next 'posthuman' phase," arguing that Gilbert Simondon shows us the presence of "the *nonhuman* at the 'dephased' heart of every individuation, human and otherwise."[4] Simondon's argument for the coevolution of humans and technology has been restated from a different perspective by philosopher and cognitive scientist Andy Clark, who characterizes humans as "natural-born cyborgs" in order to underscore how (at least since the invention of language) human cognition has been interdependent with embodied, nonhuman technologies.[5]

To name a conference "The Nonhuman Turn in 21st Century Studies," then, was first and foremost to make a historical claim about a certain set of not always entirely compatible developments in academic discourse in the humanities and social sciences at the end of the twentieth and beginning of the twenty-first centuries.[6] Intended as a macroscopic concept, the nonhuman turn is meant to account for the simultaneous or overlapping emergence of a number of different theoretical or critical "turns"—for example, the ontological, network, neurological, affective, digital, ecological, or evolutionary. As something of a theoretical or methodological assemblage, the nonhuman turn tries to make sense of what holds these various other "turns" together, even while allowing for their divergent theoretical and methodological commitments and contradictions. Each of these different elements of the nonhuman turn derives from theoretical movements that argue (in one way or another) against human exceptionalism, expressed most often in the form of conceptual or rhetorical dualisms that separate the human from the nonhuman—variously conceived as animals, plants, organisms, climatic systems, technologies, or ecosystems. Among the features that loosely link these turns is that they were all opposed, in one way or another, to the more linguistic or representational turns of the 1970s through 1990s—such as the textual, cultural, ideological, or aesthetic turns—in a rough adherence to what Nigel Thrift has characterized as "non-representational theory." Similarly, these very different methodologies shared a resistance to the privileged status of the autonomous male subject of the Western liberal tradition, especially in their refusal of such fundamental logical oppositions as human/nonhuman and subject/object.

For practitioners of the nonhuman turn, what is problematic about these dualisms is their insistent privileging of the human. The critique of social constructivism for stripping the nonhuman world of agency or inherent meaning or qualities has been widespread. Perhaps most powerfully, the nonhuman turn challenges some of the key assumptions of social constructivism, particularly insofar as it insists that the agency, meaning, and value of nature all derive from cultural, social, or ideological inscription or construction. Massumi points to the methodological dominance of constructivism in the last decades of the twentieth century in explaining why Simondon's insistence on the co-construction or ontogenesis of human and nonhuman has only begun to find an audience in the twenty-first century. Constructivism proved extremely valuable, Massumi says, for its emphasis on "becoming," its insistence

> that things can't be taken as givens, rather they come to be. . . . But the constructivism of the period played out in ways that radically diverge from the direction [Simondon] indicates. What was considered to come into being was less things than new social or cultural takes on them. What is constructed are fundamentally perspectives or paradigms, and the corresponding subject positions. Within the 1990s constructivist model these were understood in terms of signifying structures or coding, typically applying models derived from linguistics and rhetoric. This telescoped becoming onto the human plane. At the same time, it reduced the constitution of the human plane to the question of the human subject (if not its effective construction, then the impossibility of it, or if not exactly that, its subversion). A vicious circle results.[7]

Practitioners of the nonhuman turn find problematic the emphasis of constructivism on the social or cultural constructions of the human subject because, taken to its logical extreme, it strips the world of any ontological or agential status. The epistemological focus that informed much of the work of constructivism actively discouraged any discussion of ontology, by refusing to grant agency to nonhuman nature, organisms, or technologies.

Among the most recent and arguably most visible critiques of constructivism has been speculative realism, particularly its critique of Kantian correlationism, the belief that knowledge of the nonhuman world had to be correlated with or mediated by a priori human categories.[8] Throughout this book speculative realism and object-oriented ontology appear both explicitly and implicitly in relation to the nonhuman turn. Indeed, when the call for papers for the conference first circulated among various social media, it was initially taken as another conference on speculative realism or object-oriented ontology, generating a good deal of social media buzz on Facebook and Twitter.[9] But the nonhuman turn was at work long before anyone had ever heard of speculative realism or object-oriented ontology, which from a historical perspective are relative latecomers (albeit interesting ones) to this concern with the nonhuman. The Nonhuman Turn conference (along with this book) was organized not principally to make a claim about philosophical ontology but to sketch out an important methodological or conceptual development in late twentieth-century and early twenty-first-century academic scholarship.

Although the current heightened pace of academic discourse often obscures the fact, long-standing institutional formations such as the humanities and social sciences make wide and quite slow turns, more like one of the large freighters on Lake Michigan visible through the windows of the Center for 21st Century Studies than like a Twitter stream or viral video. This slow pace of change can often be hard to see in the new "digital academy" of the twenty-first century, especially for graduate students and younger scholars, for whom even blogs can sometimes seem like a slow and archaic form of academic communication. Nonetheless, the editors of *The Speculative Turn*, which presented the first comprehensive collection of essays on speculative realism, contend that in addition to its philosophical innovations, one of the self-proclaimed medialogical innovations of speculative realism was its deployment of blogs and social media to develop and circulate key texts and arguments informing the newly emergent discourse of speculative realism, object-oriented ontology, and its variants:

> As any of the blogosphere's participants can attest, it can be a tremendously productive forum for debate and experimentation. The less formal nature of the medium facilitates immediate reactions to research, with authors presenting ideas in their initial stages of development, ideally providing a demystifying sort of transparency. The markedly egalitarian nature of blogs (open to non-PhDs in a way that faculty positions are not) opens a space for collaboration amongst a diverse group of readers, helping to shape ideas along unforeseen paths. The rapid rhythm of online existence also makes a stark contrast with the long waiting-periods typical of refereed journals and mainstream publishers. Instant reaction to current events, reading groups quickly mobilizing around newly published works, and cross-blog dialogues on specific issues, are common events in the online world.[10]

One does not have to be as enthusiastic as *The Speculative Turn*'s editors about how blogs and social media accelerate the pace and intensity of academic discourse to recognize the increased role of Facebook, Twitter, and other social media in twenty-first-century academic mediality. The machinic temporality of contemporary scholarship, and the intensity created by all forms of socially networked media, exemplify how the nonhuman has altered the modes and rhythms and style of academic discourse in the twenty-first century. An important consequence of digital media technology and its nonhuman impact on academia and the humanities has been an intensification of time. It is necessary, therefore, to focus not only on the impact of our new technical media on the human, but on the nonhuman speeding up (and multiplication) of "academicky" discourse on e-mail, Facebook, Twitter, blogs, Tumblr, and other social media formats. Although a 2012 study noting that 51 percent of Internet traffic was already nonhuman garnered a good deal of media attention as marking a significant milestone in the history of the Internet, the nonhuman turn lets us recognize that Internet traffic is always both human and nonhuman. Technical mediation itself needs to be understood as a nonhuman process within which or through which humans and nonhumans relate. Because socially networked media transactions multiply and quicken with or without human intervention—in marked contrast to the more reserved and deliberate interactions enabled by a technical medium like print—new technical formats have accompanied and fostered a speeding up of academic transactions through digital media, requiring twenty-first-century academics to spend significant research time online, hence generating new categories of academic work. As opposed to an earlier generation of graduate education, where research in the humanities and social sciences most often meant time working alone at home, in libraries, or cafés, much of the digital academic work of younger scholars is spent online in social media networks, archives, or databases. These online media interactions don't replace embodied academic interactions but intensify them. Invited talks, conferences, and symposia like the Nonhuman Turn, or research labs, centers, and institutes like C21—all are much more prevalent in today's globally networked academic world than they were thirty years ago. The accelerated nonhuman rhythm of socially networked communication and exchange can serve as well to intensify the affective tones of academic debate and disagreement in ways that can be exciting and generative, but that can often lead to misunderstandings or an inflated investment in or evaluation of the present and very near future, at the expense of the achievements of the past.

The immediacy of our online academic environment both generates and is generated by the specialization or multiplication of audiences and online communities, which accelerates the pace of academic discourse within social networks of like-thinking individuals with shared interests. In part because of the numerous microcommunities that make up the nonhuman turn, neither the conference nor this book could possibly do justice to all of the diverse elements that make up the nonhuman turn in twenty-first century studies. The particular emphases of this book are undoubtedly influenced by my own "nonhuman turn," which began with the discovery of the Derridean trace or the maxim that *il n'y a pas de hors-texte*. In the Berkeley English department of the early

1980s, the recognition that literature or "the text" does not have a special ontological status, coupled with Foucault's genealogies of disciplinary apparatuses and techniques, helped to generate the "new historicism"—itself an attempt to turn critical attention toward discourses of the nonhuman, like medicine, economics, technology, or science. For the new historicism, however, language was still at the center, even if literary language had (in the best such work) been decentered or put on a level playing field with other nonliterary discourses. These methodological limitations led me to the nonhuman turn through three distinct approaches, which feature prominently in this book: science and technology studies (STS), particularly actor-network theory (ANT); new media theory; and affect theory.

The Nonhuman Turn would have looked very different without the publication of two formative works of critical STS, Donna Haraway's "Manifesto for Cyborgs" in 1985, and the English publication of Bruno Latour's *Science in Action* in 1987.[11] Haraway offered the ironic figure of the cyborg, a hybrid of human and nonhuman, as a potential replacement for the human-centered figures of "woman" and "labor" that underlay the political critiques that late twentieth-century socialist-feminism often directed at informatics and technoscience. Haraway's controversial conclusion that she would "rather be a cyborg than a goddess" was meant to counter a conception of woman that excluded the nonhuman from its purview. And for Latour, the distribution of agency across a heterogeneous network of human and nonhuman actants exploded the fundamental distinction between human science and nonhuman nature that underwrote much of the social science, history, and philosophy of science for much of the twentieth century. *Science in Action* was a crucial text in spurring actor-network theory to think intensively about the distribution of agency among human and nonhuman actors. Both of these works were instrumental in catalyzing the emerging interdisciplinary field of science and technology studies, particularly in the insistence on the need to account for the distributed or cyborg agency of humans and nonhumans in technoscientific practice.

Together, STS and ANT provided an important counter to the almost religious rhetoric of cyberspace and virtual reality that played a large role in critical cyberculture studies and early new media theory. In the enthusiasm of the emergence of cyberculture in the '80s and '90s, Latour's actor-network model provided a theory of translation with which to understand the transformative relations among textual and material mediations, human and non-human actors. Coupled with the insights of earlier nonhuman theorists like Walter Benjamin and Marshall McLuhan, actor-network theory helped in the development of theories like remediation, which took up the nonhuman implications of new media technologies, as well as media logics like immediacy, hypermediacy, and Lev Manovich's database aesthetic. Digital media function as material objects within the world, following Latour's distinction between intermediaries and mediators, in which mediators are not neutral means of transmission but are actively involved in transforming whatever they mediate. Digital media operate through what Latour characterizes as translation, not by neutrally reproducing meaning or information but by actively transforming human and non-human actants, as well as their conceptual and affective states. By the end of the twentieth century, science studies and new media theory each offered different but largely compatible ways to incorporate a concern for nonhumans into the humanities, to account for the agency of nonhuman actors, events, and mediation.

In 1995, ten years after Haraway published her "Manifesto for Cyborgs," two key essays in the field of affect theory were published: Eve Sedgwick and Adam Frank's "Shame in the Cybernetic Fold: Reading Silvan Tomkins," and Brian Massumi's "The Autonomy of Affect."[12] Sedgwick came to Tomkins and affect through her concerns with queer theory and paranoid and reparative reading, Massumi largely through his analysis and translation of Deleuze and Guattari. But despite their different accounts of and deployment of affectivity, Sedgwick and Massumi (through Tomkins and Whitehead, respectively) shared an intellectual ancestor in William James, whose monumental, two-volume *Principles of Psychology* remains a foundational work for affect psychology in the twenty-first century. Sedgwick and Massumi each argued that the representational or ideological thinking that had dominated cultural studies in the '80s and '90s needed to make way for modes of thought that paid attention aesthetically or politically to questions of embodied and autonomous affect. For Tomkins, and Sedgwick's reading of him, affect is always object-oriented. There is no affectivity without an object, even if that object is another affect. For Massumi, affect was not reducible to linguistic, symbolic, or conceptual meanings but operated as an intensity moving through human and nonhuman bodies alike. For both Sedgwick and Massumi, affect provided a way to reassert the ontological agency of the natural or the nonhuman against what Sedgwick powerfully characterizes as "paranoid reading," in which any ascription of agency, inherent qualities, or causality to nature was seen as politically reactionary.

Taken together, Sedgwick and Massumi helped to generate a critical-theoretical turn to affect—particularly but not exclusively in the emergence of a new materialism in feminist theory—that not only highlights the nonhumanness of embodied affectivity, but also provides a model to think about the affectivity of both animate and inanimate nonhumans.[13] Although it is not always readily apparent how human affect can be nonhuman, I take affect theory to be particularly important for the nonhuman turn in two respects. First, it is crucial to affect theory, both from the James-Lange theory of emotion to Silvan Tomkins and Daniel Stern, and from Spinoza, Bergson, and Whitehead to Deleuze and Guattari, that human affect systems are somatic and bodily. Affect systems operate autonomously and automatically, independent of (and according to Massumi, prior to) cognition, emotion, will, desire, purpose, intention, or belief—all conventional attributes of the traditional liberal humanist subject. Second, it is also the case that affectivity belongs to nonhuman animals as well as to nonhuman plants or inanimate objects, technical or natural. Tomkins, for example, distinguishes the cat's site-specific affect system and its purr from the greater freedom of sites or avenues for humans to maximize affective happiness. But crucially both cat and human share affect systems, suggesting that affectivity is not limited to the human. And as Deleuze notes in *Cinema 1*, affectivity is a quality of things as well as people.

> And why is expression not available to things? There are affects of things. The "edge," the "blade," or rather the "point"

of Jack the Ripper's knife, is no less an affect than the fear which overcomes his features and the resignation which finally seizes hold of the whole of his face. The Stoics showed that things themselves were bearers of ideal events which did not exactly coincide with their properties, their actions and reactions: the edge of a knife.[14]

A key challenge to the idea of affect as nonhuman comes from fields like trauma theory, which sometimes appeals to affect theory to make sense of the traumatic emotional and affective experiences of those who had been subject to objectification and dehumanization. Considered more broadly, the nonhuman turn often invokes resistance or opposition from participants in liberatory scholarly projects—for example, feminist critiques of sexual violence, critical race studies, or holocaust studies—which work precisely against the objectification of the human, its transformation into a nonhuman object or thing that can be bought and sold, ordered to work and punished, incarcerated and even killed. For scholars working on such politically liberatory projects, who have labored so hard to rescue or protect the human from dehumanization or objectification, the nonhuman turn can seem regressive, reactionary, or worse, particularly if it is identified solely with the turn to objects as fundamental elements of ontology. Motivated partly by social constructivism, many practitioners of politically liberatory scholarship share the belief that any appeal to nature, for example, as possessing causality or agential force, could only operate in service of a defense of the status quo rather than fostering a more capacious sense of becoming and construction than social constructivism imagined. But this does not have to be the case. A concern with the nonhuman can and must be brought to bear on any projects for creating a more just society. If following Latour and others we take society as a complex assemblage of human and nonhuman actors—not as an autonomous entity or realm that can be appealed to in order to explain why things are as they are, or that can be somehow changed apart from changing the way things are—then the question of political or social change becomes a question of changing our relations not only to other humans but to nonhumans as well. To extend our academic and critical concern to include nonhuman animals and the nonhuman environment, which had previously been excluded or ignored from critical or scholarly humanistic concern, should be a politically liberatory project in very much the same way that earlier, similar turns toward a concern for gender, race, ethnicity, or class were politically liberatory for groups of humans.

Having sketched out a very partial genealogy of the nonhuman turn, I conclude with a brief look at an even longer genealogy—the etymology and changing definitions of the word *turn*—as a way to return to the question of "turn fatigue." While it is true that critical "turns" have proliferated in the past few decades almost as a form of academic branding, the idea of a "nonhuman" turn provides a different perspective on what it means to name an intellectual movement a "turn." In fact, if we take a look at the definitions of the word *turn* as presented in the *Oxford English Dictionary (OED)*, we can see that nonhuman materiality and movement have been part of the meaning of the word from its inception.[15] Originating in fifteenth-century Middle English, with roots back through Anglo-Norman to Latin and Greek, *turn* is used in English as an action noun involved with nonhuman movement and change. The *OED* divides its various meanings under five main headings. The first meaning of *turn*, as "rotation," is tied to the physical technology of the wheel and entails nonhuman movement around an axis or central point, as in the turns of the hand of a clock or the phrase "as the world turns." "Change of direction or course," the second sense of *turn*, describes physical movement or change without the idea of rotating or revolving around a fixed center, as when a river turns around a bend or a rider turns his horse in a certain direction. The third meaning, "change in general," drops the sense of turn as physical movement and applies it to moments of transition, as in the turn of the season, the year, or the century. The fourth sense, which groups instances of turn as "actions of various kinds," includes the affectivity of turn in phrases like "bad turn" or "evil turn" or in sayings like "One good turn deserves another." The fifth sense of *turn* as "occasion" operates temporally—referring not to change or movement in space but to the movement of action through time. In this sense *turn* describes behavior that fosters (or counters) collectivity, especially as turn refers to the time an action comes around to an individual, or when one fulfills one's obligation to serve—as when one takes one's turn or when one's turn comes around, or conversely when one acts or speaks out of turn. In this interesting sense of the word, it is agency or action, not wheels or rivers, that rotates among individuals or changes course or direction.

Describing the nonhuman turn as a shift of attention, interest, or concern toward nonhumans keeps in mind the physicality and movement involved in the idea of a turn, how the nonhuman turn must be understood as an embodied turn toward the nonhuman world, including the nonhumanness that is in all of us. Rehearsing these various senses of the word *turn* lets me defend and reclaim its use to account for the change of direction or course in twenty-first century studies toward a concern with nonhumans. This nonhuman turn could be said to mark in one sense the rotation or revolutions of academic fashion. But in another sense this turn could also help to provoke a fundamental change of circumstances in the humanities in the twenty-first century. Insofar as a turn is an action, movement, or change, it also functions as a means of translation or mediation in the Latourian sense, indeed as a means of remediation or premediation. A turn is invariably oriented toward the future. Even a turn back is an attempt to turn the future around, to prevent a future that lies ahead.

Throughout I have referred to the nonhuman turn as a concept. But in thinking of it as a movement of embodied thought, a rotation or shift of attention toward nonhumanness, I also underscore the way in which the nonhuman turn operates on what Deleuze and Guattari call "the plane of immanence." Most crucially, then, the embodied sense of a turn as a movement should be understood as what Deleuze and Guattari call a "turning toward": "truth can only be defined on the plane by a 'turning toward' or by 'that to which thought turns.'" In distinguishing the plane of immanence from the verticality of the concept, they emphasize repeatedly the sense of embodied movement in turning toward, and also emphasize that turning toward something is "the movement of thought toward truth" and the turning toward truth of thought. "To turn toward does not imply merely to turn away but to confront, to lose one's way, to move aside."[16] To turn toward the nonhuman is not only to confront the nonhuman but to lose the traditional way of the human, to move aside so that other nonhumans—animate and less animate—can make their way, turn toward movement themselves. I hope that this book, if not the nonhuman turn itself, might in some small way mark the occasion for a turn of fortune, an intensified concern for the nonhuman that might catalyze a change in our circumstances, a turn for the better not for the worse, in which everyone who wants to participate, human and nonhuman alike, will get their turn.

Remediating the plenary addresses from the 2012 Nonhuman Turn in 21st Century Studies conference, the chapters collected in this book cover only small swaths of the scholarly terrain of the nonhuman turn. The conference's selection of plenary speakers was, as is true of any conference, in part a product of accident and contingency—including the availability of invited speakers, limitations of funding, and the critical climate in which the conference occurred. As I have already suggested, the concerns of this book are shaped in part by the intensity of interest in speculative realism and object-oriented ontology that was near its zenith at the time of the Nonhuman Turn conference. But as I have also suggested, the conference was not explicitly organized to address speculative realism but to explore more broadly the late twentieth- and early twenty-first-century turn toward the nonhuman. Although invited speakers were not asked explicitly to address the question of the nonhuman turn, all of their chapters exemplify that turn and some reflect on it explicitly. To frame the collection I introduce each chapter in terms of its relation to the nonhuman turn, trying in the process to draw some loose connections among them.

The book opens with Brian Massumi's chapter because Massumi has been a practitioner and theorist of the nonhuman turn more extensively and for a longer period of time than any of the book's other contributors, and because his thought has been crucial for my own involvement with the nonhuman turn. "The Supernormal Animal" takes as its starting point a critique of the utilitarian account of instinct as a quality that has been deployed historically to distinguish humans from nonhuman animals. Building upon an insightful reading of Niko Tinbergen's analysis of the supposedly instinctive behavior of herring gulls, Massumi develops a concept of the "supernormal" to account not only for the unpredictability of such supposedly automatic behaviors as feeding but also for the animality of desire and excess that generate such quintessentially human activities as art making. Near the end of the chapter, Massumi glosses the relation between animality and humanity: "Take it to heart: animal becoming is *most* human. It is in becoming animal that the human recurs to what is nonhuman at the heart of what moves it. This makes it surpassingly human. Creative-relationally *more-than* human." It is this more-than-humanness of the human that Massumi alludes to in the concept of "the supernormal animal."

Steven Shaviro also takes up the continuity of humans and nonhumans in his chapter on "Consequences of Panpsychism." Shaviro's argument for panpsychism is directed squarely at some of the key debates in speculative realism and object-oriented ontology, unlike Massumi, who does not take up these debates explicitly (even while offering an ontogenetic account of objects that implicitly counters the insistence by Graham Harman and some of his followers that objects are ontologically originary).[17] Running the risk of taking seriously the claims of panpsychism, which is often dismissed as something like a new age fantasy, Shaviro traces out its philosophical pedigree "from the pre-Socratics, on through Baruch Spinoza and Gottfried Wilhelm von Leibniz, and down to William James and Alfred North Whitehead." Shaviro dismisses the question of consciousness in favor of a more limited idea of sentience, developing an account of the continuity of human and nonhuman minds and values. After a discussion of Rudy Rucker's playful 2007 science fiction story "Panpsychism Proved," Shaviro unfolds an account of panpsychism built upon three key sources: Thomas Nagel's 1974 article "What Is It Like to Be a Bat?"; Wittgenstein's philosophical investigations of inner sensations and other minds; and Galen Strawson's 2006 defense of panpsychism. The payoff for Shaviro, or one of them, is to find fault with one of the key points of Harman's object-oriented ontology, the claim that all objects are in the final analysis "withdrawn" from access. Invoking Whitehead's more processual ontology, Shaviro insists "that the inner and outer, or private and public, aspects of an entity always go together," but that we have no more cognitive access to human thought or sensation than we do to that of nonhumans.

Erin Manning joins Shaviro and Massumi in refusing any categorical distinctions between human and nonhuman. Manning cites David Lapoujade's assertion, "At the heart of the human is nothing human" (also cited in Massumi's piece) as a way to take up the question of "artfulness," particularly the intuitive artfulness through which the relationality of the world is activated and made available to humans and nonhumans alike. At the heart of Manning's chapter is what might be called a kind of philosophical case study, the participatory exhibition *Stitching Time*, which she installed at the 2012 Sydney Biennale. Manning takes her experience in creating and managing the exhibit for the three weeks of the Biennale as an opportunity to think about a variety of interesting concerns—artfulness, time, sympathy, intuition, contemplation— many of which initially seem to belong to the human, not the nonhuman, subject. She addresses this concern in the penultimate section of the chapter, explaining that "Artfulness is always more than human":

> Despite my focus on human participation here, the art of participation does not find its conduit solely in the human. Art also does its work without human intervention, activating fields of relation that are environmental or ecological in scales of intermixings that may include the human but don't depend on it. How to categorize as human or nonhuman the exuberance of an effect of light, the way the air moves through a space, or the way one artwork catches another in its movement of thought. This is surely the force of curation: its choreographic capacity to bring to life the lingering nonhuman tendencies that bridge fields activated by distinct artistic processes.

Like Manning, Ian Bogost takes up the relations among art and philosophy in "The Aesthetics of Philosophical Carpentry." And like Manning, he draws upon his own creative practice—in Bogost's case as a writer and game designer—to articulate an aesthetics of nonhuman philosophy. Like Manning, but in a very different style and to different ends, Bogost's prose both exemplifies and describes an aesthetic ethics of what he calls "carpentry," which focuses less on relationality or process and more on objects and things. Bogost's piece takes up the question of what it means to write philosophy, to deliver an academic paper, to make an argument. He draws upon Graham Harman and Alphonso Lingis in developing his idea of philosophical carpentry, which is meant to underscore the materiality of writing, or lecturing, or computing, or gaming, or participating in online social media. But carpentry is meant also to assert the ontological and agential status of objects or things in making their and our world. Most of all, however, Bogost makes philosophical carpentry (and the textual objects it constructs) seem like great fun. He eschews (or playfully remediates) academic argumentation in favor of an autobiographical, whimsical romp through the geographical and cultural landscape of Milwaukee and the digital landscape of such whimsical (and intentionally pointless) games like his *Cow Clicker* or La Molleindustria's *The McDonald's Videogame*. More than any piece in the collection, Bogost's chapter captures the flavor of an academic conference, of the Nonhuman Turn conference itself.[18]

In "Our Predictive Condition; or, Prediction in the Wild," Mark B. N. Hansen takes up the role of prediction in our contemporary historical moment. Hansen is concerned with the technical, computational, or medial nonhuman, specifically the way in which the administration of President Barack Obama has deployed a logic and politics of prediction that replaces the ideological "unknown unknown" of the George W. Bush administration's logic of preemption with the analysis of imminent threats. Hansen's chapter adds to and modifies the related concepts of preemption and premediation. Unlike what he sees as the event-driven focus of Massumi's account of preemption or my own account of premediation, Hansen understands "prediction in the wild" as operating independently of "human understanding and affectivity": "The discoveries of predictive analytics are discoveries of micrological propensities that are not directly correlated with human understanding and affectivity and that do not cohere into clearly identifiable events: such propensities simply have no direct aesthetic analog within *human* experience." Because the predictive logic of the Obama administration depends upon probabilistic analysis of possible future security threats made visible only through the nonhuman analysis of data, Hansen sees the logic of prediction to be based on reality rather than the allegory or fantasy of the Bush administration's doctrine of preemption. Hansen cites the current television series *Person of Interest* and the predictive news service Recorded Future as exemplary of the current "predictive condition" of the twenty-first century.

Wendy Hui Kyong Chun sees our contemporary new media condition as one of crisis, not of prediction, providing an instructive counterpoint to Hansen's piece. In "Crisis, Crisis, Crisis; or, The Temporality of Networks," Chun deconstructs the contemporary mythos of computer code as *logos,* arguing that crisis both exceeds and is structurally necessary to networks. In part because both hardware and software operate according to a nonhuman, machinic temporality, network technologies must be repeatedly cared for in response to (and to prevent) crises that would disrupt connectivity. Stability and continuity on the network are the proof not of its permanence but of its fragility. Chun cites Friedrich Kittler to declaim the fact that human agency in computing has been surrendered to "data-driven programming," much as Hansen underscores the nonhuman technical analysis of data to predict the future. But for Chun what is most interesting about predictive data analyses like climate models is what she calls their "hopefully effective deferral of the future: these predictive models are produced so that, if they are persuasive and thus convince us to cut back on our carbon emissions, what they predict will not come about. Their predictions will not be true or verifiable." This "mode of deferring a future for another future" characterized by Chun would also be true of the Obama administration's data-mining analysis of security threats that Hansen describes—if these predictions prove persuasive in the present and the imminent threats are eliminated, then "what they predict will not come about." Chun sees this "gap between the future and future predictions" not as "reason for dismissal" but for "hope."

In "They Are Here," Timothy Morton provides a rambunctious and sustained reading of the music video that Toni Basil made for the Talking Heads' song "Crosseyed and Painless." Morton takes on the potentially controversial task of linking the objectification and dehumanization experienced by African American youth in urban

Southern California with their involvement with nonhuman technologies, by way of object-oriented ontology's erasure of the human/
nonhuman divide. Morton links the oppression of the urban black
community not with its history of slavery but with such factors as
environmental and economic racism. As such, he argues through
an extended reading of the *Crosseyed and Painless* video that "the
story of race, the story of environment, the story of things, are intertwined." Deploying a discussion of the broken tool in Heidegger,
by way of the quantum operation of the cathode ray tube, Morton
explains a key moment in the video as revealing the continuities
between human and nonhuman sentience, of people and things.

In "Form / Matter / Chora: Object-Oriented Ontology and Feminist New Materialism," Rebekah Sheldon takes up a question implicit in Morton's chapter: What does an ontologically informed
critical reading of an aesthetic artifact look like? Choratic reading,
Sheldon suggests, might be a way to make sense of texts as assemblages, to account for "the agency of human and nonhuman
bodies, organic and nonorganic vitalities, discourses and the specific material apparatuses those discourses are." Beginning with
the welcome observation that speculative realism has in some
sense been anticipated by feminist materialism, Sheldon provides
a cogent explanation of both the feminist and the speculative realist critiques of correlationism. She convincingly shows how the
feminist critique of correlationism invokes the agency of matter
while the object-oriented critique focuses on the formal features
of objects, citing in support Harman's claim that object-oriented
ontology is "'the first materialism in history to deny the existence
of matter.'" Sheldon invokes Jane Bennett's account of vital materialism in *Vibrant Matter* as an example of how to acknowledge
both the persistence of things and their relationality. She ends her
chapter by calling for a practice-based model of "choratic reading,"
which draws on a highly theorized conceptualization of the chora
as generating "an ontology of material-affective circulation" that
preserves both the independence of objects from human correlation and their relationality.

More directly than any of the chapters in this book, Jane Bennett takes up the significance of the nonhuman turn in the opening paragraphs of "Systems and Things: On Vital Materialism and

Object-Oriented Philosophy." She offers the theory of "vital materialism" both as a supplement to historical materialism and as a corrective to some of the key assumptions of object-oriented ontology, particularly its insistence on rejecting relationality. Bennett sees the nonhuman turn as a continuation of a long-standing philosophical project: "The nonhuman turn, then, can be understood as a continuation of earlier attempts to depict a world populated not by active subjects and passive objects but by lively and essentially interactive materials, by bodies human and nonhuman." Bennett places this sense of the vitality of objects against the claim made by Graham Harman that all objects withdraw from relations, as well as against Morton's concept of "hyperobjects." She offers her own theory of assemblages as a way to hold on to objects and relationality both, arguing for the importance of relationality for the nonhuman turn. To underscore the liberatory tendencies of the nonhuman turn referred to earlier in this introduction, Bennett ends her chapter (and the book) with a brief discussion of the historical materialism of literary texts as "special bodies," which "might help us live more sustainably, with less violence toward a variety of bodies," human and nonhuman alike. Although she is the last author to take her turn in this book, Bennett's chapter is by no means the final word on the nonhuman turn. Like the intense and animated conversations sparked by the conference from which this book is drawn, the chapters in this book should work to open the possibility for others to take their turn at making sense of the increasingly complex interrelations among humans and nonhumans both before and after the twenty-first century.

Notes

1. For a discussion of the revitalization of Lucretius in the early modern period, see Stephen Greenblatt, *The Swerve: How the World Became Modern* (New York: Norton, 2012).

2. William James, *The Principles of Psychology* (Cambridge, Mass.: Harvard University Press, 1890; rpt. 1983).

3. The most complex treatments of the posthuman, each of which exemplifies the two different senses of the term, include N. Katherine Hayles, *How We Became Posthuman: Virtual Bodies in Cybernetics, Literature, and Informatics* (Chicago: University of Chicago Press, 1999); Cary Wolfe,

What Is Posthumanism? (Minneapolis: University of Minnesota Press, 2009); and Rosi Braidotti, *The Posthuman* (Cambridge: Polity, 2013).

4. Brian Massumi, "'Technical Mentality' Revisited: Brian Massumi on Gilbert Simondon," interview with Arne De Boever, Alex Murray, and Jon Roffe, *Parrhesia* 7 (2009): 45.

5. Andy Clark, *Natural-Born Cyborgs: Minds, Technologies, and the Future of Human Intelligence* (New York: Oxford University Press, 2003).

6. Perhaps because of this diversity and incompatibility, as late as the summer of 2011, when our conference on the nonhuman turn was first imagined, there were no substantive instances of this phrase to be found on Google, and only a handful of passing and qualified references to the phrase. This discovery was quite surprising, particularly because it seemed so clear to me that this "turn" had been well underway for some decades.

7. Massumi, "Technical Mentality," 37.

8. See Rebekah Sheldon's chapter in this book for an excellent description of the critique of correlationism by speculative realism and object-oriented ontology.

9. On November 29, 2011, the day that the initial call for papers (CFP) for C21's conference on the Nonhuman Turn in 21st Century Studies was circulated among various social media, a lively and at moments testy series of exchanges broke out in the Facebook comment streams of Alexander Galloway and McKenzie Wark, each of whom had graciously shared the CFP on their Facebook walls. The lively comments manifested two main concerns. First there was some general expression of "turn" fatigue, which I take up later in the introduction. But more intense, and initially more perplexing, were the majority of comments that assumed that a conference on the Nonhuman Turn in 21st Century Studies was ipso facto a conference on the burgeoning school of thought called "speculative realism" or "object-oriented ontology." What made these comments a matter of concern was that this debate was taking place on the Facebook walls of two prominent New York–based media and political theorists, underneath the CFP for C21's conference on the nonhuman turn, with the tacit implication that this was a conference devoted to, or advocating, recent developments in object-oriented ontology. One reason for this assumption was undoubtedly the (unintentional) resemblance between the name of the conference and the title of a recent collection of essays called *The Speculative Turn.* Another reason for this assumption, as I soon realized, was that the CFP for the Nonhuman Turn conference reactivated some prior debates from the third New York Object-Oriented Ontology symposium in September 2011, which featured presentations by several of the speakers at the C21 conference, including Jane Bennett, McKenzie

Wark, Tim Morton, Steve Shaviro, Aaron Pedinotti, and Ian Bogost. Although social media are global in their scope, they do not completely do away with regionalism; in light of the New York locations of Galloway and Wark, the identification of our CFP with object-oriented ontology was not altogether unreasonable.

10. Levi Bryant, Nick Srnicek, and Graham Harman, "Towards a Speculative Philosophy," in *The Speculative Turn: Continental Materialism and Realism*, ed. Bryant, Srnicek, and Harman (Melbourne: re.press, 2011), 6–7.

11. Donna Haraway, "A Manifesto for Cyborgs: Science, Technology, and Socialist Feminism in the 1980's," *Socialist Review* 2 (1985): 65–107; and Bruno Latour, *Science in Action: How to Follow Engineers and Scientists through Society* (Cambridge, Mass.: Harvard University Press, 1987).

12. Eve Kosofsky Sedgwick and Adam Frank, "Shame in the Cybernetic Fold: Reading Silvan Tomkins," in *Shame and Its Sisters: A Silvan Tomkins Reader*, ed. Sedgwick and Frank (Durham, N.C.: Duke University Press, 1995), 1–35; and Brian Massumi, "The Autonomy of Affect," *Cultural Critique* 31 (1995): 83–109.

13. Jonathan Flatley provides a helpful overview of the various twentieth- and twenty-first-century variations of affect theory in *Affective Mapping: Melancholia and the Politics of Modernism* (Cambridge, Mass.: Harvard University Press, 2008), 11–27. For a useful survey of recent work in affect theory, see Melissa Gregg and Gregory J. Seigworth, *The Affect Theory Reader* (Durham, N.C.: Duke University Press, 2010).

14. Gilles Deleuze, *Cinema 1: The Movement-Image*, trans. Hugh Tomlinson and Barbara Habberjam (Minneapolis: University of Minnesota Press, 1986), 118.

15. *Oxford English Dictionary*, 2nd ed., s.v., "turn."

16. Gilles Deleuze and Félix Guattari, *What Is Philosophy?*, trans. Graham Burchell and Hugh Tomlinson (New York: Columbia University Press, 1994), 38.

17. For further discussion of the relations between Massumi and Harman, see Richard Grusin, "Reading *Semblance and Event*," *Postmodern Culture* 21, no. 3 (2011), http://muse.jhu.edu/.

18. What is most interesting or ironic about the close relationship between Bogost's chapter and his conference presentation is that he was the only one of the plenary speakers to deny us permission to video stream and archive his talk on the C21 YouTube site. In a sense, the style of the chapter remediates the conference presentation so effectively that it stands in for the absent video record.

The Supernormal Animal

BRIAN MASSUMI

> Instinct is sympathy. If this sympathy could extend its
> object and also reflect upon itself, it would give us the
> key to vital operations.
>
> —Henri Bergson, *Creative Evolution*

THE ATHLETIC GRACE of the pounce of the lynx. The architectural feats of the savanna termite. The complex weave of the orb spider's web. We admire these accomplishments as marvels of the natural world. The wonder resides as much in the automatic nature of these animal accomplishments as in their summum of technical perfection. Instinct: an innate condensation of ancestral wisdom passed from generation to generation, acquired through random mutation, retained through adaptive selection, unfolding with such regularity and efficiency as to rival the most skilled of human artisans (and in the case of certain social animals, apt to put the most well-oiled human bureaucracy to shame). Standard stimulus, normative output. Signal, triggering, performance, following one another in lockstep, with no second thoughts and without fail. Pure mechanism, all the more trustworthy for being unreflective. Instinct: the instrumentality of intelligence wrapped into reflex. So masterful it is in its functionality that it gives luster to utility. The productive beauty of the hive. The automatic aesthetics of adaptive stereotype.

Such is instinct . . . by repute. But instinct has always been hard pressed to live up to its reputation. From the very first systematic investigations dedicated to it by the nascent science of ethology, it has betrayed a most disconcerting tendency. The same drive that so naturally leads it through to its normative accomplishments seems to push it, just as naturally, to overshoot its target. Instinct seems called upon, from within its very own movement, following its own momentum, to outdo itself. Its instrumentality envelops an impulse to excess. This suggests a very different natural aesthetic—or a different nature of the aesthetic—than the beauty of utility.

It is not for nothing that for thinkers such as Gilles Deleuze, Félix Guattari, Raymond Ruyer, and Étienne Souriau the theory of the animal is bound to the theory of art. The link between animality to artfulness necessitates a reevaluation of the neo-Darwinian notion that selective adaptation, consolidated by instinct, is the sole motor of evolution. Deleuze and Guattari replace adaptive evolution under pressure of selection with the concept of becoming as the pilot concept for the theory of the animal. Becoming is taken in the strongest sense, of emergence. "Can this becoming, this emergence, be called Art?"[1]

Called "art," the formative movement of animal life is no longer analyzable exclusively in terms of adaptation and selection. Another name is called for: expression. In what way do the animal and the human, each in its own right, as well as one in relation to the other, participate in this expressive becoming? Together in what natural animal "sympathy"? If this natural sympathy is moved by an instinctive tendency to outdo itself in expressive excess over its own norms, what does this say about the nature of the animal? The nature of nature? And if this sympathy could extend its object and also reflect upon itself, providing the key to vital operations, what would prevent us from finding, at the self-extending core, something that could only be described as a primary consciousness? A germinal consciousness flush with life's continuance? Might it be instinct that, against all expectations, obliges us to say, with Raymond Ruyer, that "consciousness and life are one"? That "morphogenesis is always consciousness"?[2] A consciousness flush with the unfolding genesis of forms of life: a creatively lived dynamic abstraction. Abstraction? How is that animal? How animal is that?

It is only possible here to stage a first move in the direction of these questions, through a replaying of instinct.[3]

It was Niko Tinbergen, one of the pioneers of ethology, who first noticed that all was not right in the automatism of instinct. Tinbergen was researching the instinctive behavior of the herring gull.[4] A red spot on the female beak serves as signal or "trigger" for feeding behavior. It attracts the peck of the chick. The execution of the peck intensifies the chick's begging behavior and triggers the corresponding behavior in the adult, namely the regurgitation of the menu. Tinbergen was interested in knowing what precise perceptual quality constituted the trigger. He built decoy gull beaks presenting variable characteristics in an attempt to isolate which characteristics were essential to triggering the instinctive behaviors.

His method was guided by four assumptions: (1) the signal as such is a discrete stimulus (the colored spot); (2) the stimulus stands out in its discreteness against a supporting background, the form of which is imprinted in the young gull as an innate schema (the geometry of the adult's beak and head); (3) the hungry chick's response follows mechanically from the appearance of the spot against the background of an actual shape formally resembling the schema; and (4) the response is a sequence of purely automatic actions operating as a reflex. The assumed mechanism was the triggering of an automatism by an instinctive recognition following a principle of formal resemblance.

What Tinbergen found was quite different. Against expectations, the decoys most resembling actual seagull beaks and heads exerted the *least* force of attraction. The most "natural," or naturalistic, forms left something to be desired. Tinbergen decided to push the experiments further by extending the range of variation of the presented forms "beyond the limits of the normal object." This included decoys that "did not look like a good imitation of a herring gull's bill at all."[5] Certain decoys exhibiting a noticeable deficit of resemblance were among the most effective of all. Tinbergen himself was forced to recognize something: that instinct displays an inherent tendency to snub good form and overshoot the limits of the normal in the direction of what he dubbed "supernormal stimuli." The question then became, Precisely what perceptual qualities press beyond the normal?

There was a strong correlation between the color red and the triggering of feeding behavior. The absence of red, however, did not necessarily block the instinctive activity. A spot of another color—even black or gray—could do the job, provided that there was high enough contrast between the spot and its background. High-contrast red proved the surest signal. But the fact that black or gray could also do the job meant that the effect didn't hinge on a discrete color quality, not even red. What the effectiveness of the presentation hinged on, Tinbergen concluded, was an *intensification* effect, in this case produced by the relation of contrast. The color red exerted a supernormal force of attraction to the extent that it lent itself to this intensification *relation*. Gull chicks may have a predilection for red, but even where red was present, there was supernormal pressure toward forcing red into an intensifying relation of immediate proximity with another color, the more contrastive the better. It was this proximity of differences in quality, this qualitative *neighborhood*, that dynamized the force of attraction, pushing the instinct to surpass what had been assumed to be its natural target.

The term *supernormal* thus does not connote a simple opposition between what is normal and what is not, or between the natural and the artificial. What it connotes is a plasticity of natural limits, and a natural disrespect of good form. It indicates a tendency toward deformation stretching behavior out of shape from within its own instinctive operation—a transformational movement naturally pushing animal experience to artificially exceed its normal bounds. Supernormal stimuli express a natural tendency toward an affirmation of excessiveness. "Supernormal dynamism" is a better term than "supernormal stimulus" because it better reflects this tendential movement and the relational tenor of its triggering.

The term *trigger* needs revisiting as well. If the signal functioned purely to trigger an automatic sequence of actions, it would be naturally resistant to the intervention of the supernormal dynamism. It would be firmly under the jurisdiction of the laws of resemblance governing good form and its well-behaved representation. The supernormal dynamism would come in contravention of the laws, relegating it to the status of a simple negative—an infraction— rather than recognizing it as an affirmation of what exceeds the bounds of behavioral norms. It also consigns it to that status of an externality, like an accident whose occurrence doesn't rightfully belong to the nature of the situation, and simply intrudes. But the supernormal tendency clearly pushes from within, as a dimension of the situation. It does not accidently come up against. It pushes across, with a distinct air of exaggeration. It doesn't just throw the behavioral functioning off its form. It makes the form of the functioning behaviorally vary. It twists the situation into a new relational variation, *experientially* intensifying it. What is in play is an immanent experiential excess by virtue of which the normal situation presents a pronounced tendency to surpass itself. That Tinbergen was unable to predict which characteristics were determining testifies to the fact that what is at stake is not resemblance to a specific schema serving as a model. The triggering "stimulus" was not in fact isolatable, and was not subject to the necessity of corresponding to a model. The most that can be said is that red as "stimulus" is *bound* to contrast. The same applies to other qualities ingredient to the situation. If they are likewise treated as linked or indissociably bound variables—in other words as relata—the bounds of potential variation are stretched. The plasticity of the situation is complicated with additional dimensions. The unpredictability grows with the complexity. For example, the geometric variables of length and thickness of beak, and beak size in comparison to head size, enter into relation with contrast, yielding a color-linked geometry in motion. The rhythm and pattern of the movement express a collective covariation, shaken into further variation by changes in aspect accompanying the quasi-chaotic movements of the hungry chick. The sum total of the qualities ingredient to the variation do not add up to a gestalt. There is no reliable background, any more than there is a fixed figure to stand out against it. When one quality changes, its proximity to others in the directness of their linkage entails a simultaneous variation affecting them all, in something like a relativist curvature of the space-time of behavior. Any variation reverberates across them all with a contagious force of deformation. "Such 'relational' or 'configurational' stimuli," Tinbergen observes, "seem to be the rule rather the exception."[6] There is no privileged element capable of extracting itself from its immediate neighborhood with the totality of linked qualities. The color red may well be a favorite of the gulls. But its preeminence can even be endangered by mousy grey. An element that is normally foregrounded is perpetually at risk of sinking back into the gregarity of the moving ground from which it distinguished itself. Any discrete quality may be swallowed back up at any time in the tide of collective variation. Given this general condition of covariant link-age between qualities in immediate experiential neighborhood, it is no wonder that the ethologist was rarely able to predict the response to models including a supernormal element. Even after the fact, it is impossible to identify with certainty which linkage the relational intensification was due to. "So far," Tinbergen writes, "no one has been quite able to analyze such matters; yet somehow, they are accomplished."[7]

At most, it is possible to discern passages toward plastic lim-its, with periods of relative stasis along the way: vectors of super-normality punctuated by stases in the unfolding of instinct's inter-nal dynamic. In Deleuze and Guattari's terms, it is more a question of "consistency"—that is to say, processual "self-consistency"—than it is a question of a gestalt or perceptual form in any nor-mal sense. Philosopher of science Raymond Ruyer uses the word *auto-conduction,* which again has the advantage of connoting the dynamism.[8]

The upshot is that there is an inexpungible element of unpre-dictability in instinct that pertains not to the outside intervention of accidents, but to the self-consistency of its experiential dy-namic. Self-consistency, as distinguished from the accidental, is not a synonym for predictable, regularized, or law abiding. Ruyer makes much of the fact that instinct may trigger in the absence of any stimulus because it demonstrates a capacity for *spontaneity.* The difference is that spontaneity is not slave to external circum-stance. If it is as unpredictable as the accident, it is because it is auto-conducting to excess. Ruyer holds that the capacity for spon-taneity, which he qualifies as "hallucinatory," must be considered a necessary dimension of all instinct.[9] Although the spontaneity of instinct cannot be reduced to the accidental, accidents neverthe-less play a role. According to Ruyer:

> We must consider that an animal in a complex, accident-rich environment would have little chance of survival if it could only avail itself of stereotyped movements, even if they were corrected by orienting stimuli. Of far greater importance are responses that are improvised directly upon the stimulus . . . acting as a kind of irritant rather than as a signal.[10]

The lesson of the accident: if instinct really lived up to its reputation as a reflex mechanism, it would be downright maladaptive. For this reason, Ruyer replaces the notion of the trigger-signal. The "stimulus" irritates, provokes, stirs. It is a processual "inducer." It jump-starts an active process, inducing the performance of an "improvisation." If we put the two terms together, we get a replacement for both "trigger" and "accident" in one terminological stroke: *induced improvisation*. The improvisation is an integral modification in the tendential self-consistency of animal experience, correlated to the externality of an accident-rich environment but governed by its own stirring logic of qualitative variation. An improvisation is a modification rising from within an activity's stirring, bringing a qualitative difference to its manner of unfolding. It is immanent to the activity's taking its own course.

The animal's observable behavior change in the environment is the external face of this immanent modification. In the immanence of its stirring, the modification is hallucinatory: it is "improvised *directly*" on the percept. It operates in all immediacy in the experiential domain of qualitative neighborhood. The physical environment and the qualitative neighborhood are in close processual embrace, but their dynamics remain distinct. Their difference in nature is never erased. The environment, or external milieu, does in the end impose selective constraints. Its selective principle is and remains that of adaptation. And yet, instinct opposes to the law of adaptation an auto-conducting power of improvisation that answers to external necessity with a supernormal twist. The improvised modification of the instinctive tendency, although externally induced, takes its own spontaneous form. As an improvisation, it is formally self-causing. Evolution is and remains subject to selective pressure. But that is not the question this episode from Tinbergen's research raises for ethology and by extension for the philosophy of science.

Conceptually, the question pertains to relation. Adaptation concerns external relations between an animal and its environment. Selective pressure exerts an external judgment on the fitness of a modification. By contrast, what an improvisation concerns directly, in the tendential neighborhood of its ownmost activity, are *"internal" relations*: covarying experiential qualities that come of a block, indissociably linked.[11] For Deleuze and Guattari, as for Ruyer and Bergson, there is another dynamic generative of variation besides the accident (on the accident of genetic mutation, more later). There is a positive principle of form-generating selection operating in its own neighborhood, autonomously of selective adaptation to external conditions. The peck of the herring gull expresses an inventive power of artifice immanent to the nature of instinct, no less than instinct is immanent to nature.

To the adaptive imperative of conformity to the demands of selective pressure, instinct opposes an immanent power of supernormal invention. Faced with a change in the environment, like the sudden appearance of a red-spot-sporting beak on a head, it turns tail, folding back on itself to return to its own neighborhood, there to renew the ties of its native tendency. The accident-rich environment preys upon the instinctive animal. In answer, animal instinct plays upon the environment—in much the sense a musician plays improvisational variations on a theme. Bergson made the point: instinct, he said, is *played* more than it is represented.[12] The ludic element of instinct pries open a margin of play in the interaction between individuals and between the organism and the environment. The blind necessity of mechanistic adaptation selecting schema of automatism is just half the story. Instinctual behavior is ringed, in Ruyer's words, by a "fortuitous fringe" of induced improvisation.[13] Deleuze and Guattari refer to a "creative involution" occurring on that fringe, a phrase itself playing on Bergson's "creative evolution."

Involution: "to involve is to form a block that runs its line 'between' the terms in play and beneath assignable relations" (which is to say, external relations).[14] Between individuals, and between the organism and the milieu, runs a tendential line in the direction of the supernormal. It plays directly in the unassignable register of internal relations: immediate qualitative linkages in a solidarity of variation, mutually deforming as a plastic block. The tracing of this "line" of plasticity is unpredictable, but is not strictly speaking accidental or aleatory, being oriented: toward a spontaneous excess of creative self-consistency.

The tendency toward the supernormal is a vector. It is not only oriented, it carries a force. For example, a cuckoo chick possesses supernormal traits encouraging the female of another species whose nest the cuckoo parasitizes to take it under its wing and nourish it. The host female, Tinbergern says, isn't "willing" to feed the invader. No, she positively "loves" to do it.[15] She does not just do it grudgingly. She does it positively with passion. The force of the supernormal is a positive force. It is not a force in the mechanistic sense. A mechanical force pushes up against a resistance to deliver an impulse determining a commensurate movement in reactive conformity with the quantity of applied force. What we have with the supernormal is a force that pulls forward from ahead, and does so qualitatively: an attractive force. Supernormality is an attractor that draws behavior in its direction, following its own tendency, not in conformity but deformedly and, surpassing normality, without common measure. Supernormality is a force not of impulsion or compulsion, but of *affective propulsion*. This is why it is so necessary to say that instinct involves the inducement of an effect rather than the triggering of an automatism. It is more stirringly about effecting from within than being caused from without. To do justice to the activity of instinct, it is necessary to respect an autonomy of improvised effect with respect to external causation.[16] Instinctive is spontaneously *effective*, in its affective propulsion. It answers external constraint with creative self-variation, pushing beyond the bounds of common measure.

Deleuze and Guattari have a favorite word for affective force that pulls deformationally, creatively ahead, outside common measure: *desire*. Desire is the other, immanent, principle of selection. Deleuze and Guattari define desire as a force of liaison, a force of linkage conveying a transformational tendency. Desire has no particular object. It is a vector. Its object is before it, always to come. Desire vectorizes being toward the emergence of the new. Desire is one with the auto-conducting movement of becoming. Becoming bears on linked experiential qualities in a solidarity of mutual modification, or what Deleuze and Guattari call "blocks" of sensation.[17] It plays upon unpredictable relational effects. It is the improvisation of these deformational, relational effects that constitutes the new. As Deleuze writes, "Form is no longer separable from a transformation or transfiguration that . . . establishes 'a kind of linkage animated by a life of its own.'"[18]

Creative life of instinct: vital art. Ruyer remarks that it is of the nature of instinctive activity to produce an "aesthetic yield."[19] After all, what is a force of mutual linkage if not a force of composition?[20] Deleuze and Guattari ask, "Can this becoming, this emergence," this composition animating the genesis of new forms with a life of their own and producing an aesthetic yield, be called "Art"?

We've entered another immediate neighborhood, that of art, the animal, and becoming (evolution played upon by creative "involution"). In this immediate proximity, Deleuze and Guattari write, "What is animal . . . or human in us is indistinct."[21] For if we can call this Art, it is because the human has the same self-animating tendency to supernormality. Only when we experience it in our own desiring lives we arrogantly tend to call it culture as opposed to nature, as if the animal body of human beings was somehow exempt from instinctive activity. As any biologist will tell you, the human body is on the animal continuum.

Instinctively, as Deleuze and Guattari might say, we humans are in a "zone of indiscernibility" with the animal.[22] Paradoxically, when we return most intently and intensely to that neighborhood "we gain singularly in distinction."[23] It is when the human assumes its immanent excess of animality that it becomes all the more itself. Brilliantly so. "The maximum determination issues from this block of neighborhood like a flash."[24]

Addendum: Project Notes

A preliminary indication of the direction in which this replaying of the theory of instinct might move, along lines suggested by the opening quotation from Bergson, can be provided by glossing the concept of desire in relation to Gabriel Tarde's notions of "belief" and "appetition."

Belief for Tarde has no content in the sense of fundamentally referring to an external object. It is a force of liaison binding a multiplicity of lived qualities into a primary perception that is self-effecting (Ruyer's "hallucinatory" activity). It does not belong to a subject. It is a belonging conditioning the subject's emergence. The subject does not have or possess belief. Rather, belief is a "possession." It is the possession of a multiplicity of life-qualities *by each other.* It is this immediate qualitative linkage that constitutes the real conditions of emergence of a subject of experience.

In Bergsonian terms, this immediate possession of life qualities by each other can be considered a primary sympathy. Once again, sympathy is not something that is had by a subject. It is not a subjective content of animal life. It is a self-effecting qualitative movement constitutive of the life of the animal. *The animal does not have sympathy; it is sympathy.*

"Appetition" for Tarde is the movement from one such sympathetic perception to another, following a tendency toward expansion. The tendency toward expansion is an "avidity," corresponding in the present account to the "passion" of the supernormal tendency to excess. The passion of animal life is its creatively outdoing itself. It is the vital movement of animality's self-improvising, energized by the sympathy that it is. Because this moves animality to surpass what it normally is, it would be more precise to say not that the animal "is" sympathy, but that its becoming is sympathetic.

Together, belief and appetition constitute a pulse of "pure feeling." This feeling is pure in the sense of not yet belonging to a subject, but rather entering actively into its constitution. This is the "block of sensation" for Deleuze and Guattari, or William James's "pure experience."

The concepts of belief, desire, and pure feeling ground Tarde's thinking in always-already ongoing *minimal activity,* rather than any a priori foundation, objective anchoring in external relation, or substance. The possession of belief and the movement of desire that orient sympathetic becoming are immanent to this minimal germinal activity. This is what I call elsewhere "bare activity."[25] The subject *issues* from this immanence: it is, in Whitehead's terms, a "superject."

Tarde uses *desire* as a synonym for *appetition.* In this essay, desire refers to the co-operation of belief and appetition in Tarde. As employed here, the concept of desire also includes an essential reference to Ruyer's definition of consciousness as an experiential solidarity between perceptual qualities indissociably bound in "primary liaison." Primary liaisons are nonmechanistic and, as Deleuze and Guattari emphasize, "non-localizable." There are not therefore "connections" in any usual sense of the term. At the level of life's minimal (germinal) activity, consciousness is one with the desiring movement of pure feeling.[26]

It is only when this primary consciousness comes to fold back onto itself—"reflect" on itself as Bergson had it in the opening quotation—that it secondarily "extends its object." More precisely, life's folding back on itself recursively *constitutes* an object. The object emerges as an effect of this recursivity. The object, Whitehead says, is *that which returns.*[27] This should not be taken to imply that there is a preconstituted object that returns for a subject. It is not so much that the object returns, but rather that life recurs. It cycles back to an already improvised block of sensation, periodically reiterated with a negligible degree of variation—a variation within the bounds of what, for practical purposes, can be treated as the "same."

Thus the object, as it happens, is not one. It is a recursively emergent, reiterative *event*. What distinguishes an object-event from other species of event is that its reiterability enables it to stand as what William James calls a "terminus": an attractor for life-composing movements of appetition.[28] When the object is not actually present, it has not "withdrawn," as object-oriented ontology would have it. It is attractively present as a virtual terminus. It is quietly exerting a force of potential.

The objective movement of return of events to negligible variation settles in as a countertendency to the supernormal tendency. The already-improvised gels into a nodal point. In tendential orbit around points of return, life's movement can take on regularity. The "sameness" of the object is the harbinger of this regularization. Through it, the object-event becomes a pivot for life reexpressing itself, with a higher quotient of repetition than variation. Thus it is less that "consciousness extends its object." It is more that life extends its own activity into objective-event mode. A plane of regularization bifurcates from life's self-expressive coursing. Life activity settles into a reiterative ordering of itself, a level organization holding variation to an orbit of negligible variation. Regularization, normalization: it is on this object-oriented level that life's activity comes to *function.*

This object-oriented normalization of life constitutes what Deleuze and Guattari call the "plane of organization." The plane of organization of function is in reciprocal presupposition with the "plane of consistency" of desire.[29] This gives life a *double-ordering*. Pure feeling is doubled by object-oriented perception, in a play of supernormal tendency and normalizing countertendency: of qualitative excess in vectored becoming, and objective leveling in recursive return; of passion-oriented "minimal" activity, and regularized object-oriented action; of creative spontaneity, and organized function. Always both, in a complexity of mutual imbrication.

Evolution cannot be thought apart from this mutual imbrication of contrasting planes of life, and the dynamic tension of their always coming together, never dissolving into each other, never resolving their difference. Evolution is differential. Functional adaptation is only half the story. The other half is spontaneous and creative. On this side lies the primary origination of forms of life (which are nothing if not intensely qualitative, tending to excess in an immediacy of germinal activity).

This double-ordering implies that what we normally call "consciousness" is a derivative of a primary, nonreflexive, non-object-oriented consciousness corresponding to a radically different mode of life activity, as yet in no subject's possession. This primary consciousness is not *of* something. It *is* something: sympathy. It "is" the immediacy of sympathetic becoming—also called intuition.[30] From primary consciousness's recurrent becoming comes, paradoxically, its countertendency. The mode of this derivative, or secondary consciousness, is *recognition*. Recognition takes recursive return for identity. It constrains recurrence to the same. Organization and normalization are predicated on object-oriented countertendency running circles around desire.

Project:

- Index the animal to its unrecognizability.
- Find in the human the passion of the animal.
- Induce human being to recur to its animal becoming.
- Take it to heart that "at the heart of the human there is nothing human."[31] For it is in the eminently objectless, immediately relational, spontaneously variation-creating activity flush with instinctive animality—this tendency

the human shares with the gull—that the human "gains singularly in distinction," attaining its own "maximum determination" in a passionate flash of supernormal becoming.

- Take it to heart: animal becoming is *most* human. It is in becoming animal that the human recurs to what is nonhuman at the heart of what moves it. This makes its surpassingly human. Creative-relationally *more-than* human.[32]
- Put that in writing.
- Remembering that supernormal becoming is a "minimal activity" of life's exceeding itself. It is modest, to the point of imperceptibility. In the nest or in writing, it is a modest gesture, vanishing even, no more than a flash. Yet vital. Potentially of vital importance. Because it may resonate and amplify and shake life's regularities to their object-oriented foundations.
- Consider that in the primary consciousness of the immediate intuition of animal sympathy "the act of knowledge coincides with the act that generates the real."[33] Not: correlates to. *Coincides* with. Thought-matter.[34] The reality of animality *as* abstraction. Abstraction *as* the movement of the real.
- Improvise on that.

Notes

1. Henri Bergson, *Creative Evolution*, trans. Arthur Mitchell (New York: Henry Holt and Company, 1911), 238.

2. Raymond Ruyer, *La genèse des formes vivantes* (Paris: Flammarion, 1958), 260, 238. Translations mine.

3. For a more extended consideration of these questions, see Brian Massumi, *What Animals Teach Us about Politics* (Durham, N.C.: Duke University Press, 2014).

4. Niko Tinbergen and A. C. Perdeck, "On the Stimulus Situation Releasing the Begging Response in the Newly Hatched Herring Gull Chick," *Behavior* 3, no. 1 (1950): 1–39. The same effect had been observed by O. Köhler in 1937.

5. Niko Tinbergen, *Animal Behavior* (New York: Time-Life Books, 1965), 67.

6. Ibid., 68.

7. Ibid. "There is no absolute distinction between effective sign-stimuli and the non-effective properties of the object. . . . The full significance of supernormal stimuli is not yet clear." Niko Tinbergen, *The Study of Instinct* (Oxford: Oxford University Press, 1951), 42, 46. Tinbergen, however, does not integrate these observations into his theory of instinct overall. They remain isolated musings. Deleuze and Guattari critique the predominance of the stimulus-trigger-automatism model in Tinbergen's thinking; see Gilles Deleuze and Félix Guattari, *A Thousand Plateaus*, trans. Brian Massumi (Minneapolis: University of Minnesota Press, 1987), 327–28.

8. "This is a question of consistency: the 'holding-together' of heterogeneous elements. At first, they constitute no more than a fuzzy set." Deleuze and Guattari, *A Thousand Plateaus*, 323. They characterize life itself in terms of a "gain in consistency," for which they use "self-consistency" *(auto-consistance)* as a synonym (335). They go on to define consistency as a "surplus-value of *destratification*" (emphasis in original, 336). For Ruyer on auto-conduction, see *Genèse des formes vivantes*, 65.

9. Ruyer, *Genèse des formes vivantes*, 146–47.

10. Ibid., 149. Ruyer says the same of internal "signals" such as hormones, which according to his account induce a relational effect of covariation that is in every respect analogous to what occurs in the case of fields of external perception.

11. On expressive qualities and internal relations, see Deleuze and Guattari, *A Thousand Plateaus*, 317–18, 329.

12. Bergson, *Creative Evolution*, 145, 180. *Joué* is translated as "acted."

13. Ruyer, *Genèse des formes vivantes*, 142.

14. Deleuze and Guattari, *A Thousand Plateaus*, 239.

15. Tinbergen, *Animal Behavior*, 67.

16. On cause and effect as belonging to different orders, see Gilles Deleuze, *Logic of Sense*, ed. Constantin V. Boundas, trans. Mark Lester with Charles Stivale (New York: Columbia University Press, 1990), 6–7. Deleuze ties the independence of effects to language. The present account does not follow him in this regard.

17. On blocks of becoming, see Gilles Deleuze and Félix Guattari, ch. 10, "Becoming-Intense, Becoming-Animal, Becoming-Imperceptible . . . ," in *A Thousand Plateaus*, 232–309; and Gilles Deleuze and Félix Guattari, ch. 8, "Blocks, Series, Intensities," in *Kafka: For a Minor Literature*, trans. Dana Polan (Minneapolis: University of Minnesota Press, 1986), 53–62.

On the associated concept of blocks of sensation, see Gilles Deleuze and Félix Guattari, ch. 7, "Percept, Affect, Concept" in *What Is Philosophy?*, trans. Graham Burchell and Hugh Tomlinson (New York: Columbia University Press, 1994), 163–99.

18. Gilles Deleuze, *Francis Bacon: The Logic of Sensation*, trans. Daniel W. Smith (Minneapolis: University of Minnesota Press, 2003), 104. In the English translation, the French phrase *une liaison animée par une vie propre* is rendered as "a love affair kindled by a decent life." I take the phrase much more literally. The word *liaison* is used throughout Deleuze and Deleuze/Guattari's work in reference to and in resonance with Ruyer's thought to mean an unassignable (nonlocal) "linkage," and the idea of an immanent life of form ("animated by a life of its own") fits the context of this passage, which is working from the thought of Wilhelm Worringer.

19. Ruyer, *Genèse des formes vivantes*, 142.

20. Deleuze, *Francis Bacon*, 104.

21. Deleuze and Guattari, *What Is Philosophy?*, 174.

22. Deleuze and Guattari, *A Thousand Plateaus*, 273, 279, 293–94, 305.

23. Deleuze and Guattari, *What Is Philosophy?*, 174 (translation modified).

24. Ibid., 174 (translation modified).

25. Brian Massumi, *Semblance and Event: Activist Philosophy and the Occurrent Arts* (Cambridge, Mass.: MIT Press, 2011), 1–3, 5, 10–11, 22, 23, 27; and Brian Massumi, "Perception Attack: Brief on War Time," *Theory & Event* 13, no. 3 (2010), http://muse.jhu.edu/journals/theory_and_event/v013/13.3.massumi.html.

26. For an analysis of belief, appetition, avidity, and pure feeling in Tarde, see Didier Debaise, "La métaphysique des possessions: puissances et société chez G. Tarde," *Revue de métaphysique et de la morale* 4, no. 60 (2008): 447–60. On consciousness as transspatial liaison, see Raymond Ruyer, *Le néo-finalisme* (Paris: PUF, 1952), 113. On non-localizable liaison and becoming, see Deleuze and Guattari, *A Thousand Plateaus*, 413.

27. "Objects are the elements in nature that can 'be again.'" Alfred North Whitehead, *Concept of Nature* (Cambridge: Cambridge University Press, 1964), 143.

28. William James, *Essays in Radical Empiricism* (Lincoln: University of Nebraska Press, 1996), 39–91.

29. On the plane of organization and the plane of consistency, see Deleuze and Guattari, *A Thousand Plateaus*, 9, 21, 70–73, 251–52, 265–72.

30. For an excellent analysis of intuition and sympathy in Bergson (which in Bergson's texts are not actually as synonymous as they are presented to be here), see David Lapoujade, *Puissances du temps. Versions de Bergson* (Paris: Editions Minuit, 2010).

31. Lapoujade, *Puissances du temps*, 62.

32. Erin Manning develops the concept of the more-than-human as a relational "ecology of practices" in *Always More Than One: Individuation's Dance* (Durham, N.C.: Duke University Press, 2013).

33. Henri Bergson, *Mélanges* (Paris: PUF, 1972), quoted in Lapoujade, *Puissances du temps*, 35.

34. On the plane of consistency as matter, see Deleuze and Guattari, *A Thousand Plateaus*, 43.

2

Consequences of Panpsychism

STEVEN SHAVIRO

WHAT IS IT LIKE TO BE A ROCK? Rudy Rucker's science fiction short story "Panpsychism Proved" (2007) provides one possible answer. An engineer at Apple named Shirley invents a new "mindlink" technology, which allows people to "directly experience each other's thoughts." When two individuals swallow "microgram quantities of entangled pairs of carbon atoms," they enter into direct telepathic contact. Shirley hopes to seduce her coworker Rick by melding their minds together. Unfortunately, he has other plans. She ingests a batch of entangled carbon particles; but Rick dumps his corresponding batch on a boulder. Instead of getting in touch with Rick, Shirley finds that "the mind she'd linked to was inhuman: dense, taciturn, crystalline, serene, beautiful. . . ." She fails in her quest for sex and deeper human contact. But she finds solace through intimacy with a "friendly gray lump of granite. How nice to know that a rock had a mind."[1]

Panpsychism is the thesis that even rocks have minds. More formally, David Skrbina defines *panpsychism* as "the view that all things have mind or a mind-like quality. . . . Mind is seen as fundamental to the nature of existence and being."[2] Or in the slightly different words of Thomas Nagel, who entertains the notion without fully endorsing it, panpsychism is "the view that the basic physical constituents of the universe have mental properties, whether or not they are parts of living organisms."[3] Most broadly, panpsychism makes the claim that mind, or sentience, is in some manner, as Rucker claims, "a universally distributed quality."[4] In opposition to idealism, Cartesian dualism, and eliminativist physicalism alike, panpsychism maintains that thought is neither merely epiphenomenal nor something that exists in a separate realm from the material world. Rather, mind is a fundamental property of matter itself. This means that thinking happens everywhere; it extends all the way down (and also all the way up). There are differences of degree in the ways that entities think, but no fundamental differences of kind.

Because it makes such seemingly extravagant claims, panpsychism is easily subject to derision and ridicule. The most common response to it is probably the one epitomized by the philosopher Colin McGinn, who calls it "a complete myth, a comforting piece of utter balderdash. . . . Isn't there something vaguely hippyish, i.e., stoned, about the doctrine?"[5] Even Galen Strawson, the best-known contemporary analytic philosopher to embrace panpsychism, admits that the doctrine "sounded crazy to me for a long time"; he finally got "used to it," he says, only when he became convinced that there was "no alternative."[6]

However stoned or crazy it might sound, panpsychism in fact has a long philosophical pedigree, as Skrbina amply demonstrates in *Panpsychism in the West*. From the pre-Socratics, on through Baruch Spinoza and Gottfried Wilhelm von Leibniz, and down to William James and Alfred North Whitehead, panpsychism is a recurring underground motif in the history of Western thought. It was under eclipse in the second half of the twentieth century, but in recent years it seems to have returned with a vengeance. No less than three anthologies of essays on panpsychism have been published in the past decade, with contributions by analytic and continental philosophers alike.[7] Panpsychism seems especially relevant today, in the light of the "nonhuman turn" in critical discourse, and the new philosophical movements that are gathered under the rubric of "speculative realism." In any case, panpsychism has never been a mainstream philosophical doctrine. But it has persisted as a kind of countertendency to the anthropocentrism, and the hierarchical ontologies, of dominant philosophical dogmas. Panpsychism offers a rebuke both to extravagant idealism on the one hand, and to reductionism and eliminativism on the other.

The problem with panpsychism, for most people, is evidently one of *extension*. What can it mean to attribute mentality to all entities in the universe, without exception? Modern Western philosophy, from the Cartesian *cogito* through the Kantian transcendental subject and beyond, is grounded upon an idealization of the human mind—or more narrowly, upon the rationality that is supposed to be one of the powers of the human mind. And much of this tradition has sought to overcome the apparent problem of solipsism, or skepticism regarding "other minds," by appealing to a *sensus communis*, or a linguistic ability, that all human beings share. In this way, our minds are the guarantors of our commonality. But how far can the ascription of mentality be extended beyond the human? To begin with, can I rightly say that my cat thinks and feels?

Many philosophers have in fact said no. Descartes notoriously argued that animals were nonthinking automata. Heidegger maintained that animals (in contrast to human beings) were intrinsically "poor in world." Recent thinkers as diverse as Richard Rorty, Jacques Rancière, and Slavoj Žižek continue to endorse human exceptionalism, because they all insist upon the centrality of linguistic forms (conversation for Rorty, linguistic competence for Rancière, or the Symbolic order for Žižek) as the basis for a sort of Kantian universal communicability. Even today, it is still often argued that nonhuman animals do not *really* think, because they are incapable of language, or because they do not have an awareness of mortality, or because they supposedly lack the capacity to make rational inferences. Robert Brandom, for instance, distinguishes mere *sentience*, or "mammalian sensuousness," such as my cat might feel, from the *sapience* that supposedly human beings alone possess; for Brandom, only the latter is "*morally* significant."[8] Following Brandom, Pete Wolfendale argues that "nothing has value for animals, because there's no sense in which their behaviour could be justified or unjustified. This is the essence of the difference between us and them: animals merely *behave*, whereas we *act*."[9]

In spite of such arguments, both philosophical claims and common opinion have shifted in recent years more fully in favor of recognizing the mentality of at least the higher animals (mammals and birds, and possibly cephalopods). I presume that most people today would agree that dogs and cats have minds. That is to say, these animals think and feel; they have inner qualitative experiences, they register pleasure and pain, and they make decisions. But does a lobster similarly think and feel? Does a jellyfish? Does a tree? Does the slime mold *Physarum polycephalum*? In fact, there is good scientific evidence that *all* living organisms, including such brainless ones as plants, slime molds, and bacteria, exhibit at least a certain degree of sentience, cognition, decision making, and will.[10] But what about things that are not alive? How many non-stoned people will agree with Rudy Rucker that a rock has a mind? Or for that matter, a neutrino? According to Whitehead, Leibniz "explained what it must be like to be an atom. Lucretius tells us what an atom looks like to others, and Leibniz tells us how an atom is feeling about itself."[11] But who today is Leibnizian and Whiteheadean enough to assert that an atom, or a neutrino, feels anything whatsoever about itself?

Few advocates of panpsychism would expect that the doctrine could literally be verified by scientific experiment, as happens in Rucker's whimsical story. For panpsychism makes an ontological claim, rather than a necessarily empirical one. Even if we were able, as Whitehead once put it, to "ask a stone to record its autobiography," the results would probably not be very edifying or exciting.[12] It is not a question, therefore, of actually getting a rock or a neutrino to speak; but rather one of recognizing that mentality, or inner experience, is not contingent upon the ability to speak in the first place. Indeed, direct telepathic contact—like that portrayed in Rucker's story—is not likely to be possible, even between speaking human subjects. This is because any such contact would end up being public and external, precisely in the way that speech already is. Inner experience—sensations, qualia, and the like—would remain untouched. Panpsychism is not predicated upon the possibility of what Graham Harman calls "human access" to other entities and other minds, whether they be human or nonhuman.[13] To the contrary, panpsychism's insistence upon the mentality of other entities in the world also implies the autonomy of all those entities from our apprehension—and perhaps even from our concern.

When panpsychism insists upon the mentality of lobsters, neutrinos, and lumps of granite, what it is saying in the first instance is that these entities exist *pour soi* as well as *en soi*. They are autonomous centers of *value*. By this, I mean that it is not just a matter of how *we* value lobsters, or neutrinos, or lumps of granite, but also of the ways in which these entities *value themselves*—and differentially value whatever other entities they may happen to encounter. For entities do indeed value themselves. In the first instance, they do so by the very act of persisting through time, and establishing themselves as what Whitehead calls "enduring objects" (PR, 35, 109). This active persistence is more or less what Spinoza calls *conatus*, or what Levi Bryant calls the "ongoing auto-poiesis" of objects.[14] I am not entirely happy with these terms, however. *Conatus* and *autopoiesis* seem to me to put too exclusive an emphasis upon the entity's self-reproduction and maintenance of its identity, or upon what Bryant calls its "endo-consistency."[15] But the value activity of an entity that persists through time is not just a matter of self-perpetuation, or of the continually renewed achievement of homeostatic equilibrium. It may well also involve growth or shrinkage, and assimilation or expulsion, or an active self-transformation and becoming-other. All these can be characterized as what Whitehead calls "conceptual initiative," or "the origination of conceptual novelty" (PR, 102). Such processes are more akin to what Gilbert Simondon calls "individuation," and to what the Whiteheadian poet Charles Olson calls "the will to change," than they are to conatus or autopoiesis.[16]

In any case, the active self-valuation of all entities is in fact the best warrant for their sentience. For value activity is a matter of feeling, and responding. Whitehead defines value, or worth, as an entity's "sense of existence for its own sake, of existence which is its own justification, of existence with its own character." Each cat or dog has "its own character," and so does each lobster, and even each neutrino. For Whitehead, "the common fact of value experience" constitutes "the essential nature of each pulsation of actuality. Everything has some value for itself, for others, and for the whole. . . . Existence, in its own nature, is the upholding of value intensity. . . . [Every entity] upholds value intensity for itself. . . ."[17]

In other words, each entity has its own particular needs and desires, which issue forth in its own affirmations of value. These are bound up in the very being of the entities themselves. Rather than saying (with David Hume) that values cannot be derived from facts, or (with the early Ludwig Wittgenstein) that value "must lie outside the world," we should rather say that multiple values and acts of valuation are themselves irrefutable facts within the world.[18] These values and valuations all *belong* to "a common world," as White-head says—indeed, they are immanent to the very world we live in.[19] But each of these values and valuations also exists in its own right, entirely apart from us; and the values of other entities would still continue to exist in the world without us. The problem, then, is not to derive an "ought" from an "is," but to see how innumerable "oughts" already *are*. Contra Wolfendale, nonhuman animals *do* continually ascribe value to things, and make decisions about them—even if they do not offer the sorts of cognitive justifications for their value-laden actions that human beings occasionally do. And contra Brandom, this is indeed a morally significant fact; for as Whitehead puts it, "We have no right to deface the value experience which is the very essence of the universe" (*MT*, 111).

The standard retort to the Whiteheadian value argument that I have just been making is, of course, to accuse it of anthropomorphism. When Whitehead claims that nonhuman entities have values and experiences, that they have particular points of view, and that they think and make decisions, is he not imputing human categories to them? I argue, however, that making such a charge is begging the question. For the accusation of anthropomorphism rests on the prior assumption that thought, value, and experience are essentially, or exclusively, human to begin with. And I can see no justification for this. Our own value activities arose out of, and still remain in continuity with, nonhuman ones—as we have known at least since Darwin. We perpetuate anthropocentrism in an inverted form when we take it for granted that a world without us, a world from which *our own* values have been subtracted, is therefore a world devoid of values altogether. After all, even Cthulhu has its own values—however much we may dislike them and (rightly) feel threatened by them. The same goes for the anopheles mosquito, and for the (recently exterminated) smallpox virus. I think that this persistence of nonhuman values is a serious problem for the "eliminativist" versions of speculative realism, such as those of Quentin Meillassoux and Ray Brassier.[20] There is no reason why overcoming what Meillassoux calls "the correlation between thinking and being" should require the extirpation of thought (or knowledge, or experience) altogether.[21]

For a more nuanced approach to the question of nonhuman

minds and nonhuman values, I turn to Thomas Nagel's famous 1974 article "What Is It Like to Be a Bat?" Nagel argues that "the fact that an organism has conscious experience *at all* means, basically, that there is something it is like to *be* that organism." He further explains that "what it is *like*," as he uses the term, "does not mean 'what (in our experience) it *resembles*,' but rather 'how it is for the subject himself.'"[22] A bat's sonocentric experience—or for that matter, a dog's olfactocentric one—is so different from the oculocentric experience of human beings that we will never be able to literally feel, or entirely understand, "what it is like" to be a bat or a dog. The best we can do is to create metaphors and similes—or as I would rather say, aesthetic semblances—that *allude* in some way to chiropteran or canine existence. Graham Harman rightly remarks that "allusion and allure are legitimate forms of knowledge," but also that they are necessarily partial and incomplete.[23] Likeness-in-human-terms, if it is projected imaginatively enough, may work to dislocate us from the correlationist position of understanding these other entities only in terms of their resemblance, and relationship, to ourselves. But it can never actually attain the inner being of those other entities.

Nagel therefore argues for a much stronger sense of "likeness." For him it is not just a matter of our trying to explain what being a bat might be like in human terms. It is also, and more important, a question of what being a bat is like *for the bat itself.* Such is the project of what Ian Bogost, following up on Nagel, calls "alien phenomenology."[24] As Nagel puts it, "The experiences of other creatures are certainly independent of the reach of an analogy with the human case. They have their own reality and their own subjectivity."[25] In affirming this, Nagel moves from the problem of access to the problem of being: from epistemology (the question of how we can know what a bat is thinking) to ontology (grasping that the bat is indeed thinking, and that this thinking is an essential aspect of the bat's own being, even though we cannot hope to comprehend it). It is evidently "like something" to be a bat; but we will never be able to imagine, or to state in words, just what that "something" is. The point is a double one. The bat's thinking is inaccessible to us; we should not anthropomorphize the bat's experience by modeling it on our own. But we also should not claim that, just because it is nonhuman, or not like us, the bat cannot have experiences at all. These are really just two sides of the same coin. We need to accept both that the bat *does* have experiences and that these experiences are radically different from ours, and may have their own richness and complexity in ways that we will never be able to understand.

The bat's inner experience is inaccessible to me; but this is so in much the same way (albeit to a far greater extent) that any other person's inner experience is inaccessible to me. It is even similar to the way that *my own* inner experience is in fact also inaccessible to me. This is because of the strange ontological status of "experience." I think that the later Wittgenstein is surprisingly relevant here—in spite of the fact that he is usually taken to be rejecting the very notion of mental states and inner (private) experiences. Wittgenstein does indeed say that the representations we make of our inner sensations are "not informative," and that it is incoherent to speak of such sensations in the same ways that we speak of physical things.[26] A toothache is not an object of perception in the way that a tooth is: you can see or touch my tooth, but you cannot see or touch my toothache. Indeed, the way that I feel a toothache *in* my tooth is vastly different from the way that I apprehend the tooth itself by touching it with my tongue or finger, or looking at it in the mirror, or even knowing its place through proprioception.

This line of argument has often been used, in post-Wittgensteinian analytic philosophy, in order to deny the existence, or the meaningfulness, of "qualia" or inner sensations altogether. But Wittgenstein himself does not do this. Rather, he explicitly warns us against denying or discounting the reality of inner experience on such a basis: "Just try—in a real case—to doubt someone else's fear or pain!" (*PI*, #303). After all, he asks, "What greater difference could there be" than that between "pain-behaviour with pain and pain-behaviour without pain"? (*PI*, #304). Inner sensation, Wittgenstein concludes, is "not a Something, but not a Nothing either!" (*PI*, #304). What he means by this is that first-person experience cannot possibly be a matter of third-person, objective knowledge. First-person experience is not a Something, because—in contrast to the behavior that expresses it—it cannot be pointed to, or isolated by an observer, or made subject to scientific experimentation. But since this inner sensation, or first-person experience, is "not a Nothing either," it also cannot be eliminated, or dismissed as meaningless.

This is why it is wrong to regard Wittgenstein as a behaviorist or an anti-internalist—although he has most commonly been interpreted this way. Thus Daniel Dennett conceives himself to be completing the Wittgensteinian revolution in philosophy, by striving to "extirpate" the very notion of "qualia that hide forever from objective science in the subjective inner sancta of our minds." Dennett takes the final reductionist step that Wittgenstein himself refuses to take—and he seems unable to understand Wittgenstein's refusal. Indeed, Dennett goes so far as to accuse Wittgenstein of trying "to hedge his bets" with the escape clause that inner sensation is "not a Nothing either." In moving toward a full-fledged eliminativism, however, Dennett throws out the baby with the bathwater. He destroys Wittgenstein's very point, in the act of trying to extend it.[27]

Wittgenstein's critique in the *Philosophical Investigations* is in fact directed as much against the functionalism and scientism that Dennett so uncritically embraces, as it is against the old idealist metaphysics of the likes of, say, F. H. Bradley. Where idealism seeks to transform qualia into objectifiable facts, scientism seeks to eliminate qualia altogether, on the ground that they cannot be transformed into objectifiable facts. But Wittgenstein opposes both of these moves, for the same reason. He argues that not everything in the world is a matter of fact. That is to say, he explicitly contradicts the claim, from his own earlier *Tractatus*, that "the world is all that is the case," and that "the world divides into facts" that are entirely separate from one another (sec. 1 and 1.2). The point of Wittgenstein's later thought in the *Philosophical Investigations* is precisely to grasp the peculiar, yet ontologically positive, status of nonthings or nonfacts (such as qualia or inner sensations). And this can only be done by disabusing us of the notion, either that such experiences are "facts" like all the others, or that they can be "explained away" by reduction to facts. Wittgenstein thus resists the imperialistic pretensions of global idealism and global scientism alike, both of which wrongly seek to encompass everything within their own theoretical constructions.

Wittgenstein further develops his point about inner sensations in a deliberately paradoxical formulation: "I can know what someone else is thinking, not what I am thinking" (*PI*, #315). Since I *have* feelings like fear and pain, it is either redundant or misleading to say that I *know* I have them. The use of the word *know* in such a case implies a confusion. For there is really no epistemological issue here at all. I do not need to "know" what I am thinking in order to think it. If I am in pain, I do not need to provide grounds for proving to myself that I am so. My being in pain is therefore not a matter of "justified true belief." It is a kind of category error, to think that my actual experience of fear or pain is somehow dependent upon the question of how I have "access" to it, or how I am able to *know* that I am experiencing it. At the same time, I *can* rightly say that I know what you are thinking; for here I *am* able to cite grounds in order to justify my belief. Perhaps I know what you are thinking because you have told me; or perhaps I gather it from your facial expression, or from the way that you are acting (laughing uproariously, or doubling over in pain). Of course, I may in fact be mistaken as to what you are thinking; indeed, you may be acting in the way you are with the deliberate aim of deceiving me. But these sorts of errors can always be cleared up, at least in principle, through additional empirical evidence.

When it comes to my own case, the question of knowledge plays out in much the same way. I cannot be directly mistaken about being in pain. However, I *can* deceive myself about my own mental state; recent psychological experiments suggest that this happens more often than not. In this way, I might not *know* that I am in pain. Also, I may well be in error when I try to analyze my pain in discursive terms and specify to myself just *what it is* that I am thinking and feeling. This is because, to the extent that I *do* know what I myself am thinking, I am making inferences about my own thinking from the outside, in the same way that I make inferences about the mental states of others.

If we try to extend Wittgenstein's line of questioning to non-human others, then the problem is evidently one of language—since Wittgenstein is so concerned with forms of speech in particular. Nagel expresses a certain uneasiness with Wittgenstein's account, because "it depends too heavily on our language. . . . But not all conscious beings are capable of language, and that leaves the difficult problem of how this view accommodates the subjectivity of *their* mental states."[28] However, Nagel goes on to alleviate this difficulty:

> We ascribe experience to animals on the basis of their behavior, structure, and circumstances, but we are not just ascribing to them behavior, structure, and circumstances. So what are we saying? The same kind of thing we say of people when we say they have experiences, of course. . . .
>
> Experience must have systematic connexions with behavior and circumstances in order for experiential qualities and experiential similarity to be real. But we need not know what these connexions are in order to ask whether experience is present in an alien thing.[29]

Evidently, my cat does not tell me what she wants in words—as another human person would be able to do. Nonetheless, I can often rightly say that I know, from observation, what my cat is thinking. (She wants dinner, she wants me to brush her, she wants to be left alone.) More important, even when I cannot tell what my cat is thinking, I can at least tell that she *is* thinking. I know that the "connexions" are there, even if I don't know what they are; and I know that "experience" requires such connexions, but also that it cannot be reduced to them. My cat's inner experiences are in no way dependent upon my ability to "translate" them into my own terms; nor are they vitiated by her inability to justify them by means of predicative judgments, or to articulate the "inferential relations" implied by the conceptualization of these experiences.[30]

All this implies that language should not be accorded too privileged a place in our inferences about inner experience; much less should language be necessary, in order for some sort of inner experience to exist. What David Chalmers calls the "hard problem" of consciousness indeed plays out the same way in relation to a bat, or a cat—or for that matter, in Chalmers's notorious example, to a thermostat—that it does in relation to another human being.[31] In the latter case, species similarity and the common ability to speak allow us to describe "what it is like" for the other person a bit more extensively; but this is only a difference of degree, not one of kind. An extreme behaviorist will deny the existence of interiority in speaking human beings as well as in nonspeaking animals and nonliving thermostats. But there is no justification for inferring interiority on the basis of linguistic behavior, while at the same time refusing to make such an inference in the case of other sorts of observed behavior.

With or without language, therefore, we are observing the behavior of others (or even of ourselves), in order to infer the existence of an inner experience that, in its own right, is irreducible to observable behavior. Following Wittgenstein's suggestions, we must say that this inner experience indeed exists; but it does so in a quite particular manner. Inner mental states, such as sensations and experiences, are not reducible to discursive language, for the same reason that they are not objectifiable as "facts" that can be observed directly in the third person. "What it is like to be a bat" is not a Something: for it is not specifiable as a *thing* at all. But the bat's inner experience is not a Nothing either. This means that it is indeed "like something" to be a bat, even though "what it is like" is not *a* Something. This distinction is not a mere play on words, but a basic ontological condition. The mentality of a bat cannot be displayed objectively, but it also cannot simply be dismissed, or explained away. A bat's experience—or a human being's, for that matter—is indubitable and incorrigible; but at the same time, it is spectral, impalpable, and incommunicable.

Indeed, this is the reason why the very attempt to discuss subjective experience in terms of qualia, precise sensations, and the like, is—as Wittgenstein suggested—not very useful. As Whitehead continually points out, most experience is vague and indistinct. We largely confront "percepta which are vague, not to be controlled, heavy with emotion." Primordial experience involves

> a sense of influx of influence from other vaguer presences
> in the past, localized and yet evading local definition, such
> influence modifying, enhancing, inhibiting, diverting, the
> stream of feeling which we are receiving, unifying, enjoying,
> and transmitting. This is our general sense of existence,
> as one item among others, in an efficacious actual world.
> (*PR*, 178)

Or, as Whitehead puts it in an earlier passage in *Process and Reality*, "The primitive experience is emotional feeling"; but "the feeling is blind and the relevance is vague" (*PR*, 163). Very few aspects of our experience are clear and distinct; we can only obtain "a clear-cut experience by concentrating on the abstractions of consciousness" and excluding everything else (*MT*, 108).

Whitehead suggests that the fatal mistake of philosophers from Descartes through Hume was to restrict themselves to such abstractions, by taking "clear and distinct ideas" as their starting point. We may say much the same about analytic philosophers today who argue about qualia. For the problem with speaking of "qualia" at all—pro or con—is that, by invoking them in the first place, we have already distorted them by extracting them from the Jamesian stream of consciousness in which they occur. Once we have done so, it is easy enough to take the further step that Dennett does, and "prove" that they do not exist at all. In other words, Dennett's eliminativism is merely the reductio ad absurdum of the premises that he shares with his opponents. Most of our experience is already lost, once it has been analyzed in detail and divided into discrete parts. All these discussions in the philosophy of mind miss the point, because mentality is both far more diffuse, and far more widespread, than these thinkers realize. Such is Whitehead's version of the claim that mentality is neither a Something nor a Nothing.

I think that Galen Strawson's argument for panpsychism makes the most sense if it is read in the light of these considerations. Strawson argues that mentality of some sort—whether we call it "experience, 'consciousness,' conscious experience, 'phenomenology,' experiential 'what-it's-likeness,' feeling, sensation, explicit conscious thought"—is "the phenomenon whose existence is more certain than the existence of anything else." Everything that we know about the world, and everything that we do in fact experience, is dependent upon the prior condition that we are able to *have experiences* in the first place. The mental, for Strawson, is therefore not something that we can point to: we have already pre-assumed it, even before we look for it explicitly. Therefore, he says, we must reject "the view—the faith—that the nature or essence of all concrete reality can in principle be fully captured in the terms of physics." Indeed, according to Strawson, the *only* way to explain "the nature or essence of experience" in "the terms of physics" is to explain it away, eliminating it almost by definition. Reductionists like Dennett end up trying to "deny the existence of experience" altogether—a move that Strawson regards as absurd and self-refuting.[32]

In insisting that we are more sure of our own conscious experience than of anything else, Strawson knowingly echoes the Cartesian *cogito*. But he gets rid of the dualism, and the reification, that have always been seen as the most problematic parts of Descartes's argument. For Strawson, "experiential phenomena" are real in their own right, and there cannot be an experience without an experiencer. But at the same time, Strawson makes no particular claim about the nature of the "I" that thinks; and he certainly does not pronounce himself to be "a thinking *thing*." Where Descartes posited mind as entirely separate from matter or extension, Strawson makes precisely the opposite move. Given the evident reality of the mental, together with a basic commitment to what he calls "real physicalism," he says that we must reject the common assumption "that the physical, in itself, is an essentially and wholly non-experiential phenomenon."[33] If we reject dualism and supernaturalism, then mentality itself must be entirely physical.

This might seem to be altogether reasonable once we have accepted—as Whitehead already urged us to do, nearly a century ago, and as many speculative realists and "new materialists" now assert—that matter is not inert and passive, but immanently active, productive, and formative. However, this is not quite Strawson's claim. For he is not arguing for the vibrancy of matter on the basis of quantum theory, as Whitehead did, and as Karen Barad currently does, nor is he arguing for it on the basis of the new sciences of complexity and emergence, as Jane Bennett, Manuel De Landa, and other "new materialists" tend to do.[34] Rather, Strawson's position is radically anti–systems theory and anti-emergentist. He rejects the idea that anything nontrivial can emerge on a higher level that was not already present in, and linearly caused by, microconstituents at a lower level. Wetness can arise from the agglomeration of water molecules that are not in themselves wet; this is something that physics has no trouble explaining.[35] And, although we do not know for sure how life originally came out of nonlife, we are able at least to develop plausible and coherent physico-chemical scenarios about how it might have happened. The emergence of life—which seemed so mysterious to the nineteenth-century vitalists—does not trouble us *metaphysically* any longer. But Strawson insists that "one cannot draw a parallel between the perceived problem of life and the perceived problem of experience in this way, arguing that the second problem will dissolve just as the first did, unless one considers life completely apart from experience."[36] According to Strawson, physics cannot even begin to explain how sentience could arise out of some initially nonsentient matter. Even if we discover the neural correlates of consciousness, that holy grail of contemporary neuroscience, this will not tell us anything about how and why inner experience is materially *possible* in the first place.

Strawson's rejection of what he calls "brute emergence" rests on an unquestioned scientific reductionism, or on what Sam Coleman calls "smallism": "the view that all facts are determined by facts about the smallest things, those that exist at the lowest 'level' of ontology."[37] This is a position that most new materialists, and non-eliminativist speculative realists, would never accept. Yet I think that we would do well to entertain Strawson's position to a certain extent, if only because it offers some resistance to our facile habit of using "quantum indeterminacy" and "higher-level emergence" like magic wands to account for whatever it is that we do not know how to explain. As Strawson puts it, "It is built into the heart of the notion of emergence that emergence cannot be brute in the sense of there being absolutely no reason in the nature of things why the emerging thing is as it is (so that it is unintelligible even to God)."[38] Of course, Quentin Meillassoux, with his notion of *the necessity of contingency*, maintains precisely this.[39] Radical or brute emergence reaches the point of its reductio ad absurdum in Meillassoux's claim that life and thought both arose miraculously, by pure contingency, out of a previously dead and inert universe.[40]

Meillassoux in fact argues for *the origin of pure novelty* out of nothing.[41] But if we are to reject miracles, and maintain—as Meillassoux emphatically does not—some version of the principle of sufficient reason, or of Whitehead's ontological principle (which states that "there is nothing which floats into the world from nowhere" [*PR*, 244]), then we must accept that novelty cannot emerge ex nihilo. Whitehead indeed says that creativity, or "the principle of *novelty*," is "the universal of universals characterizing ultimate matter of fact" (*PR*, 21). But he also insists that novelty is only possible on the basis of, and in response to, "stubborn fact which cannot be evaded" (*PR*, 43). Newness always depends on something prior. It's a bit like the way a DJ creates new music by sampling and remixing already existing tracks. A similar logic leads to Strawson's insistence that sentience must already have been present, at least potentially, from the very beginning.

What's most interesting about Strawson's argument is how it leads him into a paradoxical tension, or a double bind. Strawson, like most analytic philosophers, is a scientific reductionist, and yet he maintains that subjective experience is irreducible. He insists that everything is "physical" and reducible to its ultimate micro-components; and that mentality is as real, and therefore as "physical," as anything else. And yet Strawson also asserts that mentality is entirely inaccessible to scientific explanation. The very phenomenon of being able to have experiences—the phenomenon that alone makes objective, third-person knowledge possible in the first place—cannot itself be accounted for in science's objective, third-person terms. There is no way to bridge the gap between first-person and third-person perspectives.

Strawson refuses to alleviate this tension by adopting any of the usual philosophical dodges (dualism, emergentism, and eliminativism). Instead, he adopts the ontological postulate that mentality must *already* be an aspect, or a basic quality, of everything that exists. This is why "experience" cannot be limited to human beings, or even to living things in general. Panpsychism is the necessary consequence of respecting the *self-evidence* of phenomenal experience, without trying either to hypostasize it or to extirpate it. Thought is not a specifiable, separable Something, but neither is it a mere vacancy, a Nothing. It is rather the inner, hidden dimension of everything. "All physical stuff is energy, in one form or another," Strawson says, "and all energy, I trow, is an experience-involving phenomenon."[42]

In this regard, Strawson's position is not far from Whitehead's.

In discussing how his own philosophy of process (or of "organism") relates to the discoveries of twentieth-century science, Whitehead writes:

> If we substitute the term "energy" for the concept of a quantitative emotional intensity, and the term "form of energy" for the concept of "specific state of feeling," and remember that in physics "vector" means definite transmission from elsewhere, we see that this metaphysical description of the simplest elements in the constitution of actual entities agrees absolutely with the general principles according to which the notions of modern physics are framed. (*PR*, 116)

He adds that "direct perception [can] be conceived as the transference of throbs of emotional energy, clothed in the specific forms provided by sense" (*PR*, 116). In this way, Whitehead, like Strawson, locates the coordinates of "experience" entirely within the natural world described to us by physics, even though such experience cannot itself be accounted for by physics. This is why subjective consciousness is spectral and unqualifiable, but nonetheless entirely actual.

How is this possible? The next step in the argument is taken by Sam Coleman, who radicalizes Nagel's formulation in the "Bat" essay. Nagel himself proposes the "What is it like?" question as a kind of test, a way of determining whether or not an entity is conscious. It is evidently "like something" to be a bat, but for Nagel it might well not be like anything at all to be a rock. Coleman, however, transforms Nagel's epistemological criterion into a foundational ontological principle. Coleman argues that "absolute what-it-is-likeness" does not just apply to living things in particular; rather, it must lie "at the heart of ontology."[43] Following Bertrand Russell and Arthur Eddington, Coleman suggests that "the concepts of physics only express the extrinsic natures of the items they refer to. . . . The question of their intrinsic nature is left unanswered by the theory, with its purely formal description of micro ontology."[44]

That is to say, contemporary physics—no less than the physics of Lucretius—only "tells us what an atom looks like to others": it describes an atom in terms of its extrinsic, relational qualities. The study of these relations is what physical science is all about. But Lucretian, nor Newtonian, nor modern (relativistic and quantum) physics has ever pretended to tell us what an atom actually *is*, intrinsically, for itself. And this is the gap that panpsychism today seeks to fill—just as Leibniz sought to fill a similar gap in the physics of Newton. Coleman claims, therefore, that "the *essence* of the physical . . . is experiential"; all of the causal interactions tracked by physics must necessarily involve, as well, "the doings of intrinsically experiential existents: causality as described by physics, as currently conceived, captures the *structure* of these goings on, but leaves out the real loci of causal power."[45]

In other words, physical science gives us true knowledge of the world, but this knowledge is exclusively external, structural, and relational. Physics can help me to know what someone else is thinking; but it is powerless to explain what I am thinking. And the most hard-edged contemporary philosophy of science indeed insists upon this distinction. For James Ladyman and Don Ross, the lesson of contemporary physics is that "there are no things; structure is all there is." Physical science can only describe relational properties. Ladyman and Ross tell us that we must "give up the attempt to learn about the nature of unobservable entities from science." They conclude that, because "intrinsic natures" are not known to science, they simply do not exist. As far as Ladyman and Ross are concerned, nothing has an irreducible inside; to posit one is to make an illegitimate inference as a result of what they scornfully describe as "prioritizing armchair intuitions about the nature of the universe over scientific discoveries." In Ladyman and Ross's vision, physical science is exclusively relational; anything not determined by these relations must be eliminated.[46]

Anyone who has followed recent discussions in speculative realism is likely to be aware of Graham Harman's critique of Ladyman and Ross.[47] But Harman's is only one of many voices to have found its sort of "radical relationism" untenable and to insist instead that entities *must* have intrinsic natures of some sort. William Seager summarizes various forms of the "intrinsic nature" argument and claims that, without it, one cannot offer anything like an adequate treatment of the problem of consciousness—much less maintain panpsychism. "We are forced to postulate an intrinsic ground for the relational, structural, or mathematical properties" of which physics informs us—even if physics itself cannot provide this ground.[48] Seager and Harman alike insist, rightly, that entities must have something like intrinsic properties, because relations cannot exist without relata.[49] Therefore, as Harman puts it, "the world swarms with individuals."[50] Whitehead, for his part, says much the same thing: "The ultimate metaphysical truth is atomism. The creatures are atomic" (*PR*, 36). If we are to account for this irreducible "plurality of actual entities" (*PR*, 18), and if we are to take seriously Coleman's demand that actually existing things (from neutrinos through houses and trees and on to galaxies) be understood intrinsically, as "real loci of causal power," then the crucial ontological question is the following: how we are to identify these individuals, or ultimate relata? In just what does a thing's intrinsic nature consist?

The answer, I think, can only be that all entities have insides as well as outsides, or first-person experiences as well as observable third-person properties. A thing's external qualities are objectively describable; but its interiority is neither a something nor a nothing, as Whitehead puts it:

> In the analysis of actuality the antithesis between publicity and privacy obtrudes itself at every stage. There are elements only to be understood by reference to what is beyond the fact in question; and there are elements expressive of the immediate, private, personal, individuality of the fact in question. The former elements express the publicity of the world; the latter elements express the privacy of the individual. (*PR*, 289)

Everything in the universe is both public and private. A neutrino is extremely difficult to detect: it is only affected by the weak nuclear force, and even then, its presence can only be inferred indirectly, through the evidence of its rare interactions with atomic nuclei. Nonetheless, this is enough to define the neutrino as an interactional and relational entity, or what Whitehead calls "a public datum" (*PR*, 290). The neutrino cannot exist in the first place, apart from the fluctuations of the quantum fields within which it is so elusively active. At the same time, we must also conceive the privacy of the neutrino, its status as an "unobservable entity" with its own intrinsic experiencings, strange as that might seem. For it is indeed "like something" to be a neutrino.

Now, Graham Harman claims that all objects are "withdrawn" from access. As far as I can tell, this withdrawal is nothing more (but nothing less) than the "what-is-it-likeness," or private interior, of a thing that is *also* outwardly public and available. My problem with Harman is that he seems to me to underestimate this latter aspect. "Things exist not in relation," Harman writes, "but in a strange sort of vacuum from which they only partly emerge into relation."[51] This necessarily follows, he argues, from the fact that an object can never be equated with, or reduced to, our knowledge of it:

> Let's imagine that we were able to gain exhaustive knowl-
> edge of all properties of a tree (which I hold to be impos-
> sible, but never mind that for the moment). It should go
> without saying that even such knowledge *would not itself be
> a tree.* Our knowledge would not grow roots or bear fruit or
> shed leaves, at least not in a literal sense.[52]

The example is a good one, and Harman indeed scores a point here against the exclusively "structural realism" of Ladyman and Ross. But what leads Harman to assume that one entity's *relation* with another entity is constituted and defined by the *knowledge* that the first entity has of the second entity? Such an approach reduces ontology to epistemology. In fact, knowledge is just one particular sort of relation—and not even an especially important one, at that. Most of the time, entities affect other entities blindly, without knowledge playing a part at all.

To cite one of Harman's own favorite examples: when fire burns cotton, it only encounters a few of the properties of the cotton. In the course of the conflagration, "these objects do not fully touch one another, since both harbor additional secrets inaccessible to the other, as when the faint aroma of the cotton and the foreboding sparkle of the fire remain deaf to one another's songs."[53] That is to say, the cotton has many qualities—like its texture, its aroma, and its color—that the fire never comes to "know." Harman therefore concludes that "one object never affects another directly, since the fire and the cotton both fail to exhaust one another's reality"; or again, "fire does not exhaust the reality of cotton by burning it."[54]

Now, I cannot disagree with the *epistemological* argument that Harman is making here. I find it legitimate for him to describe the interaction of fire with cotton in the same way as he does the interaction of a human mind with either the fire or the cotton; and I agree with him that neither the mind nor the fire apprehends, or "knows," *all* of the qualities of the cotton. And yet, that is not the entire story. For there is a level of being beyond (or beneath) the epistemological one. As the cotton is burned, even those of its properties to which the fire is wholly insensitive are themselves also altered or destroyed. That is to say, fire affects even those aspects of the cotton that it cannot come to "know." And such is the case with all interactions between entities, when one thing affects, or is affected by, another. So, while I agree with Harman that the encounter between fire and cotton does indeed involve a sort of limited knowledge, I do not think that this dimension of the encounter is in any sense definitive.

Whitehead reminds us that the inner and outer, or private and public, aspects of an entity always go together. "There are no concrete facts which are merely public, or merely private. The distinction between publicity and privacy is a distinction of reason, and is not a distinction between mutually exclusive concrete facts" (*PR*, 290). Whitehead also makes this "distinction of reason" between public and private in temporal terms. Each actual occasion occupies a particular position within the flow of time; for it is causally dependent upon the other occasions in its light cone that have preceded it. However, "contemporary events . . . happen in causal independence of each other. . . . The vast causal independence of contemporary occasions is the preservative of the elbow-room within the Universe. It provides each actuality with a welcome environment for irresponsibility" (*AI*, 195). In the thick duration of its coming-to-pass, each actual entity enjoys the freedom of its own inner experience. It *feels,* in a way that is scarcely expressible. The "withdrawal" of objects can have no other meaning. At the same time, each actual entity is open to causal influences: it has been shaped by the influence of other entities that preceded it, and it will itself go on to exert causal influence upon other entities that succeed it. In this way, grounded in the past and reaching toward the future, every actual entity has an immense capacity to affect and to be affected: this is what defines its outward, public aspect.

In this sense, relationalism is true. No entity is fully determined, or entirely defined, by its relations; "there is nothing in the real world which is merely an inert fact" (*PR*, 310). But it is equally the case that no entity is altogether free from the web of influences and affections, extending thorough time, that are its very conditions of existence. "All origination is private. But what has been thus originated, publically pervades the world" (*PR*, 310). This is a situation that can be read in both directions. As the Stoics observed so long ago, I am inwardly free and outwardly in chains. But it is equally accurate for me to say that I am inwardly isolated and imprisoned, while outwardly I am able to make affiliations and pursue enlivening relations. Panpsychism is the recognition that this duality of privacy and relationality is not just a human predicament, but the condition of all entities in the universe.

As a coda, I quickly outline some consequences of what I have said.

- Evidently, I have no *proof* of the inner life of a neutrino. But strictly speaking, I also have no proof of the inner life of a bat or a cat, or indeed of another human being. This absence of proof is unavoidable, given the spectral nature of inner, private experience. But because I nevertheless do acknowledge and respect the inner lives and values of other human beings, I can potentially do the same with other entities of all sorts. What's needed, perhaps, is an extension of sympathy.
- Panpsychism allows us to overcome "the correlation of thinking and being" without the necessity of eliminating the former. We step outside the correlationist circle when we acknowledge both that other entities think and that their thinking is, even in principle, inaccessible to us.
- My own panpsychist position is in fact quite close to Harman's by virtue of being its symmetrical inverse. Harman argues that things think when they interact, or enter into

relations, with other things; he rejects universal panpsychism because he argues that entities are "dormant" and unthinking whenever they are entirely withdrawn and free of all relations. Although (unlike Harman) I do not believe that absolute non-relationality is possible, the real difference between us is that I attribute mentality precisely to the "withdrawn" or entirely private aspect of entities rather than to their public, relational side.

- Experience, or mentality, or spectral interiority is always a matter of what Whitehead calls "feeling" before it is a matter of cognition.

- Sentience is a more basic category than life or vitality. Life is possible *because* there is already sentience, rather than the reverse. (A difference between Whitehead and Deleuze, as noted by Brassier.)[55]

Notes

1. Rudy Rucker, "Panpsychism Proved," in *Futures from Nature,* ed. Henry Gee (New York: Macmillan, 2007), 250.

2. David Skrbina, *Panpsychism in the West* (Cambridge, Mass.: MIT Press, 2005).

3. Thomas Nagel, *Mortal Questions,* Canto ed. (Cambridge: Cambridge University Press, 1991; first published 1979), 181. Citations are to the 1991 edition.

4. Rudy Rucker, "Mind Is a Universally Distributed Quality," *Edge,* www.edge.org/q2006/q06_3.html#rucker.

5. Colin McGinn, "Hard Questions: Comments on Galen Strawson," in *Consciousness and Its Place in Nature: Does Physicalism Entail Panpsychism?,* ed. Anthony Freeman (Exeter, U.K.: Imprint Academic, 2006), 93.

6. Galen Strawson, "Realistic Monism: Why Physicalism Entails Panpsychism," in *Consciousness and Its Place in Nature,* 25.

7. See Anthony Freeman, ed., *Consciousness and Its Place in Nature*; David Skrbina, *Mind That Abides: Panpsychism in the New Millennium* (Amsterdam: John Benjamins, 2009); and Michael Blamauer, ed., *The Mental as Fundamental: New Perspectives on Panpsychism* (Piscataway, N.J.: Transaction Books/Rutgers University, 2012).

8. Robert Brandom, *Reason in Philosophy: Animating Ideas* (Cambridge, Mass.: Belknap Press of Harvard University Press, 2009), 148. See also Jon Cogburn, "Brandom on (Sentient) Categorizers versus (Sapient)

Inferers," *Jon Cogburn's Blog*, March 6, 2010, http://drjon.typepad.com/ jon_cogburns_blog/; and Pete Wolfendale, "Brandom on Ethics," *Deontologistics: Researching the Demands of Thought* blog, February 27, 2010, http://deontologistics.wordpress.com/.

9. Pete Wolfendale, "Not So Humble Pie," *Deontologistics*, http://deontologistics.files.wordpress.com/2012/04/wolfendale-nyt.pdf.

10. Anthony Trewavas and František Baluška, "The Ubiquity of Consciousness," *EMBO Reports* 12, no. 12 (November 18, 2011): 1221–25. See also Steven Shaviro, ed., *Cognition and Decision in Nonhuman Biological Organisms* (Ann Arbor, Mich.: Open Humanities Press, 2011).

11. Alfred North Whitehead, *Adventures of Ideas* (New York: Free Press, 1967; first published 1933), 132. Citations are to the 1967 edition and are hereafter indicated parenthetically in the text as *AI*.

12. Alfred North Whitehead, *Process and Reality* (New York: Free Press, 1978; first published 1929), 15. Citations are to the 1978 edition and are hereafter indicated parenthetically in the text as *PR*.

13. Graham Harmon, *Prince of Networks: Bruno Latour and Metaphysics* (Melbourne: re.press, 2009), 152–53.

14. Levi Bryant, *The Democracy of Objects* (Ann Arbor, Mich.: Open Humanities Press, 2011), 143.

15. Ibid., 141.

16. Gilbert Simondon, *L'individuation à la lumière des notions de forme et d'information* (Grenoble: Éditions Jérôme Million, 2005); and Charles Olson, "The Kingfishers," in *The Collected Poems of Charles Olson: Excluding the Maximus Poems*, ed. George Butterick (Berkeley: University of California Press, 1987), 86.

17. Alfred North Whitehead, *Modes of Thought* (New York: Macmillan, 1938), 109, 111. Hereafter indicated parenthetically in the text as *MT*.

18. Ludwig Wittgenstein, *Tractatus Logico-Philosophicus*, trans. D. F. Pears and B. F. McGuinness (London: Routledge and Keegan Paul (RKP), 1961; first published 1922), sec. 6.41. Citations are to the 1961 edition and appear hereafter parenthetically in the text.

19. Alfred North Whitehead, *Science and the Modern World* (New York: Free Press, 1967; first published 1925), 90. Citations are to the 1967 edition.

20. Quentin Meillassoux, *After Finitude: An Essay on the Necessity of Contingency*, trans. Ray Brassier (London: Continuum, 2008); and Ray Brassier, *Nihil Unbound: Enlightenment and Extinction* (New York: Palgrave Macmillan, 2009).

21. Meillassoux, *After Finitude*, 5.

22. Thomas Nagel, *Mortal Questions*, Canto ed. (Cambridge: Cambridge University Press, 1991; originally published 1979), 166, 170. Cita-

tions are to the 1991 edition. "What Is It Like to Be a Bat?" originally appeared in *Philosophical Review* 83, no. 4 (October 1974): 435–50.

23. Harman, *Prince of Networks*, 225.

24. Ian Bogost, *Alien Phenomenology, or What It's Like to Be a Thing* (Minneapolis: University of Minnesota Press, 2012).

25. Nagel, *Mortal Questions*, 191.

26. Ludwig Wittgenstein, *Philosophical Investigations*, trans. G. E. M. Anscombe (New York: Macmillan, 1953), #298. Hereafter cited as *PI* in parenthetical citations in the text.

27. Daniel Dennett, "Quining Qualia," in *Consciousness in Modern Science*, ed. A. Marcel and E. Bisiach (Oxford: Oxford University Press, 1988), http://ase.tufts.edu/cogstud/papers/quinqual.htm.

28. Nagel, *Mortal Questions*, 191.

29. Ibid., 191–92.

30. Here I am drawing on—and expressing disagreement with—Pete Wolfendale, "Phenomenology, Discourse, and Their Objects," *Deontologistics*, December 20, 2009, http://deontologistics.wordpress.com/.

31. David Chalmers, "Facing Up to the Problem of Consciousness," *Journal of Consciousness Studies* 2, no. 3 (1995): 200–219, http://consc.net/papers/facing.html; and David Chalmers, *The Conscious Mind: In Search of a Fundamental Theory* (New York: Oxford University Press, 1996).

32. Strawson, "Realistic Monism," 3, 4, 7.

33. Ibid., 4, 11.

34. See Karen Barad, *Meeting the Universe Halfway: Quantum Physics and the Entanglement of Matter and Meaning* (Durham, N.C.: Duke University Press, 2007); Jane Bennett, *Vibrant Matter: A Political Ecology of Things* (Durham, N.C.: Duke University Press, 2010); and Manuel De Landa, *Intensive Science and Virtual Philosophy* (London: Continuum, 2002).

35. Strawson, "Realistic Monism," 13–14.

36. Ibid., 20.

37. Ibid., 18. Sam Coleman, "Being Realistic: Why Physicalism May Entail Panexperientialism," in *Consciousness and Its Place in Nature*, 40.

38. Strawson, "Realistic Monism," 18.

39. Meillassoux, *After Finitude*, 65, 71.

40. Graham Harman, *Quentin Meillassoux: Philosophy in the Making* (Edinburgh: Edinburgh University Press, 2011), 182–87.

41. Ibid., 179.

42. Strawson, "Realistic Monism," 25.

43. Sam Coleman, "Mind under Matter," in *Mind That Abides*, 97.

44. Coleman, "Being Realistic," 52.

45. Ibid.

46. James Ladyman and Don Ross, with David Spurrett and John Gordon Collier, *Every Thing Must Go: Metaphysics Naturalized* (Oxford: Oxford University Press, 2007), 130, 92, 10.

47. Graham Harman, "I Am Also of the Opinion That Materialism Must Be Destroyed," *Environment and Planning D: Society and Space* 28, no. 5 (2010): 772–90.

48. William Seager, "The 'Intrinsic Nature' Argument for Panpsychism," in *Consciousness and Its Place in Nature*, 135.

49. Ibid., 140. Harman, "I Am Also of the Opinion," 786.

50. Harman, "I Am Also of the Opinion," 788.

51. Harman, *Prince of Networks*, 132.

52. Harman, "I Am Also of the Opinion," 788.

53. Graham Harman, *Guerrilla Metaphysics: Phenomenology and the Carpentry of Things* (Chicago: Open Court, 2005), 170.

54. Ibid., 188. Harman, *Prince of Networks*, 143.

55. See Ted Chiang, *The Lifecycle of Software Objects* (Burton, Mich.: Subterranean Press, 2010).

3

Artfulness

ERIN MANNING

Thanks to art, instead of seeing a single world, our own, we see it multiply. . . .
—Gilles Deleuze, *Proust and Signs*

Part 1. The Art of Time

The word *art* in German *(die Art)* continues today to carry one of the earliest meanings of the term: "manner" or "mode." In the early thirteenth century, art was still connected to this qualifying notion, attuned less to an object than to a skill or craft of learning.[1] A way of learning. To speak of a "way" is to dwell on the process itself, on its manner of becoming. It is to emphasize that art is before all else a quality, a difference in kind, a technique, that maps the way toward a certain attunement of world and expression.

Art, understood along these terms, is not yet about an object, about a form, or a content. It is still on its way, in its manner of becoming. It is intuition, in the Bergsonian sense. As Henri Bergson defines it, intuition is the art—the manner—in which the very conditions of experience are felt. Beyond the state (and the status quo), across the force of the actual, intuition touches on the decisive turn within experience in the making that activates a difference within time's durational folds: intuition activates the proposition at the heart of the as yet unthought.

In its feeling-forth of future potential, intuition draws on time. It touches the sensitive nerve of time. Yet intuition is not duration per se. "Intuition is rather the movement by which we emerge from our own duration, by which we make use of our own duration to affirm and immediately to recognize the existence of other durations."[2] Intuition is the relational movement through which the present begins to coexist with its futurity, with the quality or manner of the not-yet that lurks at the edges of actual experience.[3] This is art: the intuitive potential to activate the future, to make the middling of experience felt where futurity and presentness coincide, to invoke the memory not of what was, but of what will be. Art, the memory of the future.

Duration is lived only at its edges, in its commingling with actual experience. In the time of the event, what is known is the mobility of experience, experience in the making. To actually measure the time of the event, a backgridding activity is necessary. This activity "after the fact" tends to deplete the event-time of its middling, deactivating the relational movement that was precisely event-time's force. Backgridded, experience is reconceived in its poorest state: out of movement.

Out of movement is out of act. For Alfred North Whitehead, all experience is in-act, variously commingling with the limits of the not-yet and the will-have-been. Experience is (in) movement. Anything that stands still—an object, a form, a being—is an abstraction (in the most commonsense notion of the term) from experience. It is not the image of the past (for the past cannot be differentiated from the in-act of the future-presenting), but a cutout from a durational field already elsewhere. "Object and objective denote not only what is divided, but what, in dividing, does not change in kind."[4]

Everything changes in kind. This is the paradox: for there to be a theory of the "object," the "object" has to be conceived as out of time, relegated beyond experience. For in experience, what we call an object is always, to some degree, not-yet, in process, in movement. We know it not in its fullness, in its ultimate form, but as an edging into experience. What resolves in experience is not, as Whitehead would argue, first and foremost a chair, but the activity of "sitability." It is only after the fact, after the initial entrainment the chair activates, that the movement into the relational field of sitability, that the chair as such is ascertained, felt in all its "object-like" intensity. But even here, Whitehead would argue, what stands out is not its three-dimensional form, but its quality of form-taking. Form is held in abeyance. "Chair" is not an object so much as a feeling.

To hold in abeyance does not mean that the form is contained in an unreachable elsewhere. The object is this abeyance—the not-quite-form that cannot be separated out from the milieu, from the field that it coactivates. Whether sitability or the plushness of comfort, the experience of chair is never a finite one, and it is never contained by the dimensions of the object (or the subject) itself.

The art of time makes this more-than of the object felt, and it does so by activating the differential of time in the making, the difference between what was and what will be. For all actualization is in fact differentiation. The in-act is the dephasing of the process toward the coming into itself of an occasion of experience. In this dephasing, the differences in kind between the not-yet and the will-have-been are felt, but only at the edges of experience. They are felt in the moving, activating the more-than.

To feel in the moving, to activate the more-than that coincides both with object likeness and relational fielding, is to experience the nonlinearity of time where nothing is: everything acts. There is no succession in the metric sense. To act is to activate as much as to actualize, to make felt the schism between the virtual folds of duration and the actual openings of the now in its quality of passage. On its way.

The emphasis on the ontogenesis of time is important: the quality of the way depends on there not being a notion of time or space that preexists the event of expression that art creates. This is not to deny the past, but to say instead that what exists in experience is not a linear timeline but "various levels of contraction."[5] The manner of existence is how it contracts, dilates, expands.

The manner of experience is its quality, and outside of this quality there is nothing. The "objective" does not preexist it, and does not justify it. Quality is how the world comes to expression, how it is felt, how it is lived, and how it does its living. How the quality quantifies is analogous to the question of how time is counted: it does so after the fact, abstracted from the force of movement-moving.

The quality, the manner, the art of time is, as I suggested above, intuition. *Intuition* is a good term here because it reminds us that experience demands a taking, a making of time. It insists: Take time before stopping at the object, before defining art as genre, as historical marker, as form or content.

The art of time is not about definitions so much as about

sensations, about the affective force of the making of time where "we are no longer beings but vibrations, effects of resonance, 'tonalities' of different amplitudes."[6] Nor is the art of time about economy, about marking the worthiness of a given experience, the usefulness of time spent. "We must become capable of thinking . . . change without anything changing."[7] Duration as time felt in the beyond of apparent change, independently of any notion of linear succession.

Intuition never stems from what is already conceived. It introduces into experience a rift in knowing, a schism in perception. It forces experience to the limits not only of what it can imagine, but what it has technically achieved. For intuition is never separate from technique. It is a rigorous process that consists in pushing technique to its limit, revealing its technicity—the very outdoing of technique that makes the more-than of experience felt. Bergson calls it a long encounter, a mode of work, that has nothing to do with synthesis or recognition.

Intuitively, a memory of the future is crafted, a memory for the future. A memory of the future is the direct experience of time's differential. "It is a question here of something which has been present, that has been felt, but that has not been acted."[8] A memory not only of and for the human: a memory active in duration itself, a memory inseparable from duration's movement, a movement always relational. Not only of and for the human because duration is not for the human—"Duration does not attach itself to being—or to beings—it coincides with pure becoming."[9]

A memory for the future activates the smallest vibrational intervals—human and nonhuman—that lurk at the interstices of experience. It intuits them, activating their force of becoming such that their movements begin to make a difference. This is intuition: the captivation of the welling forces that activate the dephasing of experience into its more-than. A memory of the future because this more-than cannot quite be captured, cannot be held within the matrix of representation. It is an attunement, an affective tonality, a sensation of what has already come to be. Déjà-felt.

Bergson calls the mechanism by which this future-feeling arises "sympathy." Sympathy not "of" the human but "with" experience in the making. "We call intuition that sympathy by which we are transported to the interior of an object to coincide with what it has that is unique and, consequently, inexpressible."[10] Sympathy as the motor of excavation that allows the movement to be felt, that opens experience to the complexities of its own unfolding.

What is intuited is not matter per se: "There is therefore no intuition of matter, of life, of society *in and of themselves,* that is, as nouns."[11] There is intuition of forces, of qualities that escape the superficial interrogation of that which has already taken its place. Intuition is always and only compelled by what is on its way.

Deleuze might speak of intuitions or the art of time as essence. In his early work on Proust, Deleuze speaks of essence as the force of the as-yet-unfelt in experience. Essence is here everything it usually isn't: it is not truth, or origin. Essence is the ultimate difference in kind. Linked to art, essence for Deleuze speaks of the unquantifiable in experience, of that which exceeds the equivalence between sign and sense. "At the deepest level, the essential is in the signs of art."[12] The signs of art do not convey meaning, they make felt its ineffability.

The essential, the sign that does not have sense so much as it creates, or undoes sense, is a species of time, a durational fold in experience. This quality of time—the art of time—is not abstracted from its coming-into-formation. The field it creates is analogous to its time, a time not of change or succession—a time of difference in itself. Time—as Deleuze says, *le temps*—is plural.

A plurality of time in time multiplies experience in the now. This, Deleuze suggests, is what art can do. Art not as the form an object takes, but as the manner in which time is composed. A composition that has effects, for it activates the difference at the heart of being: what is activated here is not a subject or an object, but a field of expression through which a different quality of experience is crafted. What art can do is to bypass the object as such and make felt instead the dissonance, the dephasing, the complementarity of the between, of what Deleuze calls the "revelatory" or refracting milieu.[13] The refraction produces not a third object but a quality of experience that touches the edgings into form of the material's intuition. Matter intuits its relational movement, activating from within its qualitative resonance an event that makes time for that which cannot quite be seen but is felt in all its uncanny difference.

Tuning into the art of time involves work. It requires an atten-tiveness to the field in its formation. "An artist 'ages' when 'by ex-haustion of his brain' he decides it is simpler to find directly in life, as though ready-made, what he can express only in his work, what he should have distinguished and repeated by means of his work." The mechanical cannot be confused with the art of time, for the mechanical repeats what has already come to pass, playing the tune of Friedrich Nietzsche's last men, the men who dwell in the swamp of time past. Intuition, in its amplification of the technicity of a process, in its capacity to think the more-than in a memory of the future, forecasts what Deleuze calls "an original time" that "surmounts its series and its dimensions," a "complicated time" "deployed and developed," a time devoid of preconceptions, of di-rections, a time that makes its own way.[14]

The art of time makes apparent the complexity of relation, re-lation as the field in which creativity dwells, creativity in the name of potential, of the more-than. For relation is not solely between-two. Relation is the force that makes felt the how of time as it co-composes with experience in the making. It is out of relation that the solitary is crafted, not the other way around: relation is what an object, a subject is made of.

This is what David Lapoujade means when he writes that "at the heart of the human there is nothing human." The world is made of relation activated by intuition, felt sympathetically on the edges of experience, touching its nonhuman tendencies. "We must move beyond the limits of human experience, sometimes inferior, some-times superior, to attain the pure material plane, the vital, social, personal, spiritual planes across which the human is composed."[15] What is at stake in the intuiting of the more-than that art requires is not the requalification of subject and object, artist and work, but the shedding of all that preexists the occasion in which the event takes place. Only this, Lapoujade suggests, makes the unrealizable realizable.

For we must be clear: the memory of the future, the art of time—these are not quantifiable measures. These are speculative propositions, forces within the conceptual web that lurks on the edges of the thinkable. They rejoin Michael Taussig's provocative suggestion that we ask unanswerable, impossible questions such as "What color is the sacred?" that we engage in a sayability that exceeds the known and the knowable.[16]

The art of time is the proposition art can make to a world in continual composition. Instead of immediately turning to form for its resolution, it can ask how the techniques of relation become a conduit for a relational movement that exceeds the very form-taking art so often strives toward. Instead of stalling at the object, it can explore how the forces of the not-yet co-compose with the milieu of which they are an incipient mode. It can inquire into the collective force that emerges from this co-composition. It can develop techniques for intuiting how art becomes the basis for creating new manners, new modes of collaboration, human and non-human, material and immaterial. It can touch on the technicity of the more-than of art's object-based propositions. It can ask, as Deleuze does throughout his work, how the collective iteration of a process in the making itself thinks. It can ask what forces it to think, to become. It can inquire into the forces that do violence to the act of making time, and it can create with the unsettling milieu of a time out of joint, intuiting its limits, limits that often have little to do with form. And in so doing, it can create a time for thought "that would lead life to the limit of what it can do" complicating the very concept of life by pushing life "beyond the limits that knowledge fixes for it."[17] Art, then, as a manner, a technique, a way.

This way is relational. It is of the field, in the milieu. Art as the intuitive process for activating the relational composition that is life-living, for creating a memory of the future that evades, that complicates form. The art of time: making felt the rhythm of the differential, the quality of relation. It is not a question of slow time, or quick time, of lingering or speeding. It is a question of moving experience beyond the way it has a habit of taking, of discovering how the edges of life-living commingle with the forces of that which cannot yet be seen, the "polymorphous magical substance that is the act and the art of seeing."[18] The art of time involves taking a risk, no doubt, but risk played out differently, at the level not of identity or being: risk of losing our footing, risk of the world losing its footing, on a ground that moves and keeps moving. Here, where movement always predates form, where expression remains lively at the interstices of the ineffable, the field of relation itself becomes "inventor of new possibilities of life," possibilities of life we can only intuit in the art of time.[19]

Part 2. The Art of Participation

My art practice is directly concerned with the art of time. Over the past decade, this has expressed itself chiefly through an exploration of how to create generative lures toward a participatory process that is capable of crafting emergent collectivities. Following from William Forsythe's notion of the choreographic object,[20] in which I see the object not as a stable form but as a lure or objectile, I have been concerned with what I have called the art of the event or event-time.[21] Both in the SenseLab and through my own artwork,[22] I have been concerned with how to create events that build on conditions that creatively delimit the participatory call even as they keep it open to surprise and invention.[23] I think of delimitation—or what Brian Massumi and I have called "enabling constraints"[24]—at once as a boundary (a structured improvisation) and as a relational platform that works as an invitation to activate the work's outside or openness, openness as an ethos of event-based hospitality rather than as a melting pot of common denominators. As I have suggested in my exploration of choreography as mobile architecture,[25] or with my concept of the dance of attention, it is not about creating an "easy" space, but about crafting an ease of entry into a complex environment itself always under modulation.

At the 2012 Sydney Biennale, I presented an ongoing participatory composition titled *Stitching Time*. It is to this artwork that I now turn my attention, focusing in particular on how the art of time co-composes with the "art" of participation.

Stitching Time is a large-scale installation made up of a textile collection called *Folds to Infinity* (Figure 3.1), which comprises two thousand serged, buttonholed, magneted, and buttoned pieces of fabric. *Folds to Infinity*'s proposition is to create an ethos of collective time that is tuned to foldings that generate both garments and environments.

Stitching Time was conceived as a site-conditioned work that attempted to bring into relational play both the environmental and the clothing-related aspects of the *Folds to Infinity* project. It

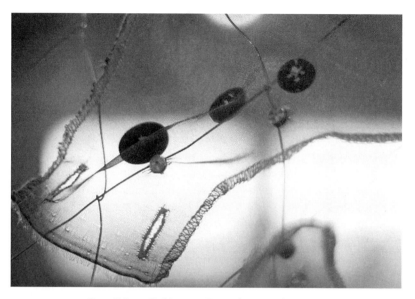

FIGURE 3.1. *Detail from* Folds to Infinity *(2003–13), Erin Manning, at 18th Biennale of Sydney (2012). Photograph courtesy of Leslie Plumb.*

was constructed with a double logic: on the one hand, using half the fabric, we created a sculpture that we hoped would activate the perception of color through light, and on the other, using baskets and other participatory cues, we invited participants to compose garments. The difference from earlier iterations of the work (particularly the series titled *Slow Clothes*) was that the sculpture, which covered almost three thousand square feet, was not malleable or "interactive" in the strict sense of the word. This time, because of the pressure of keeping the exhibition up for three months, the intention was not for the participants to fashion the environment using the sculptural surround, but for them to participate *perceptually* in its co-composition with the movement of light throughout the space. From the open invitation of previous exhibitions where dressing included dressing the environment, we narrowed the hands-on interactivity to only garment-making. But this does not mean that we only considered the hands-on component participatory: the field of light and color occasioned by the sculptural component was conceived as a choreographic object that would allow a movement-based engagement with the changing light qualities of the space.

This sculptural/perceptual experience was facilitated by a complex topology of transparent netting installed by artist and architect Samantha Spurr (Figure 3.2). The role of the netting was to provide a field for movement, both physical and perceptual, for the netting both reflected light and created passages into the color fields: sometimes hung overhead laying bare large areas of open floor space, and sometimes delimiting the space by curving across it and landing, the netting became an arena of complex movement potential from open vistas to curving small enclosures, from areas that invited a lean or a duck to areas that breathed with the height of the twenty-foot ceiling.

With the netting, and with a complex stringing of metal wire to which the fabric was connected magnetically, an experience of seeing-through-light was mapped to the movements of the sun throughout the day—from early morning seeing-through-blue to late afternoon seeing-through-orange-and-red (Figure 3.3). We hoped that, moving across the space's fourteen large windows, light might make color felt such that color itself would become a modality of perception.[26] The hope was to make felt the materiality of perception, creating not only physical opportunities for complex mobility in the space, but also conceptual mobilities, or movements of thought. This was facilitated by there being no single vista: the perceptual field was architected to be as complex as the physical field, proposing a co-composition between perception and displacement. The proposition: to perceive is already to have (been) moved. Through this experience of seeing through light, color could be experienced immersively. This was particularly palpable when the participant looked through fabric sculptures connected to the netting, seeing the vista of saturated color as though submerged underwater.[27]

This co-composition of perception and movement sought to foreground the ethos of time built into the concept of the work. With each of the two thousand pieces cut, sewn, and composed individually (a process that took approximately five hours per piece of fabric), and with many of the pieces sewn over weekly sewing circles around conversation and communal soup, *Stitching Time*

FIGURE 3.2. Stitching Time *(2012), Erin Manning, at 18th Biennale of Sydney (2012). Photograph courtesy of Brian Massumi.*

was before all else an exhibition of time shared and time given. By bringing together a sculptural sense of time with the actual time given by the collaborators in the space to assist with the creation of garments (we were present for the duration of the work, from June to September 2012), the hope was to make felt how participation is always a gift of time, be it hands-on experimentation or the experience of how perceptual shifts are occasioned by time itself.

While composing the space, much attention was given to subtraction. The tendency to fill the space was continuously counteracted by the realization that it was important to allow air and light to move through. Physical openings in the space, created by wafts of transparent fabric or densities of netting, worked to accentuate the potential for movement, both perceptual and physical, inviting the participant to linger, to sidle into or to wander comfortably through a variety of environments of color, some of them easy to reach and others more complex, inciting perhaps a slowing down, a bending or a curving. This invitation to linger was predicated not simply on the slowness of movement, but on its complexity.

FIGURE 3.3. Stitching Time *(2012), Erin Manning, at 18th Biennale of Sydney (2012). Photograph courtesy of Brian Massumi.*

To linger was to move at various speeds and slownesses, in different rhythms, a durational mobility facilitated by the lure of a chromatic arrangement, the color itself composing with the movement of light, from the early morning blues and greens to the warm reflective browns and deep oranges of the morning light, to the yellows and transparent golds of the afternoon light to the reds of sunset.

Although to some this sculptural/perceptual aspect of the work may seem nonparticipatory (which may explain why some participants were drawn to alter the sculptural installation), for me this was an intrinsically relational environment. Like most kinds of art, it was designed to activate a field of relation, inviting the participant to engage with a collective refashioning of space-time. This, an activity that sunsets inspire, as do fall walks in the woods surrounded by the colored leaves, was collective in the sense that movement was activated in an ecology that included but also exceeded me or you, movement—of light, of perception, of sound and smell—always in excess of this or that human body. To engage with a sculpture is not to be within a field of limited activity. It is, at its best, to be moved in a vista where the intensity of engagement cannot be mapped to a single object or body.

During the first month of the exhibition, much of our attention was tuned to keeping the light sculpture in place. We daily wondered whether this gesture should be encouraged, whether we should simply allow the work to fall to the ground and lose its quality of seeing-through-color, and whether it was fetishistic to try to hold to the sculpture that I built so carefully over the period of a month before the Biennale began. How important to the experience might a hands-on engagement with the sculpture prove to be? Was the participant engaging more intensely with *Stitching Time* through the dismantling or rebuilding of the sculpture, or was he or she simply territorializing the field of participation? As time went by, we came to the conclusion that, too often, interaction at this level seemed reduced to a kind of Do It Yourself (DIY) aesthetic without much of a sense of participating in the perceptual composition of the space.

With hundreds of participants in the space daily, this kind of quick interaction with the sculptural component of the work tended to unfold this way: A participant would enter the space and perhaps sense the inherent mobility of the environment (or perhaps have been told that the space was participatory). For the participant who didn't take time to encounter the environment, this perhaps translated to the idea that the space itself could be directly altered. Perhaps *Stitching Time*'s immersive quality signaled an invitation that the sculptural proposition was malleable? Or perhaps the participant tended toward immediate hands-on interactivity because the art event had been mediatized as attractive to families with an emphasis on the "fun" interactive aspect of art and its capacity to "unleash" the "inner artist" in us all?[28] Whatever the reason, this kind of entry into the space was focused on "doing," and this most often with very little attention to the wider ecology of the larger environment. Toni Pape, a collaborator onsite, called this quick interactivity "stillborn" not because it couldn't be interesting to engage this way—some of the earlier iterations of *Folds to Infinity* were conditioned for just this kind of participation—but because this kind of engagement with the environment in this context rarely occurred in a way that complexified either the vista itself or its engagement with color, light, or time. It tended instead to be more goal directed or task oriented, the participant choosing the fabric closest at hand to hang on the installation in the most rudimentary way. A space that took four weeks to compose was altered in seconds. This was rarely done to harm the space per se—it was done more in an ethos of contribution. ("This is what I thought I was meant to do" was a typical statement.) Participants had sensed the environment's mutability of transformation, but instead of responding with a sense of care for the potential of transformation, had immediately put themselves at the center.

This leads to the question of participation itself. Why assume that an environment affectively modulating must be altered in an instrumental way? Why assume that a collaboration must be material, in the sense of altering an existing work?

The issue, it seems to me, is with the concept of attention. Attention, when posited as a purely human quality, makes the human the center of any interaction. Their participation is based on what they see, and how they attend to the work's transformation. What if instead the dance of attention *of the environment itself* were what is at stake? What if instead of immediately wanting to change an environment, participation meant attending to how the space reveals itself (to the way it is composed with light, for instance, or how it attends to movement)? What if "adding" to the work were not measured in instrumental terms and were instead conceived in terms of a collective ethos of attention that included every aspect of the ecology—the work itself, the environment, the artworks surrounding it, the air, the light, the sound, and, in this case, the island, the water, the seagulls? If such a complex ecology were at stake, perhaps participation would mean to attend to the incipient composition already at work instead of bringing to the piece a haphazard addition? For almost without fail, that participant who came in and immediately altered the piece did not stay to reflect on the change, instead quickly leaving the work to move on to the next one.

Paradoxically, perhaps, it seemed that it was the participant who "did" less who participated more thoroughly, the participant who was less quick to "do." To enjoy the processual force of time, it is necessary to take time, and to give time. The participant who senses this will have lingered, less concerned with what the work is "about" than with discovering its resonances. To sense the force of time—the art of time—in any work is to have participated *in its process*, to have felt *what it seeks to give*. For *Stitching Time*, the participant who delved into the art of time was the one with whom we tended, as activators of the work, to share the most unique moments, with whom the conversation unfolded in the most surprising ways. This was the participant with whom the most intricate garments were made. Or with whom no garment was made, and no conversation was had, but whose very presence in the space altered its affective tone in a way that colored the rest of the day.

This story raises all kinds of questions, not least of which is how to refrain from making the participant the holder of the key to the work. In my writing, I have often spoken critically of this tendency of the artist to feel mistreated or misunderstood by the participatory public, and have explored the idea that when the work works it is because it has been able to create the conditions for a kind of participation that outdoes its initial proposition. But as I watched the three thousand–plus people per week move through *Stitching Time*, I wondered about the role of tending in this proposition: How responsible *is* the public for the tending of a work? How responsible are we collectively for the opening of the work to its outdoing? What is our role in the tending of the way of art, in the art of time?

Limits of Existence

As a starting point I think of participation not as something that "happens" to the work (not as something an outside does in response to an already crafted inside) but as that which is stimulated by the work's own dance of attention. The dance of attention, or a work's mobile architecture (or "diagram," in Francis Bacon's terms[29]) is felt when the work becomes capable of attuning to the force of its own potential in a way that exceeds its initial proposition. When the work works (or when it "stands up," as Deleuze and Guattari might say), it creates its own momentum, its own block of sensation, its own field of forces. When this happens, the work becomes *what it does,* and it does so in a continual process of out-doing technique. From the precision of the techniques that create its bedrock, the work evolves into a technicity that unleashes it to a becoming that could not have been mapped in advance. The work comes to life. The art of participation must begin here, it seems to me, where it is no longer a question of subject and object, of artist and participant, but a question of how the work calls forth its own potential evolution.

To explore the art of participation, it is necessary to return to a few key issues raised earlier around the notion of the art of time.

1. What is activated by an artwork is not its objecthood. (An object in itself is not art.) Art is the way, the manner of becoming, that is intensified by the coming-out-of-itself of an object. It is the object's outdoing as form or content.
2. Intuition is the work that sets the process of outdoing on its way.
3. The manner of becoming makes time felt in the complexity of its nonlinear duration. This is an activation of the future—the force of making felt what remains unthinkable (on the edge of feeling).
4. The activation of the manner of becoming is another way of talking about the work's technicity, or its more-than. This more-than is a dephasing of the work from its initial proposition (its material, its conditions of existence).
5. The relational field activated by the work's outdoing of itself touches on an ecology that is more than human. The work participates in a worlding that potentially redefines the limits of existence.

Limits of existence are always under revision, particularly when confronted with a schema that does not place the human at the center of experience. How a constellation evolves—an artwork-human constellation, or an artwork-environment-artwork constellation—always has an effect, and this effect cannot be abstracted from the question of participation. The art of participation therefore takes the notion of modes of existence as its starting point, asking how techniques of encounter modify or modulate how art can make a difference, opening up the existing fields of relation toward new forms of perception, accountability, experience, and collectivity. This aspect of the art of participation cannot be thought separately from the political, despite the fact that its political force is not necessarily in its content. This is not about making the form of art political. It is about asking how the field of relation activated by art can affect the complex ecologies of which it is part.

To address these issues, I return to the question of sympathy as it arises in Bergson's work around intuition.

Sympathy

Sympathy is not the benevolent act that follows the event. Sympathy is neither the result of, nor a response to, an already-determined action. Sympathy is the vector of intuition without which intuition would never be experienced as such. An event is sympathetic to the force of its intuition such that it opens itself to its technicity. Sympathy is how the event expresses this outdoing. The event has sympathy for its creativity, its capacity to express the novelty (the inexpressibility) intuition has inspired. To repeat, "we call intuition that sympathy by which we are transported to the interior of an object to coincide with what it has that is unique, and, consequently, inexpressible."[30]

As Lapoujade emphasizes, it is impossible to think intuition and sympathy as wholly separate from one another, but neither should we consider them as the same gesture. Intuition touches on the differential of a process, and sympathy holds the contrasts in the differential together to express the ineffable. Sympathy is the gesture of making this ineffability felt, allowing for the expression of a certain encounter already held in germ. Where intuition is the force of expression or prearticulation of an event's welling into itself, sympathy is the way of its articulation.

Sympathy is a strange term for this process, so connected is it with the sense of applying a value judgment on a preexisting process. It may therefore not hold the power as a concept to make felt the force of what it does, or can do. I use it here as an ally to concepts such as concern and self-enjoyment in Whitehead, concepts that remind us that the event has a concern for its own evolution, and that this concern, the event's affective tonality, the how of its coming-to-be, is central to any understanding of a more-than-human framework. To make sympathy the driver of expression *in the event* is to bring care into the framework of an event's concrescence, to foreground how intuition is a relational act that plays itself out in an ecology that cannot be abstracted from it. Intuition leads to sympathy—sympathy for the event in its unfolding. Without sympathy for the unfolding, the event cannot make felt the complexity of durations of which it is composed. For this is what sympathy is—a tending to the complexity of an intuition that lurks at the very edge of thought where the rhythms that populate the event have not yet moved into their constellatory potential.

Outdoing is another complex notion. What is a work in its outdoing, and why is it important for an event to be sympathetic to its outdoing? A work outdoes itself when it begins to participate with its conditions for emergence in a way that exceeds expectations, becoming a work in motion. This mobility is not necessarily spatial in an extensive sense—it is a mobility of thought, of perception, of feeling. For an event to have sympathy with its outdoing means that it is capable of being sensitive to the absolute or immanent mobility of a process—to what may be imperceptible as such but is immediately felt. Sympathy understood this way is neither comforting nor easy. A work may undermine expectation, may push boundaries, may dispel intensity or activate havoc. In the case of *Stitching Time,* there has certainly been this sense of an unleashing of the unexpected, resulting in many momentary desires to bring it back to the individual, to capture the event as though it were outside, to hold it to expectation, to harness its potential. Ultimately this desire to hold back will always fail, however, *for the event is the how of its unfolding,* and this how includes all participatory aspects in its relational movement. What is at stake therefore is never how to capture it to stop its flow but how to "allow the passage to the 'interior' of realities, to seize them from 'inside.'"[31] Sympathy: to outdo the inside, making apparent how the folds hold the germs of intuition.

The Way of Art

If the art of time is inextricably linked to art as way, as path, then *art* and *intuition* must always be seen as synonyms, for intuition is the fold in experience that allows for the staging of a problem that starts a process on its way, or curbs a process into its difference.

This raises the question of where intuition is situated when art lingers on the side of participation. Is participation also intuitive? I would say that where art is mobilized through an intuitive process that crafts and vectorizes the problem that will continue to activate it throughout its life, participation is the sympathy for this process. Participation is the yield in what Raymond Ruyer calls the "aesthetic yield." It is the yield both in the sense that it gives a sense of direction to a process already underway and that it opens that process to the more-than of its form or content. Aesthetic yield expands beyond any object occasioned by the process to include the vista of expression generated by art as event. This I call artfulness. Artfulness, the aesthetic yield, is about how a set of conditions coalesce to favor what Lapoujade calls a "seizing of the inside" that generates the field of expression we call participation. The art of participation is its capacity to activate the artfulness at the heart of an event, to tap into its yield. Artfulness as the force of a becoming that is singularly attendant to an ecology in the making, an ecology that can never be subsumed to the artist or to the individual participant. Artfulness: the momentary capture of an aesthetic yield in an evolving ecology.

All ecologies are more than human. They are as much the breath of a movement as they are the flicker of a light and the sound of a stilling. They are earth and texture, air and wind, color and saturation. In the context of an artwork, artfulness is how the complex relation between intuition and sympathy comes into contact with a worlding that itself expresses the more-than of an ecology in the making. This is not quickly or easily done: Bergson speaks of intuition in terms of the necessity of a long camaraderie engendered by a relationship of trust that leads toward an engagement with that which goes beyond premature observations and preconceived neutralizing facts.[32] Intuition is a rigorous process that agitates at the very limits of an encounter with the as yet unthought. Artfulness is the sympathetic expression of this encounter.

Tapping into the differential, artfulness opens the world to the novelty Whitehead foregrounds—a novelty that is not about the capitalist sense of the new, but about the force of mixtures that produce new openings, new vistas, new complexions for experience in the making. This is artfulness: the world's capacity to make felt the force of a welling ecology. This welling ecology is not a general fact—it is an intensive singularity, an opening onto an outside that affects each aspect of experience but cannot be captured as such. A fleeting sensation of the potential for the world to differ from itself. A captive attention to an intuition that for each occasion there remains an opening to the unsayable, the unthinkable. And a sympathy for the force of this unthinkability.

Artfulness does not belong to the artist, or to art as a discipline. Not every event is artistic, but many events are artful. The distinction made here returns us to the question of the yield and forces us to ask how intuition and sympathy coincide in the everyday. Whether in the artistic process or in the everyday, when there is artfulness it is because conditions have been created that enable not only the art of time, but also the art of participation. For it is only when there is sympathy for the complexity of the problem opened up through intuition that an event can yield to its more-than. When this happens, a shift is felt toward a sense of immanent movement—and the way at the heart of art is felt. It is not the object that stands out here, not the tree or the sunset or a painting. It is the force of immanent movement the event calls forth that is experienced, a mobility in the making that displaces any notion of subjectivity or objecthood. This does not mean that what is opened up is without a time, a place, a history. Quite the contrary: what emerges at the heart of the artful is always singular—*this* process, *this* ecology, *this* feeling. It's just that its eventness in the now of its immanent mobility in an ecology of practices is as central to it as the complexity and precision of its history.

Artfulness is an immanent directionality, felt when a work does its work, when a process activates its most sensitive fold where it is still rife with intuition. This modality is beyond the human. Certainly, it cuts through, merges with, captures and dances with the human, but it is also and always more than human, active in an ecology of resonances that cannot be mapped strictly onto the human. This is what Bergson means when he speaks of the spirituality of duration—the art process now has its own momentum, its own art of time, and this art of time, excised as it is from the limits of human volition, collaborates to create its own way. The force of art is precisely that it is more than human.

Rhythm is key to this process that flows through different variations of human-centeredness toward ecologies as yet unnamable. Everywhere in the vectorizations of intuition and sympathy are durations as yet unfolded, expressions of time as yet unlived, rhythms still unlivable. This is what makes an event artful—that it remains on the edge, at the outskirts of a process that does not yet recognize itself, inventing as it does its own way, a way of moving, of flowing, of stilling, of lighting, of coloring, of participating. For this is how artfulness is lived—as a field of flows, of differential speeds and slownesses, in discomfort and awe, distraction and attention. Artfulness is not something to be beheld. It is something to move through, to dance with on the edges of perception where to feel, to see, and to be are indistinguishable.

What moves here is not the human per se, but the force of the direction the intuition gave the event in its preliminary unfolding. Techniques are at work, modulating themselves to outdo their boundedness toward a technicity in germ. Thought, intent, organization, consideration, habit, experience—all of these are at work. But with them is the germ of intuition born of a long and patient process now being activated by a sympathy for difference, a sympathy for the event in its uneasy becoming. It is not the human but the art that has become capable of activating or generating an event-time that invents with the forces that exceed our humanness. To touch on the artful is to touch on the incommensurable more-than that is everywhere active in the ecologies that make us and exceed us.

Tweaked toward the artful in the process of making, art becomes a way toward a collective ethos. For the incommensurability it calls forth already holds the collective in germ. From the most apparently stable structure to the most mobile or ephemeral iteration, art that is artful activates the art of participation making felt the transindividual force of an event-time that catapults the human into our difference. This difference, the more-than at our core, the nonhuman share that animates our every cell, becomes attentive to the relational field that opens the work to its intensive outside, its own nonhuman share. This relational field must not be spatially understood. It is an intensive mattering, an absolute moving that inhabits the work durationally. It is the art of time making itself felt.

A fielding of difference has been activated and this must be tended. The art of participation involves creating the conditions for this tending to take place. This tending is first and foremost a tending of the fragile environment of duration generated by the working of the work. A tending of the work's incipient rhythms. I say fragile because there is so much to be felt in the process of a work's coming to resonance with a world itself in formation.

Take the example of a busy day within *Stitching Time*. When we turned our attention to the flows of interactivity within the space in order to better understand how to stop the process of the sculptural disintegration, we found that the movements of participants were contagious. One person playing with the fabric sculpture was an invitation for twenty-five more to begin dismantling it. By attending to the modulation of the field of participation, we also noticed how little it took for the quality of duration to be radically altered in a way that inflected the affective tonality of collective engagement. How to compose with this contagious energy, given that there was also, as mentioned at the beginning, a physically participatory aspect to the piece that involved making garments?

Throughout the installation, twenty-five baskets hung, each of them full with pieces of the larger *Folds to Infinity* collection (Figure 3.4). In the first few days, assuming that activation would be a challenge (based on early experiences where it was quite challenging to convince participants to engage with the fabric), we told all the participants entering the space that they were welcome to take fabric from the baskets to make a garment of their choice. Since to make a garment was a challenging proposition that took time—this despite the many buttonholes, buttons, and magnets in the *Folds to Infinity* collection—we assumed that a minority of people would stay long enough to fashion a garment. The unspoken proposition

FIGURE 3.4. Stitching Time *(2012), Erin Manning, at 18th Biennale of Sydney (2012). Photograph courtesy of Leslie Plumb.*

was that, were they to stay and compose a piece that they liked, the garment would be theirs to take home afterward, moving nodes of time from the installation into the wider world. Our implicit invitation was to assist the few who took up our proposition, and to facilitate their process of making time by offering them tea and conversation.

In the first week, we had many lovely encounters with people who stayed for cups of tea and made beautiful, carefully crafted garments. But it quickly also became apparent that there was a problem with the conditions we were setting for the space. As outlined previously, counter to our expectations, the problem was not with a lack of activation. Not only were people continuously seeking to rebuild the sculptural installation, they were increasingly moving to the baskets in a frenzy that undermined the very process *Stitching Time* was trying to create. Garments were put together hastily only to be left on the floor in a flurry of moving-on. Should we see this as part of the process and try to tune to the experience of taking and making time?

It took a few weeks to work out, but it eventually became clear that the issue was that we ourselves were honing the experience of stitching time to the object itself. Despite our best intentions, we were directing the perceptual and expressive field of the work toward garment-making (via the baskets), thus preempting a more complex durational engagement with the space. In a work that was designed to give time by creating an ethos of shared time, we were facilitating an instrumental approach reminiscent of the very interactive model we were trying to resist.

Of course, as with any environment, there were overlapping ecologies. Even when the space was at its most chaotic, people still wandered the space, engaging it on its more subtle levels, but the waves of frenetic movement were overpowering. Ten or fifteen people would be quietly wandering around, or would be sitting at the long sewing table having a cup of tea when suddenly one group would come in and reach for the baskets. Within minutes the space would be frantic with a wave of "doing" that had much less to do with taking time than it had to do with parents trying to "occupy" or "entertain" their children (make outfits, take photographs, move onto next artwork). The issue was not simply that the participants weren't acting the way I had hoped, but that we hadn't found the best conditions to facilitate a surfacing of experience that could exceed habitual responses. That the kids dressed themselves (or that the parents dressed them) was not the problem. More so was that the parents assumed that the space did not cater to them and treated it instead as a kind of day care or play space, allowing the kids to run around, cut or draw on the fabric, undo the sculpture or pull down the baskets, leaving strewn fabric on the ground in their wake. The space thus despite itself became a passive receptor for modes of engagement that seemed to us less about its own conditions of emergence than conditions rehearsed in other settings.

Habitual responses run deep. This is the force of intuition, that it is capable of building on the habitual to find the nugget of a question that opens a problem to an aspect of itself as yet untouched or unthought. Or that it finds within habitual networks an opening as yet unseen. But intuition is honed, and does not come in a frenzy. Nor does technicity. What comes in a frenzy is the habitual, and with the habitual comes its well-rehearsed techniques. For this is the force of technique, that it builds so well, and so consistently on habit. A large open space inspires running in children. A carpet inspires rolling, or resting, or feeling at home. And fabric inspires touching. All of these tendencies are absolutely necessary to *Stitching Time,* but the hope is for them to be activated in excess of the habitual. What art seeks to do, it seems to me, is modulate the habit. Work with it to tweak it. We want movement, but not simply one velocity (running). We want a sense of feeling at home, but with an ethos of care for the collective environment. We want touching but not simply for taking, for "getting something done"— but also for reaching-toward in an ethos of time shared.

Paradoxically, perhaps what an immersive participatory environment such as *Stitching Time* makes felt is the force of the habitual and its capacity to undermine the art of participation. And if this is the case, it is likely to some extent due to how art events are increasingly formulated for the public. In the case of the Sydney Biennale, this was certainly true, particularly of the works on Cockatoo Island—the "non" museum venue. Here, the exhibition was billed as a "family event" where "kids will be able to discover the artworks and history of the Island through fun, creative activities [giving] children and their families a chance to get creative and unleash their inner artist through hands-on art making activities, as well as participation in family-friendly tours."[33] How could this not activate the very habitual response associated with kid-oriented entertainment venues? The problem is not with entertainment, but with the dispelling of the modulating field of experience art can create. For children are often the most likely among us to touch on the intuitive threads unarticulated in a process. They recognize artfulness, and given the chance, are some of the keenest perceivers of art's differential. The problem is not with them but with the rhetoric, and with the expectation that every event demands the same habitual response.

Often, "fun" is linked to the quick, the easy, the immediate. In the most frenzied moments of *Stitching Time,* I too often heard a parent exclaiming "Isn't this fun!" to a distracted child. Fun is not what art can do, it seems to me. Fun is too easily linked to habit, to an experience that already has its contour and expectation. What art can do is quite different: It demands the invention of a tonality, a feeling-tone that differs from the habitual. Without this, the artful is sidelined. The irony is that children have an instinct for the artful—just watch them engage with the dance of attention of an ants' nest or with the movements of clouds. Among children left to explore the space quietly without the added excitement of "fun," this tendency is clearly apparent. Children who were invited to move slowly and discover the space tended to be some of our most patient visitors, and some of the most creative (Figure 3.5).

These children who took the time to invent were much less quick to make decisions in advance about what the environment offered. It is the rhetoric of fun, not them, that leads toward the simplification of art's process, putting art in the field of entertainment, thereby placing it right back within a capitalist ethos that is much less about taking or giving time than "getting something out of it." There is nothing to be "gotten out of art." It's all in the making, in the giving.

This is not to say that art can't be entertaining. It is to emphasize its nuance. No nuance can be perceived in the frenetic movements of "getting it" or "doing it." Nuance is not felt through rapid consumption (and "fun" is a mode of consumption). Nuance is perceived when the event of time is felt, when the art of time becomes the art of participation. It is perceived when a work resonates beyond the easily recognizable habits it engenders at first glance.

The art of making time, and the art of taking time—both of these are about continual modulation, modulation not simply on the part of the artist, but also on the part of the participants in the ecology the work occasions. Every work is metastable and requires continual tending to recalibrate it within the complex durational fields it calls forth. A painting badly hung within a museum can fall flat, as can a video piece set up in a way that does not facilitate its taking place within the wider constellation of the exhibition. The question of modulation is vital to the art of participation.

This is where the event-space of the art of time begins to compose with the notion of a choreographic object. The choreographic object is a lure for the activation of event-time toward the generation of complex forms of collective engagement. An exhibition choreographed with a sense of collective mobility makes felt the

FIGURE 3.5. Stitching Time *(2012)*, *Erin Manning, at 18th Biennale of Sydney (2012). Photograph courtesy of Leslie Plumb.*

force of time by facilitating intuitive linkages not only between works but within the relational field itself. When this happens, art becomes less an object than a conduit or vector toward a seeing-with, a sympathizing-across, a moving-through. Emphasizing choreography in this way also serves to remind us that there is no event that isn't in some regard about movement, be it a sculpture or a notebook, an immersive installation or a sound piece. The world moves us, and how it moves us matters. For how it moves us makes felt the vector quality of its conditions of entry, makes felt the way it creates and modulates space-times in the making, makes felt the way it activates the differential not only within its own canvas but across works and in the complex ecologies they call forth. Think of moving through an installation. Note how the red of a flower exquisitely cut in wood in one space resonates with the touch of light that surfaces in a video installation in an adjacent space. Note how this quality affects the entry into another environment, and how it tunes to a tonality already at play—a lightness, an airiness. These are sympathetic attunements to a generative environment. They activate its moreness by responding to it. And, by doing so, they make the intuition at the heart of the work palpable not only to themselves, but to the field of relation in its choreographic plenitude: they make felt how the work is capable of fielding the myriad problems that continuously relaunch it.

This is why Bergson speaks of sympathy as that which reveals the nonhuman in us. Sympathy makes felt how the tendency, the way, the direction or incipient mobility, is itself the subject of the work. It makes tending the subject, undermining the notion that either the work or the human come to experience fully-formed. Sympathy: that which brings the force of the more-than to the surface. That which makes felt how the force of experience always exceeds the object.

Vectors

Despite my focus on human participation here, the art of participation does not find its conduit solely in the human. Art also does its work without human intervention, activating fields of relation that are environmental or ecological in scales of intermixings that may include the human but don't depend on it. How to categorize as human or nonhuman the exuberance of an effect of light, the way the air moves through a space, or the way one artwork catches another in its movement of thought. This is surely the force of curation: its choreographic capacity to bring to life the lingering nonhuman tendencies that bridge fields activated by distinct artistic processes.[34] Artfulness is always more than human.

Whitehead's notion of vectors is useful to get a stronger sense of the more than human quality of experience artfulness holds. The vector, in Whitehead's usage, prolongs the use of it in physics as a force of movement that travels from one occasion of experience to another or within a single occasion. What is particular to Whitehead's definition, however, is the way he connects the vector to feeling. "Feelings are 'vectors'; for they feel what is there and transform it into what is here."[35] For Whitehead, feelings are not associated to a preexisting subject. They are the force of the event as it expresses itself. Understood as vectors, feelings have the force of a momentum, an intuition for direction. They are how the event expresses sympathy for its own intuitive becoming.

Whitehead's theory of feeling catapults the notion of human-based participation on its head. *What the feeling has felt* is how the event has come to expression. The subject is its aftermath. Subject here is not limited to the human—it is the marker of that which can be located as the culmination of an occasion of experience. An occasion of experience always holds such a marker—once the occasion has come to concrescence, it will always be what it was. This is what Whitehead calls the "superject," or the subject of experience. Making the subject the outcome of the event rather than its initiator reminds us that the subject of an event includes its vector quality—in Massumi's terms, its thinking-feeling. The subject can never be abstracted or separated out from the vector quality, the "feeling-tone" that co-composed it.

The artful is the event's capacity to foreground the feeling-tone of the occasion such that it generates an affective tonality that permeates more than this singular occasion. For this to happen, there has to be, within the evolution of an occasion, the capacity for the occasion to become a nexus that continues to have an appetite for its process.

This leads us back to contagion. What is complex about contagions is that they are always multiple. A frenetic contagion of garment-making can coexist with the quietness of an experience of red turning to yellow. These are independent events occurring in a wider event-space. They are contemporary but dissociated. And yet, when the conditions allow it, they can share a feeling-tone. This vector that can activate across contemporarily independent occasions fashions a wider tonality that can begin to modulate the time of the event as a whole. Activated by vectors that cross and thus co-compose, the event has created its own mobility, its own ambiance, and in so doing, it has begun to run itself: a mobile architecture. This is a transient quality, of course, continuously cut across by captures that reinstate the necessity of harnessing the now—someone steals buttons, or someone's carelessness threatens to break the tea set. Feeling-tones are not about ease, or about comfort. They are about the force of an individuation that momentarily refuses its own capture.

As feeling-tone, vectors attune to the field of relation in its becoming-event, and tune also to its more-than. This allows a becoming-event to participate in a becoming-society, a becoming of a wider field of relation that outdoes the atomicity of its initial coming into being. As Whitehead underscores, this is a rhythmic (and not a linear) process. It swings from the in-itselfness of a given actual occasion, where what is fashioned is simply what it is, to a wider field where the openness to fashioning remains rife with potential not only in the work at hand but across a wider expanse of artfulness. Nature does this well.

Whitehead talks about this in terms of the creation of worlds—"feeling from a beyond which is determinate and pointing to a beyond which is to be determined."[36] To be determined here is resolutely to be *in potentia*—for how a feeling-tone vectorizes cannot be mapped in advance, and whether it lands in a way that activates a worlding cannot be predicted. But it can be modulated, and this is the art of participation.

Contemplation

A feeling-vector contemplates its passage, attending to the dance of an occasion coming into itself. The occasion cannot be abstracted from its feeling-tone. The contemplation of its becoming cannot be separated out from how it comes into itself.

Placing contemplation, intuition, feeling-tone, and sympathy together, what emerges is an artfulness that refuses to be instrumental. There is no use-value—it does nothing that can be mapped onto a process already underway. It has no endpoint, no preordained limits, no moral codes. But it is conditioned and conditioning.

To say that a process is conditioning is to say that it is born of enabling constraints that facilitate the most propitious engagement with the problem at hand, enabling the passage toward a field that yields. It does its work—it stands up—when this yield was already present in germ in the initial problem that activated the process, in the intuition that tapped into how technique can become technicity. Without conditions, the aesthetic does not yield, and the work cannot become in excess of the techniques that brought it into being.

Conditions facilitate contemplation. Contemplation, understood as the act of lingering-with, of tending-to a process in its outdoing of technique, is not about a doing, but neither is it simply a passive modality. It is active and activating in the sense that it attends. It attends to the conditions of the work. And it attends to the way the work attends to its conditions. Contemplation is passive only in the sense that this attending provokes a waiting, a stilling, a listening, a sympathy-with that exceeds not only the work as it presents itself, but any notion of the subject as preexistent.

Contemplation, like intuition and its counterpart, sympathy, activates the differential of a work. It reveals not how the subject (the artist, the participant) feels about a work, or what a subject sees in the work, but how the field of experience a work creates itself attends to a certain singular mode of attention. Contemplation cannot be separated out from the life of the work.

Contemplation makes the artful felt. Though it may sound spiritual or otherworldly, artfulness is anything but. It is with and in the world, in the uneasy balance between dancing and thinking, leaping and writing Zarathustra strives toward. Here, in the midst of life-living, artfulness reminds us that the "I" is not where life begins, and the "you" is not what makes it art. Made up as it is of a thousand contemplations, it reminds us instead that "we speak of the self only in virtue of these thousands of little witnesses which contemplate within us: it is always a third party who says 'me.'"[37] This is why its occurrence is so rare. For artfulness depends on so many propitious conditions, so many tendings, so many contemplations, so many implicit linkages between intuition and sympathy. And more than all else, it depends on the human getting out of the way of a process underway that exceeds us, allowing art to do the work it can do within an ecology of practices that, while often directed by us, does not find its resting place solely in the world of the human.

It is in this vista of the more-than that we find pockets of artfulness. There is the artfulness of nature, or of the animal.[38] Pockets of artfulness are nodules of time caught in the sound of a bee (Alex Finlay) or in the weight of unspun wool blowing color in the wind (Cecilia Vicuna). They are the ineffable force of an assault both homely and otherworldly occasioned by Ria Verhaege's *Living with Cuddles* (Figure 3.6). They are the wonder of Ed Pien's paperworlds or the sound of the chimes in a roofless building on

FIGURE 3.6. Living with
Cuddles *(2012), Ria Ver-*
haege, at 18th Biennale of
Sydney (2012). Photograph
courtesy of Ria Verhaege.

an island (Tiffany Singh). They are the energy of the line in Emily
Kngwarreye, and the intimate and slow movement of the human
dwarfed by the icebreaker in Guido Van der Werve's *Nummer Acht:*
Everything is going to be alright.

Artfulness: the way the art of time makes itself felt, how it lands,
and how it always exceeds its landing.

Notes

1. Today, the word for *art* in German is *Kunst,* and *die Art* is used only
to convey the sense of manner or way described in the text. In French, English, and most Romance and Indo-Germanic languages, the two meanings have become separated, though the sense of "the art of" still seems
to carry that earlier definition.

2. Gilles Deleuze, *Bergsonism,* trans. Hugh Tomlinson and Barbara
Habberjam (New York: Zone Books, 1991), 33.

3. I have developed relational movement as a concept in both *Politics of Touch: Sense, Movement, Sovereignty* (Minneapolis: University of Minnesota Press, 2007) and *Relationscapes: Movement, Art, Philosophy* (Cambridge, Mass.: MIT Press, 2009).

4. Deleuze, *Bergsonism*, 41.

5. Ibid., 74.

6. David Lapoujade, *Puissances du temps. Versions de Bergson* (Paris: Editions Minuit, 2010), 9. My translations throughout.

7. Ibid., 12.

8. Ibid., 21–22.

9. Ibid., 24.

10. Ibid., 53.

11. Ibid., 56.

12. Gilles Deleuze, *Proust and Signs*, trans. Richard Howard (New York: George Braziller, 1972), 13.

13. Ibid., 47.

14. Ibid., 48, 61.

15. Lapoujade, *Puissances du temps*, 62.

16. Michael Taussig, *What Color Is the Sacred?* (Chicago: University of Chicago Press, 2009).

17. Gilles Deleuze, *Nietzsche and Philosophy*, trans. Hugh Tomlinson (New York: Columbia University Press, 1983), 101.

18. Taussig, *What Color*, 47.

19. Friedrich Nietzsche, *Philosophy in the Tragic Age of the Greeks*, trans. Marianne Cowan, Gateway ed. (Washington, D.C.: Regnery, 1962; repr., 1996), 3.

20. I have explored in detail the concept of the choreographic object both in "Propositions for the Verge: William Forsythe's Choreographic Objects" in *Inflexions* 2 (January 2009), www.inflexions.org, and in *Always More Than One: Individuation's Dance* (Durham, N.C.: Duke University Press, 2012).

21. I discuss event-time in more detail in *Always More Than One.*

22. The SenseLab is conceived as a "laboratory for thought in motion." With the collaboration of local and international philosophers, artists, and community activists, we have organized research-creation events in our Technologies of Lived Abstraction Event Series, which has also spawned a book series at MIT Press by the same name and the journal *Inflexions: A Journal for Research-Creation*, www.inflexions.org.

23. See, for instance, "Fiery, Luminous, Scary" in *Always More Than One*, 124–31. An earlier version of the same text is also available as "Fiery, Luminous, Scary" in *SubStance* 40, no. 3 (2011): 41–48.

24. Brian Massumi and I discuss the concept of enabling constraints

in *Thought in the Act: Passages in the Ecology of Experience* (Minneapolis: University of Minnesota Press, 2014). This is a concept developed with the SenseLab. It has also been explored in the writings of SenseLab members Christoph Brunner and Troy Rhoades.

25. I discuss William Forsythe's *One Flat Thing, reproduced* as an instance of a mobile architecture and explore the possibility of a choreographic object such as *Folds to Infinity* becoming a mobile architecture in "Choreography as Mobile Architecture," *Always More Than One*, 99–123.

26. This effect is facilitated by the more than ninety spotlights in the space that merge with the color, emphasizing the nuances between tone and texture.

27. Samantha Spurr designed the netting to connect to parasitical structures made of metal that enable the hanging of the collection into sculptures. Because *Folds to Infinity* is magnetic, it requires such metallic structures to become sculpture. This parasitical use of the netting creates the impression that the fabric is floating in the air. The sculptures themselves are mostly covered with translucent fabric, which further emphasizes the quality of transparency, or seeing through color into light. Further, the fabric used for these purposes has an iridescent quality composed as it is with threads of contrasting colors—blue turning to purple, green turning to yellow, orange turning to red. This creates a shimmering effect that brings out its complementarity, contrasting it with the more opaque colors—the reds, oranges, and greens of the wider hanging installation. Our hope is that this creates a complexity in the field of color itself, whereby color is perceived less as an object (as a piece of fabric, or as a pigment) that as an effect of light.

28. See, for example, "Biennale of Sydney Caters for Families and Kids," *artshub*, June 18, 2012, www.artshub.com.au/.

29. See Gilles Deleuze, *Francis Bacon: The Logic of Sensation*, trans. Daniel W. Smith (Minneapolis: University of Minnesota Press, 2003).

30. David Lapoujade, "Intuition et Sympathie chez Bergson," *Eidos* 9 (2008): 11. My translations throughout.

31. Ibid., 12.

32. Ibid.

33. "Biennale of Sydney Caters for Families and Kids."

34. The Sydney 2012 Biennale, titled *All Our Relations,* is a good example of this kind of curatorial practice. Catherine de Zegher and Gerald McMaster not only chose artists whose works complement one another, they also installed the exhibition in a way that created implicit connections between works. These connections are not simply content based or form reliant. They are connections at the level of resonance that make felt a field of relation that is itself artful.

35. Alfred North Whitehead, *Process and Reality* (New York: Free Press, 1978).

36. Ibid., 163.

37. Gilles Deleuze, *Difference and Repetition,* trans. Paul Patton (New York: Columbia University Press, 1978), 75.

38. See Brian Massumi, *What Animals Teach Us about Politics* (Durham, N.C.: Duke University Press, 2014).

[4]

The Aesthetics of
Philosophical Carpentry

IAN BOGOST

THIS IS A CHAPTER about the practice of philosophy in the near future, based on a talk about the practice of philosophy in the near future. This is a chapter about the objects out of which philosophy is made as much as the objects of philosophy. Its form matters. It lives here now, in print, where once it did in speech—and in space: Shorewood, Milwaukee—and in time: early May 2012. It was invented for a room and now it finds itself on these pages instead. Some residue of its forcible relocation might be found, as is the case with most things wrest from their dwelling.

I. Enjoying This Chapter

A note on enjoying this chapter: Imagine a plate of artisanal meats and cheeses. Imagine lardo, Sainte-Maure-de-Touraine, cornichons with spicy mustard, Shropshire blue, pickled cauliflower, and house-made blood sausage. The thing that makes them a plate is that they are all on a plate. No one sends an assiette de charcuterie back to the kitchen because it doesn't make an argument.

II. The Things We Do

The tarmac atop airport runways and aprons and taxiways isn't really tar-penetration macadam. Instead of bound coal tar and ironworks slag, these days airports are coated with asphalt or concrete, like cupcakes are frosted with buttercream instead of confectioner's sugar.

It's a misunderstanding your airplane didn't notice when its rubber wheels glanced against the concrete runway of Milwaukee's Mitchell Airport, stretching its surface imperceptibly, like this week's raindrops against the nylon of tents thrown near Pewaukee Lake twenty miles to the west. The flights cleared behind and in front of you were similarly oblivious, no less than the precipitation or the Goodyear Flight Radials.

You weren't listening, either, to the grooved concrete or the raindrops. You were sleeping in your leather seat or your dome tent, dreaming about Kopp's Frozen Custard or reading Alfred North Whitehead or fretting over your presentation for The Nonhuman Turn conference.

A group of philosophers in a lecture hall isn't unlike a convoy of aircraft on approach. One lone Airbus A320 or associate professor performs—nose up, flaps down, throttle up, voice screeching, exhaust droning, before the rubber meets the road. The brakes engage, the show ends. Thank you very much. Meanwhile, onlookers stare agape, ears covered or plugged or otherwise impeded by droning noise pollution. Oh thank god, it's over, they cheer silently before clutching in to proceed through the traffic light on the airport-adjacent frontage road, or while plunging a Moleskine notebook into a Tom Bihn bag.

For some performances, multiple dancers tousle the venue all at once. Close-spaced double, triple, or parallel approach at Chicago O'Hare or Atlanta Hartsfield-Jackson or the Society for Cinema and Media Studies Conference. Increased organizational apparatus is key: instrument landing systems, interstitial coffee break apparatuses, microwave landing systems, multiple lecture rooms, staggered approaches, diagonal radar separation—aircraft and lecture isolation is key. Final monitor controllers are required to ensure that the NTZ (no-transgression zone) is not entered. Overstressed, underpaid air traffic controllers and graduate students ensure order: "Delta two-eight-seven-niner cleared to land runway two-three, traffic landing runway one-zero"; or, "Ah, Professor Bogost, your session is in the Oak Room. It's just around the elevator, past the Gramsci display."

We do the things we do because they are the things we do, so we do them. We do them so as not to disturb the way things are done—traffic landing runway one-zero, after all. It is at least as unlikely that this artifact will become a conversation as it is that it will become an orgy. Presumably I will write—I was brought here to write—and you will read. Had your timing or finances been better, you would have listened, or at least performed a ritual that would have been mistaken for listening (or even for reading). Some, struck by pique, may put it down to shop for a K-Cup for Keurig coffee brewers. Others may hold their heads in their hands lamenting in the guise of concentrating. Let your mind wander.

Eventually, inevitably, soon perhaps, but not soon enough, I will stop. Had we been face to face, live, polite ovation would follow. "We do have some time for questions," someone would have said, perhaps even me. "Isn't this just art?" someone might ask, or "Aren't you committing a fatal Orientalism?" or "Interesting provocation, but I'm not sure I understand what you're suggesting we do" or in any case "Not really a question, more of a comment." Now that you're reading this instead, you can tweet about it instead: "Really unusual book chapter by @ibogost" or even just ".@ibogost is bonkers." Thank you for flying Nonhuman Turn Edited Collection. We know you have a choice when you read. We wish you a pleasant stay in object-oriented ontology or in whatever your final philosophy may be. Then coffee, or wine, or schnitzel, or blogging.

What do we do when we do philosophy? That's not a rhetorical question. I'm serious. Why am I writing at you now, instead of serving you custard? I'm not sure I can fully convey to you the degree to which I am freaked out about what a philosopher could do or ought to do. This is not an act.

III. The Nonhuman Return

Milwaukee is the only town anywhere where someone might recognize my unusual surname, and that's because the Bogost family settled here after emigrating from Russia in the nineteen-aughts, and indeed all the world's Bogosts can be traced back to the city.

My father and his two brothers grew up there during the Great Depression and World War II, attending North Division High

School before shipping off to Madison to study the newly fashionable discipline of psychology and psychiatry in the early 1960s. As my father would say, it takes one to know one.

The Nonhuman Turn was the second scholarly event I attended at the University of Wisconsin-Milwaukee, and the second time I have come to Milwaukee for reasons other than visiting family. The first was hosted by Sandra Braman and Thomas Malaby in late April 2006, conveniently timed such that I was able to attend my grandmother's ninety-fifth birthday party that week as well. For years she lived right up the street from the university in Shorewood, near Oakland and Capitol. There wasn't much to do during those visits. Sometimes we would walk down to Sendik's for oranges or Benji's Deli for corned beef, and if I were very lucky, someone would take me to Walgreens for bubblegum or Garbage Pail Kids. Eventually we would drive up to Sister Bay, where there wasn't much to do either. Oranges would be replaced by cherries, corned beef by smoked whitefish. My grandfather ate the heads off of them.

That trip in 2006 was the last time I saw her, at Jack Pandl's Whitefish Bay Inn, which first opened when she was four years old. My daughter, just barely four herself at the time, panicked as dusk settled into night over North Lake Drive. "I have to go to my hotel!" she panicked, pointing outside desperately. "There are stars!"

I last came almost exactly a year before The Nonhuman Turn conference for my grandmother's funeral—she lived less than a month past her one-hundredth birthday, just long enough so the rest of us could say she did. By happenstance, Hertz rented me a big Buick, as if they knew I would need to camouflage among the elderly.

I'm not close to my extended family, and I'll admit that I was horrified that many of them were staying in the hotel I had chosen solely for Hilton HHonors elite tier status credits. Stuart Moulthrop picked me up and we ate schwinebraten and drank Franziskaner at Mader's downtown. We foolishly overate and had no room for frozen custard, even though Kopp's was right down North Port Washington Road from the Hilton Milwaukee River. A trip to Milwaukee is not complete without somehow failing to make it to Kopp's.

I'm also not very sentimental, but so much of object-oriented ontology is, to me, a reclamation of a sense of wonder often lost in childhood, that coming to Milwaukee as an adult, a professor, perhaps a philosopher even, makes me think of the rhubarb that would grow in the summer behind the house on Marion Street, or the milk delivery door at its rear, or the tea samovar on the shelf in the dining room. It didn't used to be so strange to be interested in things, but somehow it became so. Maybe this nonhuman turn is really a return, for you as much as for me. The things were always here, waiting. The rhubarb doesn't care about actual occasions or Antonio Negri.

IV. Carpentry, Part 1

In my recent book *Alien Phenomenology*, I advance an idea I call *carpentry*. It's a theory of philosophical productivity.

I found myself at the Nonhuman Turn conference performing the very act I critique in that chapter. When philosophers and critics gather together, I wrote in the book, they commit their work to writing, often reading esoteric and inscrutable prose aloud before an audience struggling to follow, heads in hands—that's why you're excused for shopping for coffee pods. Ideas become professionally valid only if written down. And when published, they are printed and bound not *to be read* but merely *to have been written*. Written scholarship is becoming increasingly inaccessible even to scholars, and publication therefore serves as professional endorsement rather than as a process by which works are made public.

The scholar's obsession with writing creates numerous problems, but two in particular deserve attention and redress. First, academics aren't even good writers. Our tendency toward obfuscation, disconnection, jargon, and overall incomprehensibility is legendary. As the novelist James Wood puts it in his review of *The Oxford English Literary History*,

> The very thing that most matters to writers, the first question they ask of a work—is it any good?—is often largely irrelevant to university teachers. Writers are intensely interested in what might be called aesthetic success: they have

to be, because in order to create something successful one must learn about other people's successful creations. To the academy, much of this value-chat looks like, and can indeed be, mere impressionism.[1]

The perturbed prose so common to philosophers, critical theorists, and literary critics offers itself up as an easy target, but it's not alone. Many scholars write poorly just to ape their heroes, thinkers whose thought evolved throughout the linguistic turn. In any case, most of us don't write for the sake of writing, despite simultaneously insisting that literature is somehow more naturally sacrosanct than painting video games or *The Real Housewives of Waukesha*.

Second, writing is dangerous for philosophy. It's not because writing breaks from its origins as Plato would have it, but because writing is *only one form* of being. The long-standing assumption that we relate to the world only through language is a particularly fetid, if still bafflingly popular, opinion. But so long as we pay attention only to language, we underwrite our ignorance of everything else. Levi Bryant puts it this way:

> If it is the signifier that falls into the marked space of your distinction, you'll only ever be able to talk about talk and indicate signs and signifiers. The differences made by light bulbs, fiber optic cables, climate change, and cane toads will be invisible to you and you'll be awash in texts, believing that these things exhaust the really real.[2]

Bryant suggests that our work need not exclude signs, narrative, and discourse, but that we ought also to approach the nonsemiotic world "on its own terms as best we can." When we spend all of our time reading and writing words—or plotting to do so—we miss opportunities to visit the great outdoors.

V. Cows, Part 1

Recently, there have been numerous rejoinders against the armchair cogitations of traditional philosophy. One such trend has been dubbed "experimental philosophy," and it looks a lot like cognitive psychology. Philosophers like Kwame Appiah and Joshua Knobe observe participants, collect data, run cognitive experiments, and attempt to draw conclusions from their results, which primarily address issues of ethics, thought, and belief.

Even more recently, philosophers like Robert Frodeman have advanced a position called "field philosophy." Borrowing the modifier from "field science," such philosophers not only abandon the wood-lined enclaves of their offices and libraries, but also eschew the public square of experimental philosophy. Instead they begin "in the world," according to Frodeman, "drawing out specific, underappreciated, philosophic dimensions of societal problems." Field philosophy "integrates ethics and values concerns with the ongoing work of scientists and engineers."[3]

Experimental and field philosophies have their detractors. Some accuse these efforts of mere instrumentalism, of turning philosophy itself into standing-reserve, or of selling out philosophy in a barely veiled support of the neoliberal interests of global capital. But Frodeman, Knobe, and others respond that philosophy ought to serve the world, not just the mind, and not just the academy. Furthermore, they argue, given the current state of things, disciplines like philosophy must adapt and renew themselves to respond to changing times, both in the university and in the world.

I'm less bothered by the purported prostitution of philosophy as I am disappointed that such approaches prove so limited in their ambition. This isn't philosophy, really, but merely ethics, an area that, as it happens, has long filled classes and books thanks to required accreditation requirements in engineering. And ethics is still a field of human interest, an amplification of the same human-world correlate that systematically omits all other beings from philosophical consideration.

I could suggest object-oriented philosophy as an alternative, one that embraces the same orientation toward the world, but without the human-centered instrumentalism of experimental and field philosophy. Would it really be so daft to admit that the world is simply full of interesting, curious things, all living their own alien lives, bumping and jostling about, engulfing and destroying one other, every one of them as secretive and withdrawn as any other?

If field philosophy just means driving our cars past the cows to the industrial farms and then going back home to write up ethics white papers, why bother leaving the office? Cows would make better field philosophers than philosophers would, since at least they work in fields. What if instead the field *were* the philosophy, not just the place where the philosopher goes to stroke his chin and scuff his wingtips before returning to an iPad in a rental Mazda and a MacBook in a Holiday Inn Express and, two flights later, an office door left just open enough to discourage anyone from entering. I am here, but not for you.

VI. Carpentry, Part 2

In *Alien Phenomenology,* I outline two versions of carpentry, which I might now call general and special carpentry, even though I don't use those names in the book.

General carpentry extends the ordinary sense of woodcraft to any material whatsoever—to do carpentry is to make things as philosophy, but to make them in earnest, with one's own hands, like a cabinetmaker.

Special carpentry takes up a philosophical position more directly connected to the practice of alien phenomenology, that of speculating about the experience of things. Into the general sense of carpentry, this sense folds Graham Harman's idea of "the carpentry of things," an idea he borrowed in turn from Alphonso Lingis. Both Lingis and Harman use that phrase to refer to how things fashion one another and the world at large. Special carpentry entails making things that explain how things make their world.

In the book I offer several examples largely from the domain of computing, where I do most of my work. These include the *Latour Litanizer,* which fashions lists of objects in the style of Bruno Latour, a phenomenon I name "Latour Litanies," and *I Am TIA,* a device that approximates the perceptual experience of the custom graphics and sound chip in the 1977 Atari Video Computer System. The first exemplifies *ontography,* a practice of philosophical enumeration central to my version of object-oriented ontology; the second carries out *metaphorism,* a speculative process of characterizing object experience through metaphor.

Carpentry might offer a more rigorous kind of philosophical

creativity, precisely because it rejects the correlationist agenda by definition, refusing to address only the human reader's ability to pass eyeballs over words and intellect over notions they contain. Sure, written matter is subject to the material constraints of the page, the printing press, the publishing company, and related matters, but those factors exert minimal force on the *content* of a written philosophy. Although a few exceptions exist (Jacques Derrida's *Glas*, perhaps, or the Nietzschean aphorism, or the propositional structure of Baruch Spinoza's *Ethics* or Ludwig Wittgenstein's *Tractatus*), philosophical works generally do not perpetrate their philosophical positions through their style or their form. The carpenter, by contrast, must contend with the material resistance of his or her chosen form, making the object itself become the philosophy. This is aesthetics as first and last philosophy.

VII. Cows, Part 2

The Kopp's Frozen Custard's website offers a flavor forecast. On Thursday May 3, 2012, the first day of the Nonhuman Turn conference, Mint Chip and Chocolate Thunder poured from metal spouts as heavy rain poured from the Milwaukee sky. One can't help but wonder if the custard mirrors the weather, or the weather the custard. According to the forecast for Saturday, May 5—the day I once spoke many of these words instead of you reading them—those fortunate to enjoy custards instead of philosophy indulged in Dulce de Leche and Chocolate Peanut Butter Chocolate. The mere existence of "Wisconsin-style frozen custard" should be enough to make us all stop reading Hegel, but alas, we shall not do so.

I'm not sure making custard is less noble or less philosophical than making philosophy, where philosophy means words written down on paper, typeset, and glued to bindings or distributed over Whispernet instead of pasteurized egg yolk and milk fat drawn through a refrigerated hopper with low air overrun. Is the dense and creamy mouthfeel of custard less rigorous than an abstruse and elaborate system of political, ethical, or ontological thought? I have to admit, I'd rather eat custard. Not cultural studies, but custard studies. As it happens, I'm an accidental bovine philosopher, so I have a head start.

At the 2010 Game Developers Conference, a schism seemed to erupt between "traditional" game developers, who make the sorts of console and casual games we've come to know well, and "social" game developers, who make games for Facebook and other networks. It was a storm that had been brewing for a few years, but the massive success of Zynga's *FarmVille* along with the company's publicly malicious attitude had made even the most apathetic of game developers suddenly keen to defend their craft as art.

In July of that year, my colleague Jesper Juul invited me to take part in a game theory seminar he runs at NYU, which he provocatively titled "Social Games on Trial." Researcher and social game developer Aki Järvinen would defend social games, and I was to speak against them.

As I prepared for the NYU seminar, I realized that theory alone might not help clarify social games—for me or for anyone in attendance. It's nice to think that "theorist/practitioners" like myself and Aki can translate lessons from research to design and back like adept jugglers, but things are far messier, as usual. The dialectic between theory and practice often collapses into a call-and-response panegyric. This in mind, I thought it might be productive to make an example that would act as its own theory—a kind of carpentry.

In the case of social games, I reasoned that enacting the principles of my concerns might help me clarify them and, furthermore, to question them. So I decided to make a game that would attempt to distill the social game genre down to its essence. The result was *Cow Clicker,* a Facebook game about Facebook games that completely consumed my life for well over a year and a half. There was a picture of a cow, which players could click every six hours. Each time they did, they received one point, called a click. Players could invite friends to join their "pasture"; when any of one's pasture-mates clicked, the player would receive a click, too. Players could purchase in-game currency, called "mooney," which they could use to buy more cows or to skip the click timer. There was more—much more, embarrassingly more—but that's enough to get us started.

By sheer reach *Cow Clicker* is easily the most successful work I have ever produced. More than fifty thousand people played it, and in most circles I am now most easily introduced as "the *Cow Clicker* guy." I was hoist on my own petard, as compulsively obsessed with running my stupid game as were the players who were playing it. I added cow gifting; an iPhone app *(Cow Clicker Moobile)*; a children's game *(My First Cow Clicker)*; a "cowclickification" API; and cow clicktivism, which allowed players to click virtual cows to send real cows to the third world via Oxfam Unwrapped. When it came time to end it, I launched a bovine alternate reality game played on four continents that revealed the coming Cowpocalypse—*Cow Clicker's* rapture. I have spent more time making cows than reading Alfred North Whitehead.

VIII. Carpentry, Part 3

What does it feel like to make custard or cows? Making something from the ground up, participating in every process; avoiding abstraction. It is handicraft. The craftsman asks, What is involved in the creation or genesis of a thing? We philosophers consider this act only in the most cursory way. Forget the custard and the pastures for a moment, just consider once more the thing scholars usually make when we deign to make things: books.

Several years ago Eugene Thacker gave me a slim book in the hallway between our offices at Georgia Tech. When I asked him what it was, he said, It's a prototype. He and Alex Galloway were writing *The Exploit*, their weird book about network culture. The two had uploaded their work in progress to the print-on-demand site Lulu and run a few perfect bound prototypes of their book-in-progress. That's what Eugene meant by a prototype: not (just) a first go of the ideas, but also of the form of the object.

It wasn't perfect. Lulu and others trim beyond standard sizes, the paper isn't of offset quality or weight, the layout isn't typeset and endnoted professionally, and so forth. It could be, of course. I've published books as an author and as a publisher, and the process is straightforward enough. Getting a hard proof for the first time is liberating and weird, even though it's so simple. A book, not a collection of words. A book that opens and dog-ears and fits in a bag or under the short leg of a wobbly table. A book that can kill a fly or be subject to marginalia conductivity tests.

Compare Thacker and Galloway's experience to the normal publishing process. Back when his book *The Textual Life of Airports* was published in December 2011, Christopher Schaberg reported what most authors do: seeing his book for the first time. "What a weird feeling," Chris wrote on his blog. "It resembles an object from outer space. Vaguely recognizable, yet totally alien at the same time." This is the experience of most authors. We say we *write books*, but really we write words. Then we put them in a FedEx box and give them to a publisher, who performs a ritual upon them that eventually spits out a book. Writers make words, and then they sign over rights to make books to book-makers.

It's not always a bad thing. The book Continuum Publishing made for *The Textual Life of Airports* is well designed and attractive, delightful to hold, a nice size, laid out well. It's also one hundred dollars in a hardback-only edition, which means that no normal human beings will buy it until Continuum gets around to publishing a paperback edition. All of which just underscores the point: authors rarely make books, where a book is an object with certain properties meant for the lives of readers. The publishing industry is not the problem, either. Sure, self-publishing puts more apparent control in the hands of an author, but the reality of print-on-demand (POD) printing and eBooks is one of far *less* design control than was ever possible in offset printing. Books can be designed. POD books just get uploaded and pressed out. They are the lunchmeats of publishing.

Shortly before *The Textual Life of Airports* dropped, Chris and his Loyola colleague Mark Yakich put together another book, *Checking In / Checking Out.* It's a two-sided book about airports and airplanes, one written by each author. The book resembles a passport in size and shape and even texture, and the effect just makes you want to carry the thing with you when you travel. Which, of course, is the perfect time to read it. As the *Los Angeles Times* put it, "About 5 by 6 inches, small enough to tuck into a jacket pocket or a purse, it's easy to carry, doesn't take too long to read, and is quite nice to look at. And if you carry it on a plane, you don't have to turn it off."[4] To produce that effect, Schaberg and Yakich had to write, design, print, market, and distribute a book—a real object in the world. Not just a series of words on pages sent to a publisher.

I've certainly found myself thinking more and more about this over the years (and asking more and more of my publishers). Both *Racing the Beam* and *Newsgames* are books whose physical size, heft, and feel very much please me. They are readable and attractive and desirable as objects. Likewise, *How to Do Things with Videogames* was made with a particular experience in mind: short chapters, small form factor, inexpensive paperback edition from day one, and so forth. A book people read and finish. And I hope enjoy having and experiencing as much as they enjoy reading it. I put laborious effort into the creation of *A Slow Year*, which is a book despite also being a video game. Experiences like these have made me realize that books are not just boxes for ideas. They are also just boxes, like cereal is just boxes.

There is a chasm between academic writing (writing to have written) and authorship (writing to have produced something worth reading). But there's another aspect to being an author, one that goes beyond writing at all: book-making. Creating the object that is a book that will have a role in someone's life—in their hands or their purses, wrapped around their mail, in between their fingers.

IX. Materials

But beyond books, what approaches do we have? One would involve embracing the materiality of different media for their own sake, rather than insisting that we make appeals to writing and speech as the singular and definitive models for intellectual productivity.

For some time now I have been arguing for the use of models, particularly computational models, to make arguments.

For example, I've written several times about La Molleindustria's *The McDonald's Videogame*, a scathing critique of the multinational fast-food industry. The game demonstrates the abject corruption required to maintain profitability and manageability of a large global food company. It's a good example of what I've previously called *procedural rhetoric*, arguments fashioned from models.

In the game, players control fields in South America where cattle are raised and soy is grown; a factory farm where cows are fed, injected with hormones, and controlled for disease; a restaurant where workers have to be hired and managed; and a corporate office where advertising campaigns and board members set corporate policy.

As play progresses, costs quickly outstrip revenue, and the player must take advantage of more seedy business practices. These include razing rainforests to expand crops, mixing waste as filler in the cow feed, censuring or firing unruly employees, and corrupting government officials to minimize public outcry against these actions.

But many players—especially those who are technically minded and enjoy mastering their video games—find themselves lamenting the difficult job of McDonald's executives rather than being incensed by their corrupt corporate policies. I've had a number of students make this observation about the game, in fact. "I empathized with the CEO of a big company. They have it rough."

When Molleindustria released a similar game, *Oiligarchy*, about the global petroleum market, they seem to have recognized this failing, if that's the right word for it. In response, they posted a "postmortem" with text and images that explain the premise of the game: peak oil, supply and demand, imperialism, and so forth.

An obvious question, then: If the game is incapable of or insufficient to do this, if the traditional media of text and image are necessary or even better as explanations, then why are we making games? It risks becoming a purely aesthetic exercise, a kind of accessory. A bag of peanuts to go along with the "real" media of language.

Whether through convention or reception, the growth of form is short-circuited. Language reasserts itself. Procedural representation is not proven intrinsically ineffective, but subordinated to the media ecosystem in which it serves as unrealized underdog.

Consider the orrery. It's a mechanical device that illustrates the position and motion of planets and moons in the heliocentric model of the universe. It's named for the Earl of Orrery, to whom the first such example was presented in 1704. It would be possible to write or draw such an explanation of object interactions, for example, in a textbook or on a classroom poster. But no such explanation would disrupt or undermine the orrery as object, as craftwork. As a physical model, as a procedural argument. No one would make an orrery and slink off apologetically to write a pamphlet to take its place, like La Molleindustria did for *Oiligarchy*. "I'm sorry, I didn't mean to make a model, please take these words instead."

Contrast the orrery with page 87 of Jared Diamond's Pulitzer Prize–winning book *Guns, Germs, and Steel*. It's a book about the ultimate material causes of human historical progress. Diamond traces proximate factors in Eurasian global domination like guns, steel, swords, disease, politics, and writing to ultimate factors like plentiful plant and animal speciation and the east-west axis of Eurasia that allowed easier spread of animal husbandry and agriculture, which in turn facilitated food surplus, storage, population density, politics, and technology.

No matter what you think of Diamond's position on geographical and material accident underlying all of human history, you might be struck by this single page—page 87—one of more than five hundred in the book. It rather stands in for the rest. Yes, of course there's a large amount of detailed description on those five hundred pages, but the fundamental argument is here on this chart. I'd wager that W. W. Norton wouldn't have published a laminated sheet with just page 87 on it, nor would that laminated sheet have won the Pulitzer Prize in nonfiction.

Another example, one closer to home. On Wednesday evening before The Nonhuman Turn conference began, Tim Morton and I sat drinking beer at Von Trier's on Farwell and North. My ten-year-old daughter started texting me:

"Why r u in Milwaukee," she asked.
   "Conference! Nonhuman Turn," I responded.
   "Mmm," she considered.
   "Weird, right," I offered apologetically.
   "Yeah," she said, adding an alien emoji to the exchange.
   "That's nonhuman," she clarified.
   Adding my own pictogram, a slice of cake, I responded, "So is this."

This may seem harmless enough to you, if perhaps also adorable ("my daughter's first lesson in object-oriented ontology," I called it on Twitter). But there's something quite serious going on here. This exchange goes further than most philosophy, because it takes a concrete situation and makes it manifest, in the moment, with only the tools I had on hand—my iPhone and its built-in emoji set. Sometimes I wonder: Why am I writing books when I could just write text messages to my ten-year-old? That may sound flip or glib, but what if we took the daily *practice* of philosophy seriously, not just the occasional chore of it?

Or, one more: Tim Morton gave a rousing talk at The Non-human Turn conference. I have no idea how it could be effectively reproduced in this book, in print, when it was so performative, so rhythmic and throbbing. Afterward, he fielded a number of questions about his rather arresting presentation. Most were questions about the form of the presentation: What is it that you just did? On the one hand, they are reasonable questions, and there's no doubt that Tim's presentation warranted them. But on the other hand, nobody would have thought to ask Steven Shaviro a question like, "I noticed you cited numerous philosophers by reading quotations from their books, which you interspersed with various commentaries about those quotes. Why did you do that?"

We are stuck in our materials, and mostly we don't realize it. Perhaps we are too obsessed with foregrounding political ideology even to notice the ideology of materials. But even if not, the ideology that *is* our materials is perhaps one to which we are even more blinded. Ideology critique demands that we take a closer look at what we take for granted. We ourselves offer one such object of study, by means of the tools we deploy for work like ideology critique.

X. Cows, Part 3

Writing in *Wired* magazine in December 2011, Jason Tanz told the story of Jamie Clark, a student and military spouse living on Ellsworth Air Force Base outside of Box Elder, South Dakota.[5] She had made close friendships with her fellow Clickers. "I don't meet a lot of people who discuss politics and religion and philosophy, but these people do, and I like talking to them," she says. "I'd rather talk to my *Cow Clicker* friends than to people I went to school with for 12 years." It's a common refrain among dedicated Cow Clickers, who have turned what was intended to be a vapid experience into a source of camaraderie and creativity, Tanz summarized. He continues:

> It may be that *Cow Clicker* demonstrates the opposite of
> what it set out to prove and that social games, no matter
> how cynically designed, can still provide meaningful experi-
> ences. That's how Zynga's Brian Reynolds sees it. "Ian made
> *Cow Clicker* and discovered, perhaps to his dismay, that
> people liked it," Reynolds says. "Who are we to tell people
> what to like?" Gabe Zichermann, a gamification expert, also
> dismisses Bogost's critique of Zynga's games. "Other gamers
> may think *FarmVille* is shallow, but the average player is
> happy to play it," he says. "*Two and a Half Men* is the most
> popular show on television. Very few people would argue
> that it's as good as *Mad Men,* but do the people watching
> *Two and a Half Men* sit around saying, oh, woe is me? At
> some point, you're just an elitist fuck."

I had responded to this idea almost a year earlier, in a "rant" at the Game Developers Conference titled "Shit Crayons." In it, I compared *Cow Clicker* players to the imprisoned Nigerian poet Wole Soyinka, who composed poems from his cell using whatever writing material he could find. How resilient is the human spirit that it withstands so much? No matter what shit we throw, nevertheless people endure, they thrive even, spinning shit into gold.

The Cowpocalypse finally arrived in the evening of September 7, 2011. Frantically working at a makeshift desk in my den, I flip a few bits I had set up weeks earlier, and all the cows disappear—raptured. In their place, just empty grass. Tanz explains better than I could:

> They have been raptured—replaced with an image of an
> empty patch of grass. Players can still click on the grass, still
> generate points for doing so, but there are no new cows to
> buy, no mooing to celebrate their action. In some sense, this
> is the truest version of *Cow Clicker*—the pure, cold game

mechanic without any ornamentation. Bogost says that he expects most people will "see this as an invitation to end their relationship with *Cow Clicker.*"

But months after the rapture, Adam Scriven, the enthusiastic player from British Columbia, hasn't accepted that invitation. He is still clicking the space where his cow used to be. After the Cowpocalypse, Bogost added one more bedeviling feature—a diamond cowbell, which could be earned by reaching 1 million clicks. It was intended as a joke; it would probably take 10 years of steady clicking to garner that many points. But Scriven says he might go for it. "It is very interesting, clicking nothing," Scriven says. "But then, we were clicking nothing the whole time. It just looked like we were clicking cows."

XI. Idiots

Despite co-organizing it, I was unable to attend the third object-oriented ontology symposium, held in September 2011 at the New School in New York City. Georgia Tech had asked me to attend the World Economic Forum's meeting of the New Champions in Dalian, China, and I couldn't refuse. I stopped over in Seoul on the way, where in an online chat I lamented with Tim Morton having to miss the triple-O event. Tim suggested I make a video they could play in my absence, and despite massive jetlag I put together a short visual essay on the twentieth-century street photographer Garry Winogrand.

Among the surprising benefits of making a five-minute video in absentia instead of delivering a three thousand-word paper, a popular photography site featured the video and it was viewed many thousands of times. One such accidental ontologist was Tod Papageorge, director of the Yale School of Art's graduate photography program and a longtime friend and scholar of street photography in general and Winogrand's work in particular. Papageorge sent me a 1974 lecture by Winogrand that included this nugget of wisdom: "A photograph is the illusion of a literal description of what the camera saw. From it, you can know very little. It has no narrative ability. You don't know what happened from the photography. You know how a piece of time and space looked to a camera."[6]

It's a sentiment that bears fruit well beyond photography. The practice of alien phenomenology I call "metaphorism" involves amplifying rather than reducing distortion, capturing the metaphorical relation between objects by characterizing their perceptions through imperfect, speculative rendition. This is the gentle tragedy of carpentry, which Hugh Crawford has called *"working like an idiot"*: in doing what we cannot, we nevertheless must strive to make something. With enough effort and practice and attention, we can even make things that are not just sufficient but also *beautiful.*

Winogrand said that still photography is the clumsiest way to exercise imagination. "Dali can have a melted watch anytime he wants," he explained. "It's tantamount to driving a nail in with a saw, when you can use a hammer." Carpentry is worse than this. Carpentry is the process of driving a nail in with a cup of frozen custard.

I want to put my custard where my hammer is, so to speak. I have many carpentered projects planned and in progress, using many different materials. But computers and cows notwithstanding, I still fancy writing—but real writing, writing where the writing matters, not just the written matter. Writing that's not sold in bulk to a tenure and promotion committee, but pruned like bonsai.

If I were really serious about the claims I made about carpentry in *Alien Phenomenology,* then I shall have to try to make good on them. As such, the work I want to do with objects is metaphoristic, not critical. I want to write well rather than write to completion. We don't have to give up writing to be philosophical carpenters. And as I think about being a philosopher—the kind who writes, anyway, at least some of the time—I realize that I can't currently imagine writing philosophical arguments or treatises or positions. Fault me for it if you'd like, but I just don't want to interpret Whitehead or Rancière. What if we took a break from it, from philosophical history for a while? What if we stopped making arguments?

One day, I hope this might be philosophy. I hope I might write some of it, and that you might read it. If that hope conflates philosophy with poetry or fiction, then so be it. Plato was wrong about poetry anyway.

Notes

1. James Wood, "The Slightest Sardine," review of *The Oxford English Literary History. Vol. XII: 1960–2000: The Last of England?, London Review of Books,* May 20, 2004, 11–12, http://www.lrb.co.uk/.

2. Levi R. Bryant, "You Know You're a Correlationist If . . . ," *Larval Subjects* (blog), July 30, 2010, www.larvalsubjects.wordpress.com.

3. Robert Frodeman, "Experiments in Field Philosophy," *The Stone* blog, *New York Times,* November 23, 2010, http://opinionator.blogs.nytimes.com/.

4. Carolyn Kellogg, "Little Books: An Airplane Reader," Jacket Copy column, *Los Angeles Times,* December 20, 2011, http://latimesblogs.latimes.com/jacketcopy/.

5. Jason Tanz, "The Curse of *Cow Clicker*: How a Cheeky Satire Became a Videogame Hit," *Wired,* December 20, 2011, www.wired.com/magazine/.

6. UCR/CMP Podcasts: Collections Series—Garry Winogrand, University of California-Riverside, California Museum of Photography, April 3, 2008, https://itunes.apple.com/us/podcast/ucr-california-museum-photography/. Also available from http://cmplab16.ucr.edu/podcasts/2008.0009.0003/UCR_CMP_Podcasts_CollectionsSeries2.m4a.

5

Our Predictive Condition; or, Prediction in the Wild

MARK B. N. HANSEN

The Politics of Imminent Threat

The February 2013 confirmation hearings for John Brennan, President Barack Obama's nominee for CIA director, rekindled—indeed significantly ramped up—comparisons between the administration's recent policy decisions concerning collection of personal data and the fantasy of "precrime" made famous by Steven Spielberg's 2002 film *Minority Report*. Already in December 2012, following a *Wall Street Journal* article detailing Eric Holder's March 2012 decision to grant the National Counterterrorism Center (NCTC) broad rights to collect and archive private data from individual citizens,[1] Jesseyln Raddack, national security and human rights director at the whistleblower nonprofit Government Accountability Project, likened the administration's move to the fantasy at the heart of Spielberg's film:

> In the movie *Minority Report*, law enforcement has an elite squad called "Precrime," which predicts crimes beforehand and punishes the guilty before the crime has ever been committed. In yet another example of life imitating art, a blockbuster *Wall Street Journal* article describes how the National Counterterrorism Center (NCTC)—an ugly child of the Director of National Intelligence—*can now examine the government files of ordinary, innocent U.S. citizens to look for clues that people might commit future crimes.*[2]

In the wake of the Brennan hearings, the talk of precrime was again all over the media, only now with a more precise focus— the administration's position on drone killings—and a far more astute understanding of the logic informing this position. Particularly incendiary about Brennan's testimony were his clarification of the underlying logic for preemption and his specification of the concept of "imminent threat." What Brennan makes clear in his testimony is that, when assessing the danger of terrorist threats and of individuals involved in such threats, the NCTC does not operate like a court of law. Indeed, far from it, for, rather than making decisions about past guilt on the basis of past information, the NCTC must make decisions about *future* guilt, that is, guilt for activities *that have not yet occurred,* and must do so on the basis of a set of factors bearing on the likelihood of such activities indeed occurring—factors that include the seriousness of the threat, the temporal window of opportunity for intervention, and the possibility of reducing collateral damage—which taken together present preponderant or overwhelming evidence of the "imminence" of the threat at issue.

Brennan's language unequivocally marks the extrajudicial terrain of the question:

> JOHN BRENNAN: Senator, I think it's certainly worthy of discussion. Our tradition—our judicial tradition is that a court of law is used to determine one's guilt or innocence for past actions, which is very different from the decisions that are made on the battlefield, as well as actions that are taken against terrorists. *Because none of those actions are to determine past guilt for those actions that they took.* The decisions that are made are to take action so that we prevent a future action, so we protect American lives. That is an inherently executive branch function to determine, and the commander in chief and the chief executive has the responsibility to protect the welfare, well-being of American citizens. So the concept I understand and we have wrestled with this in terms of whether there can be a FISA-like court, whatever—a FISA-like court is to determine exactly whether

or not there should be a warrant for, you know, certain types of activities. You know . . .

ANGUS KING: It's analogous to going to a court for a warrant—probable cause. . . .

(CROSSTALK)

BRENNAN: Right, exactly. But the actions that we take on the counterterrorism front, again, are to take actions against individuals where we believe that the intelligence base is so strong and the nature of the threat is so grave and serious, as well as imminent, that we have no recourse except to take this action that may involve a lethal strike.[3]

With its clear distinction between the act of judging past involvement in crimes and the act of warding off the imminent threat of future crimes, Brennan's comments effectively position the NCTC as a latter-day Precrime Division: while courts "get involved when people have already committed crimes," as one astute blogger puts it, the NCTC must reserve for itself, and the government it represents, the right to declare people "imminent threats"—targets for killing—*"even before they've committed a crime."*[4]

The distinction Brennan draws between judicial process and military force would seem to place his position broadly within the logic of preemptive power that Brian Massumi has developed to characterize post-9/11 American foreign policy. For Massumi, this logic involves a fundamentally altered relationship to an objective cause:

> Deterrence revolved around an objective cause. Preemption revolves around a proliferative effect. Both are operative logics. The operative logic of deterrence, however, remained causal even as it displaced its cause's effect. Preemption is an effective operative logic rather than a causal operative logic. Since its ground is potential, there is no actual cause for it to organize itself around. It compensates for the absence of an actual cause by producing an actual effect in its place. This it makes the motor of its movement: it

converts an absent or virtual cause really, directly, into a taking-actual-effect.[5]

Like preemptive power on this account, the right to kill that Brennan claims for the NCTC would appear to exercise its dominion where there are no actual causes yet, where "causal operative logic" has yet to become applicable. Understood on the logic of preemptive power, "imminent threat" would thus play the role of "virtual cause": "a futurity," as Massumi puts it, "with a virtual power to affect the present quasicausally."[6]

What lends the virtual cause its force is the operation of the "unknown unknown," understood as a kind of ultimate final cause for the threat at issue here. This absolute unknowability renders the threat an ontological problem—the problem of how to construct a relationship to what, from the standpoint of the present, remains "objectively uncertain":

> Like deterrence, it [preemption] operates in the present on a future threat. It also does this in such a way as to make that present futurity the motor of its process. The process, however, is qualitatively different. For one thing, the epistemology is unabashedly one of uncertainty, and not due to a simple lack of knowledge. There is uncertainty because the threat has not only not yet fully formed but, according to Bush's opening definition of preemption, *it has not yet even emerged.* In other words, the threat is still indeterminately in potential. This is an ontological premise: the nature of threat cannot be specified.[7]

Despite a certain terminological wavering on Massumi's part, the argument here mobilizes what appears to be a clear, categorical distinction between two models of causality, or perhaps more precisely, between a model of causality and a model of absolute noncausality (absolute refusal of causality).[8] To the extent that it operates in relation to—indeed, in virtue of—an unknowability *that can never be overcome,* preemptive power exists orthogonally to causality, and operates—or claims to operate—independently of and beyond its scope.[9] The threat that it claims to address is beyond prediction (it "has become proteiform and it tends to proliferate unpredictably"); and it exists, if indeed it can be said to exist at all, as an empty—and thus infinitely fulfillable—form of the future (it is a "time form: a futurity" and is, as such, "nothing *yet*—just a looming").[10]

Yet despite its absolutely central role as the kernel of Massumi's account of preemptive power, the category of the unknown unknown receives little if any direct attention in his meditation. Invoking "the Architect," Donald Rumsfeld, Massumi does tell us that "we are in a world that has passed from the 'known unknown' (uncertainty that can be analyzed and identified) to the 'unknown unknown' (objective uncertainty)."[11] But what exactly objective uncertainty is—other than the negation of any figure of knowledge—remains uninterrogated. Indeed, it would appear that Massumi simply ratifies Rumsfeld's analysis—and the operation of the unknown unknown as an absolute final cause—in order to focus on the intricacies of virtual causality. What enters the scene is fear as the efficiency of a quasi-causal logic that effectively substitutes for the causal efficacy of the real: "Threat is the cause of fear in the sense that it triggers and conditions fear's occurrence, but without the fear it effects, the threat would have no handle on actual existence, remaining purely virtual."[12] Preemption mobilizes the affect of fear "to effectively trigger a virtual causality." Affect, accordingly, emerges as the very medium or materiality of the threat's exercise of power: "Preemption is when the futurity of unspecified threat is affectively held in the present in a perpetual state of potential emergence(y) so that a movement of actualization may be triggered that is not only self-propelling but also effectively, indefinitely, ontologically productive. . . ."[13] From these descriptions, we can see that fear is the strict correlate of the unknown unknown: it comprises the very mechanism by which objective uncertainty can become a quasi-causally efficacious political force.

The crucial question we must ask Massumi does not concern the coherence of this virtual quasi-causal logic, but rather the effect of positioning it as a *substitute for* the causal efficacy of the real. It is one thing to argue that Rumsfeld's rhetoric of the unknown unknown made it possible to hijack this causal efficacy and to willfully impose a factually (or causally) "unjustified" imperialistic program.

But it is quite another to claim that this program—which certainly does have real causal consequences—operates at the same level as, and indeed, as an alternate modality of, the causal efficacy of the real. Because it effectively lends credit to the inaugural move of the logic of preemption—the decision to treat absolute uncertainty as source for causal efficacy—this latter position runs the risk of ratifying the Bush doctrine of preemption.

Against such a position, we need to advance two theses:

1. There is no unknown unknown in material reality: the unknown unknown is an ideological mystification of a geopolitical phenomenon, terrorism, that gains whatever traction it has from its capacity to pose extreme difficulties for extant epistemologies.
2. There is a categorical distinction between empirical evidence and affective pseudo-evidence, and we must defend the role and autonomy of the former, and specifically its capacity to debunk any and all invocations of absolute uncertainty, against strategic attempts to subsume it under the umbrella of fear (or any other affectively sustained quasi-causality).

The Return to Reality

Let us now return to Brennan's testimony, which, I emphasize, breaks with the Bush doctrine of preemptive war over the very point at issue here: the role and existence of the unknown unknown. Although he cannot but operate within a military scenario and world situation that, to be sure, was in some sense created quasi-causally by the Bush administration's false assertion of a link between Iraq and Al-Qaeda, Brennan *does not make any appeal whatsoever to absolute uncertainty* in his claim for the right to kill. Rather, he cites more proximate factors that, even if they do not establish a clear and direct causal lineage from past to future (i.e., evidence of involvement in actual criminal activity), nonetheless furnish such a "strong . . . intelligence base" that, combined with other factors, including the gravity of the threat and its imminence, justify—and indeed, leave "no recourse except"—the use of lethal force.

Among other things, what this break with the Bush-era logic of preemption signals is a certain return to reality: decisions concerning the targeting of individuals for drone killing will be made, not in virtue of an ultimate, and ultimately unknowable, source, but rather on the basis of as thorough an analysis as the given time frame permits of all available data concerning the situation at issue.[14] Such analysis is, to be sure, causal, but with a complexity that eschews all notions of simple linear causality and that embraces indeterminacy-uncertainty-unknowability as the very aspect of reality that makes causal analysis necessary in the first place. Rather than focusing on the identification and isolation of a single cause or causal thread that makes its appearance at the macrolevel of experience, as a clearly delimitable "event," such analysis seeks to identify propensities of situations on the basis of an attention to the "totality" of a situation. Thus rather than beginning with and orienting itself in relation to the notion of actions that may be committed against citizens of the United States, such analysis operates probabilistically on the matrix of the entirety of the data available at a given moment in time that pertains to a very general situation, say terrorist activity in a given region. And rather than seeking to establish guilt for past actions, such analysis seeks to identify future windows of space-time in which terroristic activity is likely to occur and then to find ways of linking such future propensity to individuals who can be targeted for killing in the present.

When Brennan attributes the distinction between military and judicial judgment to a difference in temporal modality, he doesn't emphasize strongly enough, or indeed really at all, what I take to be the most fundamental element of the distinction: namely, the fact that predictive analysis of data for assessment of future probabilities *generates information that is not there independently of the analysis.* Such a generative dimension is a generic feature of data mining, as communications scholar Oscar Gandy Jr. observes: "Data mining is said to differ from ordinary information retrieval in that the information which is sought does not exist explicitly within the database, but must be 'discovered.' In an important sense, the relationships between measured or 'observed' events come to stand as a 'proxy' for some unmeasured relationship or influence."[15]

The generative dimension that Gandy discovers in conventional data mining procedures becomes far more fundamental in the case of military data mining, where what is being mined is information relevant to events that have not yet occurred: whereas conventional, retrospective data mining involves analysis of past behavioral data to determine probabilities of future behavior, military, prospective data mining seeks to generate likely future scenarios based on the analysis of presently identifiable propensities extending into the future.

To the extent that they operate to predict factors of situations that have not yet occurred, such future-oriented, prospective procedures of data mining and predictive analytics might be said to fill in the void of the "unknown unknown." In contrast to the Bush administration's logic of preemption, and also to Massumi's analysis of it, they address the uncertain not as an ultimate final cause, but as a domain open to probabilistic analysis—as a domain that can be *partially* known. Thus, rather than the virtual production of a quasi-cause that, as Massumi puts it, "compensates for the absence of an actual cause by producing an actual effect in its place," what is at issue in the logic of executive-military judgment sketched out by Brennan is an instrumental decision concerning an imminent threat that is real precisely to the extent that it is known—but that is known, let us be clear, *not* as something that already exists, but *as something predictably likely to come to pass.*

This kind of reality finds its philosophical name in Alfred North Whitehead's concept of "real potentiality," which conceptualizes the operation of the future in the present: "The reality of the future," says Whitehead, "is the reality of what is potential, in its character of a real component of what is actual."[16] I return to Whitehead's concept in some detail later, but let me at this point simply underscore the broad scope of real potentiality's sway: real potentiality does not qualify a given agent, but the diffuse and "total" potentiality of the world at a given moment. In this sense, Whitehead's concept can help us appreciate something fundamental about the prospective model of data mining and predictive analytics: its predictive power is a direct function of its broad grasp. Not only does prospective data mining always address a "total situation," but it does so by analyzing data at a myriad of levels (or scales); it is only subsequently, as the result of an inductive process and as a function of probability, that such broad-ranging, microscalar analysis congeals into an identifiable macroscale phenomenon, an "event."[17]

That this meditation on broadened imminence remains firmly anchored in real and concretely (if probabilistically) accessible factors marks its resistance to any assimilation into an event logic: today's imminent threat differs from the quasi-causal absolute threat of preemption *precisely because it can be qualified probabilistically, precisely because one can assess the degree of certainty that it will materialize.* And what is qualified—what actually comprises the threat—is not the likelihood of a particular event, of a single actual cause, coming to pass, but a far more complex and diffuse calculus of propensities concerning a myriad of factora that *can only be known insofar as they can be qualified probabilistically.* It is these micro-propensities, not the events they may go on to inform, that are the objects of probabilistic modeling.

Rethinking "Precrime"

With this shift in the structure, and indeed, in the ontology of threat comes a displacement of fear in favor of evidence. If that displacement is what Brennan's testimony expresses, as I am suggesting here, it inaugurates a model of "precrime" that breaks with the legacy of the notion, as it extends from Philip K. Dick's original 1956 story, through Spielberg's 2002 film, to contemporary theorizations of post-9/11 political culture. Central to all of these expressions of the preemptive logic of "precrime" is a focus on the macroscale event: in both the story and the film, what the "precogs" see is the actual scene of a murder, perpetrated by an individual in a specific place and at a specific time.

When Richard Grusin invokes *Minority Report*—and the future *vision* of the precogs—as an allegory for an operation that he calls "premediation," he takes on board this event-focused legacy:

> Steven Spielberg's *Minority Report* (2002), released less than a year after 9/11, epitomized the logic of premediation that had been intensifying over the past decade and more. . . . In *Minority Report*, rather than capturing past

neural experience for playback in the future [as in Kathryn Bigelow's 1995 film, *Strange Days*], the technology captures "precognitions" of the future for playback in the present— for the purpose of preventing the recorded *events* from becoming actual history, to prevent the future from becoming the past.[18]

Grusin understands the recordings of the precogs' visions as elements within a larger network aimed at mediating—or more precisely, *premediating*—future events prior to their occurrence. What makes these visions appropriate for this task is their status as recordings that are identical technically to other forms of cinematic recording: "Technically the recording device [in *Minority Report*] would seem to work very similarly to the wire in *Strange Days*. Even though the device in *Minority Report* is supposed to be recording murders that will be committed in the future, the sensory experience that it records is recently past experience, that is, the past mental experience of the three precogs."[19] With this astute observation, Grusin helps us to understand that the mechanism for predicting the future within the diegetic world of the film is not the media apparatus itself but some magical, never fully clarified power of the precogs to see into the near future, to experience the near future *as something implicated within the present.*

On this score, the vision of precrime depicted in Spielberg's *Minority Report* stands opposed to the vision laid out by Brennan in his recent testimony: whereas the former indulges a fantasy of cognitive pre-anticipation of the future, the latter is rooted in the power of large-scale data analysis to reveal partial propensities stretching forward from the present world to (differently weighted) possible future worlds. And if the former finds its appropriate aesthetic analogue in the media technology of cinema—which is perfectly equipped to present the precogs' visions as recordings of "future *events*"—the latter is rooted in the media technics of predictive data analysis that operates at a level of granularity and fragmentation and with an ineliminable degree of uncertainty antithetical to consolidation in the form of the "future event." The discoveries of predictive analytics are discoveries of micrological propensities that are not directly correlated with human understanding and affectivity and that do not by themselves cohere into clearly identifiable events: such propensities simply have no direct aesthetic analogue within *human* experience.

Given the broader political and (especially) technical context within which it was made, Spielberg's choice to retain the central conceit of Dick's 1956 story—the magic element provided by the precogs—immediately labels the film as an allegory. Far from being a diagnosis of the system of "preventive prosecution" that the Bush administration would soon adopt, the film presents a more open vision of a future in which the political mandate for perfect preemption has simply, if magically, been translated into reality. This openness makes *Minority Report* an ideal exemplification of the logic of premediation. Indeed, the fantasy of precognition is the perfect allegorical expression of the imperative to premediate that, in Grusin's understanding, structures post-9/11 media culture: like the precog visions, the incessant production of mediations of possible futures is designed to ensure that the "future can be remediated before it happens."[20]

With its basis in data mining and predictive analytics, the recent expansion of the government's right to kill marks a clear departure from the immunologic of premediation. What is at stake in Brennan's claim for executive authority over drone killings—especially when these target individuals who have yet to commit crimes—is the causal efficacy of data and the "right" to base life-or-death decisions on it. Where Grusin's premediation fills in (or covers over) the uncertainty of the future with a torrent of mediation, contemporary precrime mobilizes the weapons of prediction in order to face that uncertainty head-on. Clearly, the two "logics" address our contemporary situation in starkly divergent ways.

This divergence surfaces in Grusin's characterization of premediation as akin to a video game:

> More like designing a video game than predicting the
> future, premediation is *not concerned with getting the*
> *future right,* as much as with trying to map out a multiplic
> ity of possible futures. Premediation would in some sense
> transform the world into a video or computer game, which
> only permits certain moves. . . . Although within these

premediated moves there are a seemingly infinite number of different possibilities available, only some of those
possibilities are encouraged by the protocols and reward
systems built into the game. Premediation is in this sense
distinct from prediction. Unlike prediction, premediation
is *not about getting the future right.* In fact it is precisely the
proliferation of competing and often contradictory future
scenarios that enables premediation to prevent the experience of a traumatic future by generating and maintaining a
low level of anxiety as a kind of affective prophylactic.[21]

With its sustained clarification that premediation is not about "getting the future right," this passage could not express more clearly
and unequivocally *the fact that premediation operates exclusively
at the level of ideology.* Indeed, premediation marks what we might
well consider a new stage in the operation of ideology, one that
marks the transformation of affectivity into the very engine of
ideology. In this respect, premediation is remarkably similar to
Massumi's preemption: in both cases, affectivity (whether low-
level anxiety or free-floating fear) comprises a resource allowing
action to be taken in the present. That is why Grusin and Massumi
come to the same conclusion: the messy operation of material reality—an operation that takes place to a large degree *beyond* the
grasp of knowledge—is subordinated to the quasi-causality produced through a sanitized, event-focused representation of the future designed to forestall the threat of the unknowable. Whether
such forestalling occurs through the incessant proliferation of
preemptive measures or the frenzied multiplication of premediated scenarios is ultimately beside the point: the only thing that
really matters is the decision to jettison the imperfections of causal
prediction in favor of a closed, quasi-causal loop that, ultimately,
simply replaces causality with ideology. Once this decision is made,
facts about reality become strangely irrelevant, as does the very
notion that the future in fact bears differentially on our predictions
in the present (or, using Grusin's terminology: that one can get the
future *at least partially* right).

By substituting the *cultural* logic of premediation for the *material* logic of prediction, Grusin's analysis does not simply deprive

us of important tools for diagnosing our contemporary situation; more significantly, it tacitly makes common cause with a far broader operation of data gathering and predictive analytics on the part of government, military, and private industry that is predicated on a functional splitting of operationality from representation, and an obfuscation of the former by the latter. As I have argued elsewhere, today's data industries operate on the basis of a system of information gathering and analysis designed to leave citizen-consumers out of the loop.[22] A case in point is contemporary social media, where the affordances of particular platforms are ultimately nothing other than "lures" to generate activity, and hence data, that fuels a predictive engine for the production of surplus value. The key point here is that this "system" combines ideology and operationality in order to secure ever more effective command over the future, or more precisely, over the future's agency in the present.

Viewed against this broad backdrop, premediation can be seen to perform a dual role: on one hand, understood as a desire that stems ultimately from the uncertainty of the future, it operates as stimulus—as lure—for the production of ever more mediation; and on the other, understood as a proliferation of media events that take the place of causal analysis, it functions to obfuscate the underlying reality, namely that policy decisions are being made on the basis of predictive analysis, yielding what must ultimately remain uncertain, probabilistic judgments concerning the future.[23] What this means is that the two logics at issue here—of premediation and of prediction—are not incompatible, or rather only become incompatible when placed on the same level, when offered as alternative causal (or quasi-causal) logics.

By shifting the terrain upon which the notion of precrime gains meaning, Brennan's testimony offers an important opportunity to think beyond the ideological obfuscations perpetrated by the logics of premediation and preemption. Expanding on the November 2011 white paper, Brennan's claim for executive right to kill in cases involving future crimes is rooted not in a closed, circular, self-creating quasi-causal loop but ultimately in an argument about the justification of lethal force on the basis of predictively secured, though intrinsically uncertain, and inherently partial, probabilities. There are certainly serious questions that will need to be asked about such justification, as well as political resistance that will need to be wielded to prevent potential executive overreach. But the fact remains that the terms of today's discussions of "precrime" mark a wholesale break with the fetishizing of the unknown unknown that occurs, whether for strategic or sincere reasons, when it is made to function as virtual final cause of the politico-cultural logics of preemption and premediation.

Prediction as Access to Worldly Sensibility

On this score, we might well turn from *Minority Report* to the recent television drama, *Person of Interest,* to find an appropriate allegory for our contemporary predictive condition. Like *Minority Report, Person of Interest* centers on the use of data to predict and ultimately shape the happening of the future; yet whereas the film features three human precogs producing dreamlike visions of future crimes, the television series focuses on the output of a mysterious machine that processes all of the data generated by computational sensors, cell phones, and Internet activity in order to predict the involvement of individuals in situations that will somehow involve murder. For my purposes here, two main factors distinguish *Person of Interest* from its precursor. First, the depiction of the "machine" at its core explicitly recognizes the partiality of intelligence generated through predictive analytics and takes this as a key element: it requires the involvement of human protagonists in the ongoing development of events out of diverse data concerning future propensities. Second, the data generated by the machine is portrayed as absolutely inscrutable to human understanding and subject to no protocols of hermeneutic decipherment; this data function simply as a spur to solicit the future-affecting involvement of human actors. What these two differences underscore is *Person of Interest*'s explicit concern with the predictive condition of contemporary life: not only does it allegorize this condition in the form of superhero-like fantasy resolutions of predicaments involving individuals dehumanized by twenty-first-century capitalism, but it does so always in a way that embraces the uncertainty inherent to the predictive logic informing the operations of today's military-entertainment complex.

Reflecting the spillover from military to civilian surveillance documented by the November 2011 white paper, the show's diverse narratives all involve some aspect of the generalization of data mining and predictive analytics at issue in our current cultural moment: although the machine was built to identify potential terrorists, the machine's architect, a character named Finch, built in a "back door" allowing him access to the extraneous data produced by the machine—data that, while irrelevant for the machine's military purpose, predict the occurrence of crimes in the mundane domain of everyday life. In this sense, the show would appear to allegorize not simply the predictive condition of life during wartime, as does a show like *Homeland,* but the more general predictive condition of life lived within the complex networks created by twenty-first-century media.

That is why *Person of Interest,* despite being in development prior to March 2012, could be taken for a direct response to the expansion of the government's right to gather private data. In her December 2012 exposé of the leaked NCTC Guidelines, *Wall Street Journal* reporter Julia Angwin characterizes the policy shift at issue here as a marked "departure from past practice, which barred the [NCTC] from storing information about ordinary Americans unless a person was a terror suspect or related to an investigation." The new rules "now allow the little-known National Counterterrorism Center to examine the government files of US citizens for possible criminal behavior, even if there is no reason to suspect them." Even more shockingly, the rules allow the NCTC to "copy entire government databases—flight records, casino-employee lists, the names of Americans hosting foreign-exchange students and many others. The agency has new authority to keep data about innocent US citizens for up to five years, and to analyze it for suspicious patterns of behavior. Previously, both were prohibited." The new policy, as Angwin clearly discerns, effectively ensures that every American is treated as a potential "imminent threat": not only can information be used in the present "to look for clues that people might commit future crimes," but it is stored expressly as a source of potential, which is to say, with a view to its future relevance. As Angwin astutely notes, this amounts to holding individuals responsible in the present for possible activities—possible crimes—that do not exist as such in the present, for crimes that, as it were, *have yet to happen*: "A person might seem innocent today, until new details emerge tomorrow."[24]

Along with the ubiquitous operation of data tracking and gathering that increasingly informs our mundane uses of computational technologies, this expanded scope of governmental data gathering creates the predictive condition allegorized by *Person of Interest*. What is striking about the show, however, and what distinguishes it from *Minority Report* and a long history of dystopian meditations on the erosion of privacy, is the positive spin it puts on our predictive condition: despite its operation beyond the bounds of human understanding, data are figured in the show as the means for justice to be served at the level of everyday life, in relation to ordinary persons. I have elsewhere sought to characterize the use of data gathering and predictive analytics for human enrichment in terms of media pharmacology (*pharmakon*, Greek for "poison" and its "antidote"), and specifically as the pharmacological recompense for the marginalization of human modes of experience (consciousness, sense perception, etc.) that ensues with the advent of our predictive condition.[25] To do so, I correlate this recompense with the expanded domain of sensibility—what I have called "worldly sensibility"—that is made accessible to us by twenty-first-century media. Specifically, technical access to and production of data about levels of experience that remain outside our direct experience, but that nevertheless affect our experience, give us the potential to gain an expanded understanding of our own experience and its implication within larger worldly situations.

At the heart of this argument, as I announced previously, is a critical engagement with the philosophy of Alfred North Whitehead that centers on Whitehead's environmental approach to process and the fundamental role that data play in his account of the world's becoming. This engagement aims to radicalize Whitehead's own radicalization of perception. Accordingly, whereas Whitehead seeks to re-embed sense perception in the broader vectors of "causal efficacy," and introduces "non-sensuous perception" (perception "in the mode of causal efficacy") to do so, I suggest that perception in both of its modes arises within and out of a broader environmental surround that remains to a great extent opaque to its regimes of presentation. Twenty-first-century media, including data gathering and analysis, furnishes a crucial and largely unprecedented means to access this broader environmental surround—the superjectal subjectivity of objectified concrescences of "data"[26]—and to translate its data (what I call "data of sensibility") into a form that can be presented, or more precisely "fed-forward," into (future) perceptual consciousness.[27]

This focus on the broad, or as Whitehead conceives it, the "total" environmental situation informing every actual occasion shifts the terrain on which media has long been theorized; specifically, it displaces the prosthetic narrative of media technology—a narrative that stretches from Plato to McLuhan and most recently to Bernard Stiegler—in favor of a model of technical distribution that dislodges perceptual consciousness and embodiment from their privileged position as exclusive synthesizers of media's experiential impact. French writer Éric Sadin aptly characterizes this displacement as an "anthropological turning point" in our species-constitutive relation with technology:

> Historically, the relation to the technical object has been instituted and developed on the inside of a distance that aims to make good—"from the outside"—deficiencies of the body and to amplify its physical capacities; our period marks the end of this distance, to the benefit of an ever more closed-in proximity. A displacement of the conception relative to *techne* is *de facto* called for, the latter no longer being envisaged, following the Western philosophical tradition, as a palliative and "prosthetic" production, or again, in the more informed manner described and analyzed by Leroi-Gourhan, as a relation of dynamic intermixture between *instruments* and *corporeality. Techne* must from now on be understood as an *enveloping* of virtualities offered to the body, which constitutes the *fundamental anchor point* for present and future technological evolutions, and which induces an *automatized* and *fluid* relation to the milieu.[28]

Sadin's claim lends forceful expression to the contemporary shift in our experience of technics: we no longer confront the technical object as an exterior surrogate for consciousness or some other human faculty, but rather as part of a process in which technics operates directly on the sensibility underlying—and preceding—our corporeal reactivity and, ultimately, our conscious experience. To be even more precise: the "reactive corporeity" that Sadin theorizes engages contemporary technics—data gathering, microcomputational sensing, predictive analytics—as a *radical exteriority* *within* the interiority of experience.

Propensity, or "Real Probability"

To the extent that this data—"data of sensibility" that are accessible only through technical means—are in fact data about probabilities bearing on future occasions, they call for a fundamental shift in how we approach media: we must cease focusing on acts of discrete agents and seek to understand tendencies for situations to happen, tendencies that are informed by a wide swathe of (mostly) environmental data, all of which is gathered incrementally and molecularly. In his recent account of tracking technologies and urban life, media artist and critic Jordan Crandall perfectly captures this priority of tendency over actuality: not only must discrete actions be redescribed as "performatively constituted action-densities, inferred through calculative, predictive or pro-active operations," "actuality" itself must be understood to be "conditioned by *tendency*" and agency to be "embroiled in a calculative, mobilizing externality" in which it "pushes and is pulled outward, as if seeking to become the predisposition that it courts."[29]

This prioritizing of tendencies over actions is precisely what allows predictive analytics to generate meaningful probabilities even when "datasets" cannot be totalized. Scenarios in which the total situation informing an occasion cannot be known yield open-ended probabilities or "probabilities in the wild"—probabilities that differ categorically from the classical a "calculus of probability" with its basis in the equipossibility of outcomes. To grasp this distinction, one need only consider the famous definition offered by Pierre-Simon Laplace: "The probability of an event is the relation of the number of favorable outcomes to the total number of possible outcomes considered to be equiprobable."[30] As Jean-Rene

Vernes explains, the calculus of probabilities hinges on two essential principles: the possibility of defining equiprobable outcomes and the independence of each move. In his study of "aleatory reason," the aptly titled *Critique of Aleatory Reason*, Vernes goes on to characterize the knowledge of probability as a form of a priori knowledge—the "a priori possible"—that charts a very different course from Humean skepticism than the Kantian legacy we know all too well. Central to the tradition theorized by Vernes is the notion that the calculus of probability correlates with an "object of immediate certainty": "In the case of a well-made die, the six faces have an identical probability of appearing, *because they appear identical in the representation that we have of them. They are interchangeable....* The link between the structure of the die and the series of results is a logical link, although of a different kind from what is typically understood under the term."[31] The key point here is that knowledge of probability is a priori: it is rooted in an a priori understanding of the equipossibility of each outcome. To this a priori knowledge of equipossibility corresponds the experiential notion of "frequency": a frequency results when series of moves tend toward a limit value. Although they are *experiential* verifications of something known a priori, frequencies remain bound to the two essential conditions of the calculus of probabilities: they are a function of equipossibility and independence of outcomes.

It goes without saying that the operation of predictive analytics concern open and incomplete "datasets" that are vastly more complex, and less discretely articulated, than the six possible outcomes of a dice roll. Indeed, the passage from the rarified domain of pure chance (Vernes's a priori aleatory reason) to the real world would seem to yield an ontological transformation of probability itself: probability ceases to function on the basis of mere possibilities and instead comes to operate as the index of "real propensities." Such a transformation is precisely what is at stake in Karl Popper's "propensity interpretation of probability." As Popper explains in *A World of Propensities*, "There exist weighted possibilities which are *more than mere possibilities*, but tendencies or propensities to become real [or, as I would prefer to say, that are real]: tendencies or propensities to realize themselves which are inherent in all possibilities in various degrees...." Still more emphatically, Popper claims that propensities *are not mere possibilities but are physical realities. They* are as real as forces, or fields of forces. And vice versa: forces are propensities." "We live in a *world of propensities,*" and in real world situations, Popper concludes, there simply are *no equal possibilities*—and indeed, no meaning whatsoever to the notion of equal possibility; hence, "we simply cannot speak here of probabilities in the classical number sense."[32]

Whatever explanatory and causal value predictive analytics of large datasets have is, I suggest, ultimately rooted in this ontological transformation whereby probabilities are understood to be expressions of the *actual propensity of things.* In this respect, Popper's conceptualization of probability as propensity provides a bridge to link Whitehead's account of worldly propensity as causal efficacy, as an expression of the present's impinging on the future (or the future's operating in the present), with the predictive condition informing contemporary life. Indeed, Popper's conceptualization helps us translate Whitehead's understanding of data as dynamically oriented to the future into the terminology of probability theory so central to contemporary technocultural mediations of worldly process.

More than any other element of Whitehead's neutral philosophy of experience, it is the probabilistic underpinnings of "real potentiality"—the way that present data already implicate their potential future power in its present operationality—that makes him *the* preeminent philosopher of twenty-first-century media. "Real potentiality" designates the potentiality of the settled universe that informs the genesis of every new actuality along with the incessant renewal of the "societies" that make up the world's materiality (worldly sensibility); as such it instigates a *feeling of the future in the present*: an experience of the future exercising its power in anticipation of its own actuality. Because this power remains that of potentiality—and indeed of an incredibly complex network of potentiality, a network inclusive of the potentiality of *every* datum comprising the universe's current state—it can only be fixed or arrested probabilistically, though to be sure in a quite singular sense. The force of the future—the future force of every single datum informing the universe at a given moment—is felt in the present in a way that can only be represented probabilistically and where such representation designates neither a purely abstract likelihood nor a statistical likelihood relative to a provisionally closed dataset, but a properly ontological likelihood: a propensity, which is to say, a likelihood that is, paradoxically, real.

Indeed, Whitehead's striking decision to include the total situation of the universe as determinative of each and every moment of its becoming lends depth to our conceptualization of propensity; specifically, it manages to capture the open-endedness of propensity: propensity names what in the present is always-already on the way toward its own future, but crucially on its way to a future that is itself not yet determined, that remains open to multiple possibilities. In this sense, the probabilistic dimension of Whitehead's concept of "real potentiality" differs starkly not simply from the a priori calculus of probability but from all empirical probabilistic systems: because of its grounding in the total situation of the universe's becoming, it is resolutely speculative in Whitehead's understanding of the term.[33]

It is precisely because of its speculative status that Whitehead's conception of potentiality furnishes the ontological basis of prediction. Insofar as it designates the future propensity of the present, real potentiality grounds the power of probability that informs the operation of today's predictive industries and that lends a certain credibility to cultural fantasies of control over the future. This is because, in Whitehead's understanding, *probabilities are expressions of real forces,* of actual propensities rather than empty statistical likelihoods. Rather than predicting the likelihood of future events on the basis of present and past data that are effectively inert, Whitehead's account foregrounds the emergence of the future—and specifically of novelty in the future—on the basis of the real potentiality of the settled world at each moment of its becoming. If the future is felt in the present, that is precisely because the future literally is (or will be) produced from out of the real potentiality—on the basis of the superjectal intensity—of the present settled world in all of its micrological detail. The key point is that the connection between future and present proceeds by way of efficacy, or better, propensity, and not of prediction. The connection is real and not just statistical, or, in Whitehead's terms, *actual without being actualized.*

That superjective intensity explains the power of the future in the present becomes clear in Whitehead's description of the Eighth Category in *Process and Reality*:

> (viii) *The Category of Subjective Intensity.* The subjective aim, whereby there is origination of conceptual feeling, is at intensity of feeling (∂) in the immediate subject, and (ß) in the *relevant* future. This double aim—at the *immediate* present and the *relevant* future—is less divided than appears on the surface. For the determination of the *relevant* future, and the *anticipatory* feeling respecting provision for its grade of intensity, are elements affecting the immediate complex of feeling. The greater part of morality hinges on the determination of relevance in the future. The relevant future consists of those elements in the anticipated future *which are felt with effective intensity by the present subject by reason of the real potentiality for them to be derived from itself.*[34]

To understand the full force of this claim, and specifically its promise to open a novel perspective concerning prediction, let us introduce philosopher Judith Jones's account of how intensity generated by data in the present is itself the source for superjectal subjectivity.[35] For Jones, the subject referenced in the final line of the previous citation simply *is* the agency of the contrast yielding intensity: "The agency of contrast *is* the subject, the subject *is* the agency of contrast. To be a subject is to be a provoked instance of the agency of contrast, and that is all it is."[36] This important interpretation underscores how the real potentiality of the future is already felt *as intensity in the present*—is felt, that is, *prior to its actualization and in its full force of potentiality*: this feeling of potentiality *for the future* generates—indeed, simply *is*—the subject.

Jones's point here is crucial: subjectivity, insofar as it *is* the intensity produced by contrasts of settled data, simply *is* a distillation of real potentiality for the future that is felt in the present. As such, subjectivity cannot be restricted to the status of inert force in the present, but literally upsurges *in and as* the transition *from present to future*: by effectively introjecting the future—the force of historically achieved potentiality—into the present, subjectivity arises in the *in-between-present-and-future*. It is the force that makes the future arise continuously out of the present, as possibility already (partially) contained in real potentiality. This, indeed, is the deep meaning of Whitehead's assertion that by "subject" he always means "subject-superject": subjectivity always arises on the basis of the power of the settled world, from "real potentiality"— which is to say, from the superjective forces of present, the constraint the present exercises over the future. For Whitehead then, the future *is already in the present,* not simply as a statistical likelihood, however reliable, but because each new concrescence is catalyzed into becoming by the superjectal intensity or real potentiality—the *future agency*—of the universe itself!

Recording the Future?

In sketching a broad shift from preemption through fear to preemption through prediction, Brennan's testimony addresses much more than the issue of drone killings. Indeed, as I have sought to suggest, it effectively foregrounds the sweeping intrusion of predictive analytics into the daily life of ordinary citizens that comprises the mandate of the November 2011 Department of Justice white paper. To begin to grapple with this intrusion—and with how Whitehead's ontology of probability might help us understand it better—let us focus on an example of predictive technics—a "third-generation" search technology that promises, quite literally, to *record the future.* Recorded Future is a small, Swedish intelligence company that sells a data analytics service for predicting future events. Initially financed by small venture capital grants from the CIA and from Google, Recorded Future has developed algorithms that make predictions about future events entirely based on publicly available information, including news articles, financial reports, blogs, RSS feeds, Facebook posts, and tweets. Recorded Future has a client base that includes banks, government agencies, and hedge funds. What it offers is a service designed to monitor the likelihood of future events or, as the company's press puts it, a "new tool that allows you to visualize the future."[37]

What most distinguishes Recorded Future is its status as a

"third-generation" search engine. Rather than looking at individual pages in isolation, as did first-generation engines like Lycos and Alta Vista, and rather than analyzing the explicit links between Web pages with the aim of promoting those with the most links, as Google has done since the introduction of its PageRank algorithm in 1998, Recorded Future examines *implicit* links. Implicit links, or what it calls "invisible links" between documents, are links that obtain not because of any direct connection between documents but because they *refer to the same entities or event.* To access the power of *implicit* links between documents, Recorded Future does not simply use metadata embedded into documents, but actually separates the content contained *in* documents from what they are *about*; Recorded Future's algorithms are able to identify in the documents themselves references to events and entities that exist outside of them, and on the basis of such identification, to create an entirely new network of affiliations that establish relations of meaning and knowledge between documents rather than mere associations.[38]

What is most crucial here is *what* Recorded Future does with the references it identifies, *how* it manages to construct those shadow references into a meaningful knowledge network with predictive power. To do this, Recorded Future *ranks the entities and events* identified by its algorithms based on a myriad of factors, the most important of which include the number of references to them, the credibility of the documents referring to them, and the occurrence of different entities and events within the same document. The result of this analysis is a "momentum score" that, combined with a "sentiment valuation," indexes the power of the event or entity with respect to its potential future impact. For example, as journalist Tom Cheshire notes, "Searching big pharma in general will tell you that over the next five years, nine of the world's fifteen best-selling medicines will lose patent protection"; the basis for this knowledge, which of course is only a heavily weighted prediction, is the high momentum score of the event, a score due to its being supported by thirteen news stories from twelve different sources.[39]

We can perhaps best appreciate the substantial predictive power of Recorded Future by focusing on another, equally crucial feature: its temporal dynamics. Recorded Future includes a time and space dimension of documents in its evaluation, which allows it to score events and entities that are yet to happen *on the basis of present knowledge about them*—what, in Whitehead's terms, we would call data of the settled universe. "References to when and where an event . . . will take place" are crucial, observes Staffan Truvé, one of Recorded Future's cofounders, "since many documents actually refer to events expected to take place in the future."[40] By using RSS feeds, Recorded Future is able to integrate publishing time as an index for this temporal analysis. Such temporal analysis affords Recorded Future the capacity to weight opinions about the likely happening and timing of future events using algorithmically processed crowdsourcing and statistical analysis of historical records of related series of such events. The result: differentially weighted predictions about the future.[41]

The Power of the Future in the Present

What accounts for Recorded Future's specificity as a third-generation search engine—its focus on data that implicate the future in the present—is precisely what constitutes the potential pharmacological recompense of today's predictive technologies: the open-endedness of data's potentiality. Whatever power it is that allows Recorded Future to make reliable predictions of future developments is a power *that is not specific to it and that is not created by its algorithms.* Rather, it is a general power—the power of the future in the present—that operates at all levels of the universe's continual becoming. It is, in short, an ontological power—the very ontological power Whitehead seeks to explain—and as such it is rooted in the total situation of causal efficacy that is captured with such precision (though of course, only partially) by today's technical data gathering and predictive analytical systems. The crucial point here is that this causal efficacy, despite its immense complexity (remember it encompasses the superjectivity of *every* datum of the current world), is both "neutral" regarding its future use and always excessive in relation to any targeted deployment of it.

This means, to put it slightly differently, that surrounding any delimited predictive system is a larger field of data—what I elsewhere call a "surplus of sensibility"—that, viewed speculatively, indexes the causal efficacy of the total situation within which this delimited system operates.[42] (Effectively, the latter gains its reliability from closing off this larger surplus of sensibility, thereby transforming an always excessive propensity into a [provisionally] closed dataset.) Because it affords data that exceed whatever any given predictive system might include, the data of the world's causal efficacy—the data constituting its real potentiality—always and in principle facilitates knowledge that cannot be restricted to any particular agenda. In this sense, reclaiming the surplus of sensibility from today's data industries—liberating it from capture in concrete networks of predictive power—comprises the first task of a pharmacology of media that would restore data's potential to offer broad insight about future tendencies that implicate humans;[43] to the extent that it potentially counteracts the control instituted through provisionally closed predictive systems, such insight would constitute a recompense that lies at the very heart of our contemporary predictive condition.

This pharmacological recompense, let me emphasize, is an intrinsic, structural element of contemporary technical mediations of the future: any system for data gathering and predictive analytics—because it operates on a "total situation" that it cannot hope to encompass in its entirety and that it can only speculatively intend—only ever actualizes a small part of a potentiality *that continues to remain potential despite this actualization, that continues to exert its ontological power in the "environment" of this system.* Whitehead's ontology of real potentiality forms a kind of check against the imperative to close off this surplus—the very imperative driving our predictive culture—at the same time as it explains the very power that grounds prediction itself. Thus, as we seek to understand and to criticize the forms of predictive power that increasingly enframe—and constrain—our experience, it is imperative that we welcome—on this score, in concert with the very predictive industries that are at issue here—the technical interface to the data of sensibility making up the potential for our future experience. For it is only by recognizing the immense power of the data networks to which contemporary technologies afford access—and also by accepting the accompanying demotion of historically human modes of experience (sense perception, conscious awareness, etc.)—that we can make good on Whitehead's fundamental contribution toward theorizing our predictive condition.

In this context, what the example of Recorded Future underscores is the very potential of Whitehead's ontology of real potentiality: in Recorded Future's weighting of present predictions concerning the future—but also, and more fundamentally, in the ontological source of these weighted predictions, the future's status as "real component of what is actual"—we encounter the power of the future to shape the present, and with it, the power of prediction as more than a mere statistical entity.[44] With third-generation search capacities, the mining and analysis of data takes a "Whiteheadian turn" in the sense that it ceases to ground the power of prediction in a recursive analysis of past behavior, and instead—taking full advantage of recently acquired technical capacities for text analysis—channels predictive power through the reference of present data to future entities and events. In this sense, we might say that Recorded Future—and the technical innovation it exploits—concretizes or instantiates Whitehead's understanding of how the future is felt by the present, that is, by reference. Recorded Future indexes the fundamental insight of Whitehead's ontology of potentiality: "Actual fact includes in its own constitution real potentiality which is *referent beyond itself.*"[45]

A Whiteheadian understanding of Recorded Future reveals a "positive" dimension of prediction: more than a mere extrapolation of the causal force of the present and the past to future possibility, prediction concerns the potentiality *contained in* the transition from present to future. The key point is that this potentiality, despite being imperfectly reliable as a ground for prediction, has ontological power: indeed, it is precisely this power that informs Whitehead's specification of real potentiality as the mode through which the future is *felt* in the present. Whitehead's contribution thus encompasses a critical and a constructive element, both of which are crucial to our efforts to understand and to live with our predictive condition.

By furnishing a *speculative* account of the total situation informing the genesis of every new actuality, Whitehead's account in effect foregrounds the *impossibility* for any empirical analytic system—no matter how computationally sophisticated and how much data it can process—to grapple with the entirety of real potentiality, or anything close to it. Rather, systems like Recorded Future can—and no doubt will—get more reliable by including more data, but their reliability will always be purchased at the cost of inclusiveness: reliability, in short, is a function of the capacity to close off some data from the larger universe of data surrounding—and complicating—it. Accordingly, there will always be a surplus of data that remain available for the future in the mode of potentiality. In this sense, Whitehead's speculative account serves as a critical check on the totalizing impulses of today's data industries, a guarantee of sorts that the future, insofar as it can be felt in the present, can never be fully known in advance.

By facilitating a model of technical distribution of sensibility rooted in an expansion of perception beyond consciousness and bodily self-perception, Whitehead's philosophy makes room for the technical innovation at the heart of Recorded Future—the capacity to search the present for predictions about the future—to impact human experience in ways that go beyond the narrow and largely instrumental purposes that inform governmental and corporate deployments of it. The capacity to predict future events by way of present reference introduces a means to access more data that is relevant to human behavior—but that remains inaccessible through human modes of perception; as such, it makes more data available for the shaping of human behavior in the future.

Isn't this twofold investment in the power of potentiality precisely the source for the appeal of *Person of Interest*, in the sense that it features superhero-like characters who have imperfect knowledge of the predictions of an all-knowing but fully mysterious "machine" and who must become involved in situations—and must embrace the uncertainties of acting—if they are to prevent predicted future murders? With its obsessive concern for the imperfections of predictive knowledge, *Person of Interest* dramatizes both the negative and the positive elements just described. Its plots develop from the tension between the machine's knowledge and the characters' need to become involved to discover, always through a gradual and circuitous process, how the predictive information (a social security number) relates to events that are in the process of developing. In this sense, the information the machine gives is not a "premediation" of a future scenario or event, but the final output of a complex and mysterious process of predictive analysis that does not forecast a preordained event with any degree of certainty but that operates incrementally on data relevant to broader situations in which events might come to occur.

The show's ideological work is focused less on gaining public support for military surveillance than it is on acclimating us to our predictive condition, and it performs this work precisely by insisting on the relevance, indeed on the centrality, of human action and decision making in the midst of situations in which human agents would seem to have no cognitive overview or mastery whatsoever. If the show depicts prediction as intrinsically partial, it does so in relation less to the concrete limitations of any finite predictive system than to pragmatic concerns that explain the poverty of the machine's output (e.g., the need to keep the "back door" from being discovered) and at the same time serve to guarantee the continued relevance, indeed centrality, of human actors. The show would seem to assure us, at the very moment when a military predictive engine has acquired apparently total knowledge of the present, that real life will continue to require our distinctly human modes of deliberation and agency. With this assurance, we find ourselves more willing than before to allow today's predictive technologies to operate as agents in an expanded grasp of the world's sensibility: as long as they don't threaten our relevance, these technologies can be invested with the power to ameliorate human existence. We can now see why *Person of Interest* provides a counterpoint to *Minority Report*. Whereas the latter focuses on a magical technology for recording the near-future before it happens, the former focuses on the new model of distributed technical agency that, I suggest, has increasingly become the reality of our predictive condition.

From Premediation to Prediction

To conclude my exploration of the ontology of prediction, let me simply introduce *Person of Interest* into Grusin's threefold account of temporality in *Minority Report*. Grusin's characterization of the three regimes of temporality takes shape in relation to his mistaken characterization of prediction as "a future determined by the sequence of past events." Grusin deploys the "idea of prediction" to discount two forms of predictive temporality: one in which the future is simply added onto the present and past in accordance with the operation of "rules, laws, and habitual behaviors"; another in which this same schematization of time is undercut by an ineliminable margin of indetermination, the "free choice" available to individuals "at every moment." In their place, Grusin champions a regime of premediated temporality: aligned with the fictional perspective of Agatha, the precog who provides the minority report, this account invests in the "virtuality of premediation," "the idea that there are multiple potential futures, and that these future events always and already impinge upon the present."[46] Grusin telescopes the key distinction between prediction and premediation through the contrast between "majority" and "minority" positions as they are represented in the film: in the precrime version of things, "the future seen by the precogs *determines* the present in the same way that the past would"; in Agatha's version, on the other hand, "the weight or force of these futures impact the present *but do not determine* it."[47]

I would concur with Grusin as far as this contrast goes: clearly the film is an allegory of the power of the future to impact the present. But I would strongly resist Grusin's dismissal of prediction as either incompatible with or irrelevant to this indeterminate mode of impact. Indeed, I suggest that prediction, once liberated from its orientation toward static and inert past data, is in fact *necessary to make the "virtualities" of premediation "real."*

The passage from which I excerpt these key words makes clear just how much Grusin's argument depends on his dismissal of prediction:

> *Minority Report* exemplifies that to see premediation as the remediation of virtuality or potentiality is to recognize that there are always multiple competing and incomplete reals— multiple actualities which can emerge from any potential present, but which emerge not by negation or addition but by differentiation and divergence from other potential but never realized actualities. What is key here is that these virtualities are real, these premediations as virtualities have a

reality in the present, a force in the present, no matter how the future might turn out. That is, the model of possibility or prediction in scenarios, game-planning, or simulation ultimately involves the creation or determination of distinctions between false or illusory possibilities on the one hand and the real or the actual on the other—only those possible scenarios that come true are real, while the others are proved false or illusory or wrong. To think of premediation as virtual, and therefore as real, is to refuse this metaphysical distinction and to insist instead on the efficacy, or force, of the multiplicity of premediations in and of themselves—no matter how the future might actually turn out.[48]

Where Grusin goes wrong is in his characterization of prediction as bound to a repertoire of predetermined possibilities. However, before we take stock of the significance of this fundamental mischaracterization—and before we foreground the necessity for a different model of prediction here—let us follow out the logic of what Grusin does claim. If, that is, prediction can do no more than present a choice between false and real possibilities, then it is left to premediation itself—premediation as the presentation of a host of virtual futures—to explain how the future arises from the present. This seems to be precisely the position that Grusin adopts—or, as I shall claim, *is compelled to adopt*—at the end of this passage (which concludes his chapter on "Premediation"): in contrast and as an alternative to inert predictions that carve up the future as a repertoire of extensions of the past, premediations engage the future not as a single, predetermined outcome that can be known from the position of the present, but as a virtuality that can encompass different present projections, different premediations, all of which (allegedly) engage the reality of the future in the present. The ultimate culmination of this logic—one which Grusin cannot himself resist—involves the transformation of causality from the real to premediation—the substitution, *for the causal efficacy of the world,* of the "efficacy, or force, of the multiplicity of premediations *in and of themselves—no matter how the future might actually turn out.*"

Against this conclusion and the logic it culminates, let us highlight the error on which it relies: by attributing causal force *to the premediations themselves*—which are, after all, representations of the future in the form of media events—Grusin mistakes allegory for the real that it allegorizes. Even though he is right to insist on the virtuality—or, as I prefer to call it, the "real potentiality"—of the future, Grusin's decision to channel its causal force through the form of the premediated event not only imposes a particular, and in this case particularly limiting, unit (the integral event) on the causal force of the real. But it also, as a consequence of this imposition, leads him to overlook the distinction between this causal force and its expression. That is precisely why Grusin finds himself compelled to champion premediation itself *as cause*—or more precisely, to recall Massumi's argument, as virtual quasi-cause— though as cause *not* of the actual future (since it doesn't matter how the "future might actually turn out"), but rather of a host of premediations of the future, which is to say, *of nothing other than premediation itself.* With this development, we are, in effect, returned to the solipsism of Baudrillardian simulation: for what are premediations if not the circulation of representations *in the place of* an absent or unknowable real?

If, by contrast, we retain the distinction between the future-implicating causal efficacy of the real *and* the premediation of how that efficacy might produce the future, we will be able to see premediation for what it is—a representation or allegory of the future that abstracts from the actual causal efficacy Whitehead locates in the world in order to produce an immunologic designed to ward off the possibility of the unexpected. Once restored to its representational status, premediation—far from providing a causal explanation of the future—cannot help but beg the question of what grants it causal force. And the answer, as I hope my discussion here has made clear, can only be the causal efficacy (or real potentiality) of the world itself that can never be known in its entirety, but that can be partially, if imperfectly, predicted and represented as discrete probabilities in the wild.

To the extent that it allegorizes prediction *as the future's inherence in the present, Person of Interest* introduces what we can only consider to be a fourth regime of temporality that extends or supplements Grusin's threefold account. As the force at the basis of this allegory, prediction on the basis of real potentiality or "prediction in the wild" seeks to grasp the propensity that carries the present world into the future. The access that large-scale data mining and predictive analytics gives to this propensity is precisely what allows prediction in the wild to "premediate" the future, not as a set of represented media events, but as a partial glimpse into the present operation of real forces that will produce—*that are already producing*—the future to come.

Notes

1. Julia Angwin, "U.S. Terrorism Agency to Tap a Vast Database of Citizens," *Wall Street Journal*, December 13, 2012, http://online.wsj.com/. Holder's decision appears in the unclassified document, "Guidelines for Retention, Use, and Dissemination by the National Counterterrorism Center and Other Agencies of Information in Datasets Containing Non-Terrorism Information" (hereafter NCTC Guidelines 2012), which is available as a sidebar in Angwin's article.

2. Jesselyn Raddack, "Minority Report: Govt Can Now Spy on Innocent Americans for Future Criminal Behavior," *Daily Kos* blog, December 13, 2012, www.dailykos.com/.

3. John Brennan, cited in "Innocent Until Proven Guilty; Imminent Until Proven—Too Late," *Empty Wheel* blog, February 11, 2013, www.emptywheel.net/. The position outlined here marks a distinct radicalization of the policy set forth in the November 2011 Department of Justice white paper. (The white paper is available at www.documentcloud.org/documents/602342-draft-white-paper.html.) Whereas the white paper implies (although without actually requiring) that, in the case of American citizens, involvement in past crimes is important for assessing the imminence of a threat, Brennan's rationale preserves no such implication, and indeed presents the latter not simply as a key point of difference between the courts and the military, but *as a part of the threat itself!* The rationale here is quite simple: if the military were constrained to exercise its force, its right to kill, only in cases where evidence of involvement in past crimes existed, it would very possibly, indeed almost certainly, miss crucial opportunities to save American lives.

4. *Empty Wheel* blog, "Innocent until Proven Guilty."

5. Brian Massumi, "Potential Politics and the Primacy of Preemption," *Theory & Event* 10, no. 2 (2007): para. 23, http://muse.jhu.edu/journals/theory_and_event/.

6. Brian Massumi, "Fear (*The Spectrum* Said)," *Positions* 13, no. 1 (2005): 35.

7. Massumi, "Potential Politics," para. 13, emphasis added.

8. Massumi speaks, in addition to the "unknowable," of "indeterminacy," "indeterminate potentiality," and "objective uncertainty," "Potential Politics," paras. 20, 13, 24.

9. And Massumi is unequivocal on this point: "The lack of knowledge about the nature of the threat can never be overcome," "Potential Politics," para. 13.

10. Massumi, "Potential Politics," para. 13; and Massumi, "Fear," 35.

11. Massumi, "Potential Politics," para. 13.

12. Massumi, "Fear," 36.

13. Massumi, "Potential Politics," para. 23.

14. Massumi notes the Bush administration's disdain for "reality": "Truth, in this new world order, is by nature retroactive. . . . The reality-based community wastes time studying empirical reality, the Bushites said: 'we create it.' And because of that, 'we' the preemptors will always be right. We always will have been right to preempt, because we have objectively produced a recursive truth-effect for your judicious study. And while you are looking back studying the truth of it, we will have acted with reflex speed again, effecting a new reality" ("Potential Politics," para. 20).

15. Oscar Gandy Jr., "Data Mining, Surveillance, and Discrimination in the Post-9/11 Environment," in *The New Politics of Surveillance and Visibility*, eds. K. Haggerty and R. Ericson (Toronto: University of Toronto Press, 2007), 369–70.

16. Alfred North Whitehead, *Process and Reality: An Essay in Cosmology*, corrected ed. (New York: Free Press, 1979), 66.

17. One key element that the executive-military context adds to this general pattern of prospective data mining is a temporal instrumentality: it renders probability a function of time. Rather than existing in relation to a fantasized total knowability, and conversely, an equally fantasized total unknowability, information is always a compromise, an arrest of an ongoing world (the process of what I've called "worldly sensibility"), that reflects the confluence of multiple, and, to some degree or other, incongruous factors. That such a pragmatic approach becomes all the more significant in the context of today's terrorist threat is a point not lost on the Justice Department. Consider the following passage from its November 2011 white paper, which meditates on the key concept of "imminent threat": "By its nature . . . the threat posed by al-Qa'ida and its associated forces demands a broader concept of imminence in judging when a person continually planning terror attacks presents an imminent threat, making the use of force appropriate. In this context, imminence must incorporate considerations of the relevant window of opportunity, the possibility of reducing collateral damage to civilians, and the likelihood of heading

off future disastrous attacks on Americans" (www.documentcloud.org/documents/602342-draft-white-paper.html).

Interestingly enough in the present context, the white paper goes on to correlate this broadened concept of imminence to the widespread use of technology, as if to position data-gathering and predictive analytics as a new theater, or rather a new "behind-the-scenes," of war itself: "We are finding increasing recognition in the international community that a more flexible understanding of 'imminence' may be appropriate when dealing with terrorist groups, in part because threats posed by non-state actors do not present themselves in the ways that evidenced imminence in more traditional conflicts. After all, al-Qa'ida does not follow a traditional command structure, wear uniforms, carry its arms openly, or mass its troops at the borders of the nations it attacks. Nonetheless, it possesses the demonstrated capability to strike with little notice and cause significant civilian or military casualties. Over time, an increasing number of our international counterterrorism partners have begun to recognize that the traditional conception of what constitutes an 'imminent' attack should be broadened in light of the modern-day capabilities, techniques, and technological innovations of terrorist organizations." John Brennan, "Remarks of John O. Brennan, 'Strengthening Our Security by Adhering to Our Values and Laws,'" address to Harvard Law School, September 16, 2011, www.whitehouse.gov/the-press-office/.

18. Richard Grusin, *Premediation: Affect and Mediality after 9/11* (Basingstoke, U.K.: Palgrave Macmillan, 2010), 39.

19. Ibid.

20. To underscore this connection, let me cite the entire passage from which I excerpt this phrase: "Premediation insists that the future itself is also already remediated. With the right technologies—in this case the distributed cognition made possible by the hybridized institution of Pre-Crime, with its three precogs, nurtured in the appropriate physical environment and attached to the correct hardware and software—the future can be remediated before it happens. This remediation of the future is not only formal but also reformative. Insofar as capital crime can be prevented, precognition allows for the remedying of the future, the prevention of the crime of murder through premediation" (Grusin, *Premediation*, 39).

21. Ibid., 46, emphasis added.

22. In my book, *Feed-Forward: On the "Future" of Twenty-First-Century Media* (Chicago: University of Chicago Press, 2014).

23. To his credit, Grusin appears to grasp how the operation of premediation he describes ultimately forms nothing more nor less than a component in a larger system whose aim is to stimulate the production

of ever more data in the service of ever more effective prediction: "The affective life of media and the anticipatory gestures of mediaphilia operate to encourage, make possible, and proliferate an ongoing flow of everyday media transactions, which provide the raw material to be mined so that future, potentially disruptive events of terrorism or other violent attacks can be pre-empted before they ever happen" (Grusin, *Premediation,* 134).

24. Angwin, "U.S. Terrorism Agency."

25. Hansen, *Feed-Forward.* My understanding of the *pharmakon* derives from Jacques Derrida's reading in "Plato's Pharmacy," as well as Bernard Stiegler's more recent developments of the concept.

26. A much misunderstood notion, in large part due to Whitehead's own descriptions, the superject designates the mode of subjectivity that an actuality takes on when it is added to, that is, becomes part of, the objective, settled world. As such, it is as superject that a completed actuality is able to act, not on its own genesis or becoming, but on the becoming of other new actualities and societies of actualities. On this understanding, which incidentally owes much to the work of philosopher Judith Jones, the superject is the mode of subjectivity and the source of power of the "real potentiality" of the settled world, which is to say, of its power to impact the future. The crucial point here, following Jones's identification of subjectivity with intensity, is how the real potentiality of the future is felt *as intensity* in the present, *prior to its actualization and in its full force of superjective potentiality.*

27. This is the central argument of *Feed-Forward.*

28. Éric Sadin, *La Société de l'Anticipation* (Paris: Éditions inculte, 2011), 13. Translations mine.

29. Jordan Crandall, "The Geospatialization of Calculative Operations: Tracking, Sensing and Megacities," *Theory, Culture & Society* 27, no. 6 (November 2010): 75.

30. Laplace, cited in Jean-Rene Vernes, *Critique de la raison aleatoire, ou, Decartes contre Kant* (Paris: Aubier-Montaigne, 1982), 87. Translations mine.

31. Vernes, *Critique,* 88.

32. Karl Popper, ""Two New Views of Causality," in *A World of Propensities* (Bristol, U.K.: Thoemmes Antiquarian Books, 1990), 9, last two emphases added.

33. Whitehead's project in *Process and Reality* (and related texts) is to provide a speculative account of the universe that explains how it must be structured in order for experience to be what it is. One key point that often gets forgotten by Whitehead's commentators is that the speculative is not accessible from the perspective of experience.

34. Whitehead, *Process and Reality,* 27, last emphasis added.

35. Jones's important book, *Intensity*, is effectively a reading of White-head's speculative empiricism from the perspective of the Eighth Category. Judith A. Jones, *Intensity: An Essay on Whiteheadian Ontology* (Nashville, Tenn.: Vanderbilt University Press, 1998), especially chs. 1 and 3.

36. Jones, *Intensity*, 130.

37. Home page, *Recorded Future*, /www.recordedfuture.com/.

38. Journalist Tom Cheshire pinpoints the significance of this capacity for reference when he compares Recorded Future with Google: "Recorded Future *knows* who Nicolas Sarkozy is, say: that he's the president of France, he's the husband of Carla Bruni, he's 1.65m tall in his socks, he travelled to Deauville for the G8 summit in May. If you Google 'president of France,' you'll get two Wikipedia pages on 'president of France' then 'Nicolas Sarkozy.' Useful, but Google *doesn't know how the two*, Sarkozy and the presidency, *are actually related*; it's just searching for pages linking the terms." Tom Cheshire, "The News Forecast: Can You Predict the Future by Mining Millions of Web Pages for Data?," *Wired UK*, November 10, 2011, www.wired.co.uk/, emphases added.

39. Ibid.

40. Ibid.

41. Despite its superficial similarity to Bernard Stiegler's account of how today's media industries support empty protentions, the predictive mechanism at issue in Recorded Future opens to a future that is not simply a function of expectations rooted in past experiences. For Stiegler, there can be no viable future because industrially manufactured memories have taken the place of "lived" secondary memories, and thus provide a false or empty source for projections of future possibility. Whereas Stiegler's model operates in relation to a static source of fixed possibilities, a situation reinforced by his discretization of memory and the past as tertiary—that is, recorded and inert—*contents* of experience, Recorded Future operates in terms of probabilities that are generated not simply through a processing of the repository of past, inert data of experience, but—crucially—through the *power of present data* to lay claim on the future. In this sense, it invests in the future as open to possibility, even if it seeks to control how the future will be produced.

42. Hansen, *Feed-Forward*.

43. I develop such a pharmacological account of the "surplus of sensibility" in *Feed-Forward*.

44. What ensures that potentiality implicates the future in the present is the *solidarity* that Whitehead attributes to the extensive continuum: "The extensive continuum is 'real,'" he writes, "because it expresses a fact derived from the actual world and concerning the contemporary actual

world. All actual entities are related according to the determinations of this continuum; and all possible actual entities in the future must exemplify these determinations in their relations with the already actual world. The reality of the future is bound up with the reality of this continuum. It is the reality of what is potential, in its character of a real component of what is actual" (Whitehead, *Process and Reality,* 66). On this account, what implicates the future in the present is nothing less than the entirety of causal nexuses operative at any moment in the ongoing process of the universe, or more concretely, in any given settled state of the superjectal world: this is the wellspring of "real potentiality."

45. Whitehead, *Process and Reality,* 72, emphasis added.

46. Grusin, *Premediation,* 59, 60.

47. Ibid., 60, emphasis added.

48. Ibid., 60–61.

6

Crisis, Crisis, Crisis; or, The Temporality of Networks

WENDY HUI KYONG CHUN

HOW ARE CODES AND SAFETY RELATED? How can we understand the current proliferation of codes designed to guarantee our safety and of crises that endanger it?

Codes, historically linked to rules and laws, seek to exempt us from hurt or injury by establishing norms, which order the present and render calculable the future. As Adrian Mackenzie and Theo Vurdubakis note, "Code systems and codes of conduct pervade many registers of 'safe living.' . . . Many situations today become manageable or tractable by virtue of their codeability."[1] Although codes encompass more than software—they are also "cultural, moral, ethical"—computational codes are increasingly privileged as *the* means to guarantee "safe living" because they seem to enforce automatically what they prescribe. If "voluntary" actions once grounded certain norms, technically enforced settings and algorithms now do so, from software keys designed to prevent unauthorized copying to iPhone updates that disable unlocked phones, from GPS tracking devices for children to proxies used in China to restrict search engine results. Tellingly, trusted computer systems are systems secure from user interventions and understanding. Moreover, software codes not only save the future by restricting user action, they also do so by drawing on saved data and analysis. They are, after all, programmed. They thus seek to free us from danger by reducing the future to the past, or, more precisely, to a past anticipation of the future. Remarkably, though, computer systems have been linked to user empowerment and agency, as much as they have been condemned as new forms of control. Still more remarkably, software codes have not only reduced crises, they have also proliferated them. From financial crises linked to complex software programs to supercomputer-dependent diagnoses and predictions of global climate change, from undetected computer viruses to bombings at securitized airports, we are increasingly called on both to trust coded systems and to prepare for events that elude them.

This chapter responds to this apparent paradox by arguing that crises are not accidental to a culture focused on safety—they are its raison d'être. In such a society, each crisis is the motor and the end of control systems; each initially singular emergency is carefully saved, analyzed, and codified. More profoundly and less obviously, crises and codes are complementary because they are both central to the emergence of what appears to be the antithesis of both auto- mation and codes: user agency. Codes and crises together produce (the illusion of) mythical and mystical sovereign subjects who weld together norm with reality, word with action. Exceptional crises justify states of exception that undo the traditional democratic separation of executive and legislative branches.[2]

Correspondingly, as I've argued in my recent book, *Programmed Visions: Software and Memory*, software emerged as a thing—as an iterable textual program—through a process of commercialization and commodification that has made code *logos*: code as source, code as conflated with, and substituting for, action.[3] This chapter revisits code as *logos* in order to outline the fundamental role crises play in new media networks. Starting from an analysis of rhetorical and theoretical constructions of the Internet as critical, it contends that crisis is new media's critical difference: its norm and its ex- ception. Crises cut through the continuous stream of information, differentiating the temporally valuable from the mundane, offering its users a taste of real-time responsibility and empowerment. They also threaten to undermine this experience, however, by catching and exhausting us in an endlessly repeating series of responses. Therefore, to battle this twinning of crisis and codes, we need a means to exhaust exhaustion, to recover the undead potential of our decisions and our information through a practice of constant care.

Internet Critical

The Internet, in many ways, has been theorized, sold, and sometimes experienced as a "critical" machine. In the mid- to late 1990s,
when the Internet first emerged as a mass personalized medium
through its privatization, both its detractors and supporters promoted it as a "turning point, an important or decisive state" in
civilization, democracy, capitalism, and globalization.[4] Bill Gates
called the Internet a medium for "friction-free capitalism."[5] John
Perry Barlow infamously declared cyberspace an ideal space outside physical coercion, writing, "Governments of the Industrial
World, you weary giants of flesh and steel, I come from Cyberspace, the new home of Mind. On behalf of the future, I ask you
of the past to leave us alone. You are not welcome among us. You
have no sovereignty where we gather." We in cyberspace, he continues, are "creating a world that all may enter without privilege
or prejudice accorded by race, economic power, military force, or
station of birth. We are creating a world where anyone, anywhere
may express his or her beliefs, no matter how singular, without
fear of being coerced into silence or conformity."[6] Blatantly disre-
garding then-current Internet demographics, corporations similarly touted the Internet as the great racial and global equalizer:
MCI advertised the Internet as a race-free utopia; Cisco Systems
similarly ran television advertisements featuring people from
around the world, allegedly already online, who accosted the viewers with "Are you ready? We are." The phrase "We are" made clear
the threat behind these seeming celebrations: Get online because
these people already are.[7]

The Internet was also framed as quite literally enabling the
critical—understood as enlightened, rational debate—to emerge.
Al Gore argued that the Global Information Structure finally realized the Athenian public sphere; the U.S. Supreme Court explained
that the Internet proved the validity of the U.S. judicial concept of a
marketplace of ideas.[8] The Internet, that is, finally instantiated the
Enlightenment and its critical dream by allowing us—as Immanuel
Kant prescribed—to break free from tutelage and to express our
ideas as writers before the scholarly world. Suddenly we could all

be Martin Luthers or town criers, speaking the truth to power and proclaiming how not to be governed like that.[9] It also remarkably instantiated critiques of this Enlightenment dream: many theorists portrayed it as Roland Barthes's, Jacques Derrida's, and Michel Foucault's theories come true.[10] The Internet was critical because it fulfilled various theoretical dreams.

This rhetoric of the Internet as critical, which helped transform the Internet from a mainly academic and military communications network to a global medium, is still with us today, even though the daily experience of using the Internet has not lived up to the early hype. From so-called Twitter revolutions—a name that erases the specificity of local political issues in favor of an Internet application—to WikiLeaks' steady flow of information to Facebook's alleged role in the 2011 protests in Tunisia and Egypt, Internet technologies are still viewed as inherently linked to freedom. As the controversy over WikiLeaks makes clear, this criticality is also framed as a crisis, as calling the critical—and our safety/security—into crisis. This crisis is not new or belated: the first attempt by the U.S. government to regulate the content of the Internet coincided with its deregulation. The same U.S. government promoting the information superhighway also condemned it as threatening the sanctity and safety of the home by putting a porn shop in our children's bedroom.[11] Similarly, Godwin's law that "as an online discussion grows longer, the probability of a comparison involving Nazis or Hitler approaches 1" was formulated in the 1990s.[12] So, at the very same time as the Internet (as Usenet) was trumpeted as the ideal marketplace of ideas, it was also portrayed as degenerating public debate to a string of nasty accusations. Further, the same corporations celebrating the Internet as the great racial equalizer also funded roundtables on the digital divide.[13] More recently, the Internet has been linked to cyberbullying and has been formulated as the exact opposite of Barlow's dream: a nationalist machine that spreads rumors and lies. Joshua Kurlantzick, an adjunct fellow at the Pacific Council on International Policy in the United States, told the *Korea Times* in response to the 2008 South Korean beef protests, "The Internet has fostered the spread of nationalism because it allows people to pick up historical trends, and talk about them, with little verification."[14]

Likewise, critics have postulated the Internet as the end of critical theory, not because it literalizes critical theory, but rather because it makes criticism impossible. As theorists McKenzie Wark and Geert Lovink have argued insightfully, the sheer speed of telecommunications undermines the time needed for scholarly contemplation.[15] Scholarship, Wark argues, "assumes a certain kind of time within which the scholarly enterprise can unfold," a time denied by global media events that happen and disappear at the speed of light.[16] Theory's temporality is traditionally belated. Theory stems from the Greek *theoria*, a term that described a group of officials whose formal witnessing of an event ensured its official recognition. To follow Wark's and Lovink's logic, theory is impossible because we have no time to register events, and we lack a credible authority to legitimate the past as past. In response, Lovink has argued for a "running theory" and Wark has argued that theory itself must travel along the same vectors as the media event. I am, as I've stated elsewhere, sympathetic to these calls.[17] However, I also think we need to theorize this narrative of theory in crisis, which resonates both with the general proliferation of crises discussed earlier and with much recent hand wringing over the alleged death of theory. Moreover, we need to theorize this narrative in relation to its corollary: an ever increasing desire for crises, or more properly for updates that demand response and yet to which it is impossible to respond completely, from ever-updating Twitter feeds to exploding inboxes. (That is, if, as Ursula Frohne theorized in response to the spread of webcams, that "to be is to be seen," it would now seem that "to be is to be updated." Automatically recognized changes of status have moved from surveillance to news and evidence of one's ongoing existence.[18]) The lack of time to respond—brought about by the inhumanly clocked time of our computers, which render the new old and, as I contend later, the old new—coupled by the demand for response, I suggest, makes the Internet compelling. Crises structure new media temporality.

Crisis: New Media's Critical Difference

Crisis is new media's critical difference. In new media, crisis has found its medium, and in crisis, new media has found its value—its punctuating device. Crises have been central to making the Internet a mass medium to end mass media: a personalized mass device. The aforementioned crises answered the early questions: Why go online? And how can the Internet—an asynchronous medium of communication—provide compelling events for users? Further, crises are central to experiences of new media agency, to information as power: crises—moments that demand real-time response—make new media valuable and empowering by tying certain information to a decision, personal or political (in this sense, new media also personalizes crises). Crises mark the difference between "using" and other modes of media spectatorship or viewing, in particular "watching" television, which has been theorized in terms of liveness and catastrophe. Comprehending the difference between new media crises and televisual catastrophes is central to understanding the promise and threat of new media.

Television has most frequently been theorized in terms of liveness: a continuous flowing connection. As Jane Feuer has argued influentially, regardless of the fact that much television programming is taped, television is promoted as essentially live, as offering a direct connection to an unfolding reality "out there."[19] As Mary Ann Doane has further developed in her canonical "Information, Crisis, Catastrophe," this feeling of direct connection is greatly enhanced in moments of catastrophe: during them, we stop simply watching the steady flow of information on television set and sit, transfixed, before it. Distinguishing between television's three different modes of apprehending the event—information (the steady stream of regular news), crisis (a condensation of time that demands a decision: for this reason it is usually intertwined with political events), and catastrophe (immediate "subjectless" events about death and the failure of technology), Doane argues that commercial television privileges catastrophe because catastrophe "corroborates television's access to the momentary, the discontinuous, the real."[20] Catastrophe, that is, underscores television's greatest technological power: "its ability to be there—both on the scene and in your living room. . . . The death associated with catastrophe ensures that television is felt as an immediate collision with the real in all its intractability—bodies in crisis, technology gone awry." Rather than a series of decisions (or significations), televisual catastrophe presents us with a series of events that promise reference: a possibility of touching of the real. However, as in Feuer's critique of liveness, Doane points out that television's relation to catastrophe is ideological rather than essential. Televisual catastrophe is central to commercial television programming because it makes television programming and the necessary selling of viewers' time seem accidental, rather than central, to televisual time. "Catastrophe," she writes, "produces the illusion that the spectator is in direct contact with the anchorperson, who interrupts regular programming to demonstrate that it can indeed be done when the referent is at stake." Thus television renders economic crises, which threaten to reveal the capitalist structure central to commercial television's survival, into catastrophes: apolitical events that simply happen. Televisual catastrophe is thus "characterized by everything which it is said not to be—it is expected, predictable, its presence crucial to television's operation.... Catastrophe functions as both the exception and the norm of a television practice which continually holds out to its spectator the lure of a referentiality perpetually deferred."[21]

In contrast, new media is a crisis machine: the difference between empowered user and the couch potato, the difference between crisis and catastrophe. From the endless text messages that have replaced the simple act of making a dinner date to the familiar genre of "email forwarding accidents," crises promise to move us from the banal to the crucial by offering the experience of something like responsibility, something like the consequences and joys of "being in touch." Crisis promises to take us out of normal time, not by referencing the real, but rather by indexing real time, by touching a time that touches a real, different time: a time of real decision, a time of our lives. It touches duration; it compresses time. It points to a time that seems to prove that our machines are interruptible, that programs always run short of the programmability they threaten. Further, crises, like televisual catastrophes, punctuate the continuous stream of information, so that some information, however briefly, becomes (in)valuable. This value is not necessarily inherent to the material itself—this information could at other moments be incidental and is generally far less important than the contents of the *New York Times*. Their value stems from their relevance to an ongoing decision, to a sense of computers as facilitating "real-time" action.

Real time has been central to the makeover of computers from work devices to media machines that cut across work and leisure. Real-time operating systems transform the computer from a pre-programmed machine run by human operators in batch mode to "alive" personal machines that respond to users' commands. Real-time content, stock quotes, breaking news, and streaming video similarly transform personal computers into personal media machines. What is real is what unfolds in real time.[22] If before visual indexicality guaranteed authenticity (a photograph was real because it indexed something out there), now real time does so, for real time points elsewhere—to "real-world" events, to the user's captured actions. That is, real time introduces indexicality to this non-indexical medium, an indexicality felt most acutely in moments of crisis, which enable connection and demand response. Crises amplify what Tara McPherson has called "volitional mobility": dynamic changes to web pages in real time, seemingly at the bequest of the user's desires or inputs, that create a sense of liveness on demand. Volitional mobility, like televisual liveness, produces a continuity, a fluid path over discontinuity.[23] It is a simulated mobility that expands to fill all time, but, at the same time, promises that we are not wasting time, that indeed, through real time, we touch real time.

The decisions we make, however, seem to prolong crises rather than end them, trapping us in a never-advancing present. Consider, for instance, "viral" email warnings about viruses. Years after computer security programs had effectively inoculated systems against a 2005 Trojan attached to a message claiming that Osama bin Laden had been captured, messages about the virus—many of which exaggerated its power—still circulated.[24] These messages spread more effectively than the viruses they warn of: out of good will, we disseminate these warnings to our address book, and then forward warnings and about these warnings, and so on, and so on. (Early on, trolls took advantage of this temporality, with their initial volleys unleashing a firestorm of warnings against feeding the troll.) These messages, in other words, act as "retroviruses." Retroviruses, such as HIV, are composed of RNA strands that use the cell's copying mechanisms to insert DNA versions of themselves into a cell's genome. Similarly, these fleeting messages survive by our copying and saving them, by our active incorporation of them into our ever-repeating archive. Through our efforts to foster safety, we spread retrovirally and defeat our computers' usual antiviral systems.

This voluntary yet never-ending spread of information seemingly belies the myth of the Internet as a "small world." As computer scientists D. Liben-Nowell and J. Kleinberg in their analysis of the spread of chain letters have shown, the spread of chain letters resembles a long thin tree rather than a short fat one.[25] This diagram seems counterintuitive: if everyone on the Internet was really within six degrees of each other, information on the Internet should spread quickly and then die. Nowell and Kleinberg pinpoint asynchrony and replying preferences as the cause: because everyone does not forward the same message at once or to the same number of people, messages circulate at different paces and never seem to reach an end. This temporality—this long thin chain of transmission—seems to describe more than just the spread of chain letters. Consider, for instance, the ways in which a simple search can lead to semi-volitional wandering: hours of tangential surfing. Microsoft has playfully called this temporality "search engine overload syndrome" in its initial advertisement for its "decision engine," Bing. In these commercials, characters respond to a simple comment such as "We really need to find a new place to go for breakfast," with a long stream of unproductive associations, such as details about the movie *The Breakfast Club* (1985). These characters are unable to respond to a question—to make a decision—because each word unleashes a long thin chain of references due to the inscription of information into "memory."

This repetition of stored information reveals that the value of information no longer coincides with its initial "discovery." If once Walter Benjamin, comparing the time of the story and news, could declare, "The value of information does not survive the moment in which it was new. It lives only at that moment; it has to surrender to it completely and explain itself to it without losing any time," now, newness alone does not determine value.[26] Currently, news organizations charge for old information. The *New York Times*, for example, charges online for its archive rather than its current news; similarly, popular radio shows such as *This American Life* offer only this week's podcast for free. We pay for information we miss (if we do), either because we want to see it again or because we missed it the first time, our missing registered by the many references to it. (Consider, in this light, all the YouTube videos referencing *Two Girls, One Cup* after that video was removed.) Repetition produces value, and memory, which once promised to save us from time, makes us out of time by making us respond continually to information we have already responded to, to things that will not disappear. As the Bing commercials reveal, the sheer amount of saved information seems to defer the future it once promised. Memory, which was initially posited as a way to save us by catching what we lose in real time—by making the ephemeral endure and by fulfilling that impossible promise of continuous history to catch everything into the present—threatens our sanity, that is, only if we expect engines and information to make our decisions for us, only if we expect our programs to (dis)solve our crises.

Bing's solution—the exhausting of decisions altogether through a "decision engine" (which resonates with calls for states of emergency to exhaust crises)—after all, is hardly empowering. Bing's promised automation, however, does perhaps inadvertently reveal that, if real-time new media do enable user agency, they do so in ways that mimic, rather than belie, automation and machines. Machinic real time and crises are both decision-making processes. According to the *Oxford English Dictionary (OED)*, real time is "the actual time during which a process or event occurs, especially one analyzed by a computer, in contrast to time subsequent to it when computer processing may be done, a recording replayed, or the like." Crucially, hard and soft real-time systems are subject to a "real-time constraint." That is, they need to respond, in a forced duration, to actions predefined as events. The measure of real time, in computer systems, is its reaction to the live, its liveness—its quick acknowledgment of and response to our action. They are "feedback machines" based on control mechanisms that automate decision making. As the definition of real time makes clear, real time refers to the time of computer processing, not to the user's time. Real time is never real time—it is deferred and mediated. The emphasis on crisis in terms of user agency can thus be seen as a screen for the ever-increasing automation of our decisions. While users struggle to respond to "What's on your mind?" their machines quietly disseminate their activity. What we experience is arguably not a real decision, but rather one already decided in an unforeseen manner: increasingly, that is, our decisions are like actions in a video game. They are immediately felt, affective, and based on our actions, and yet at the same time programmed. Furthermore, crises do not arguably interrupt programming, for crises—exceptions that demand a suspension, or at the very least an interruption of rules or the creation of new norms—are intriguingly linked to technical codes or programs.

Logos as State of Exception

Importantly, crises—and the decisions they demand—do not simply lead to the experience of responsibility; as the phrase "panic button" nicely highlights, they also induce moments of fear and terror from which we want to be saved via corporate, governmental, or technological intermediaries. States of exception are now common reactions to events that call for extraordinary responses, to moments of undecidability. As Derrida has argued, the undecidable calls for response that "though foreign and heterogeneous to the order of the calculable and the rule, must . . . nonetheless . . . deliver itself over to the impossible decision while taking account of law and rules."[27] States of emergency respond to the undecidable by closing the gap between rules and decision through the construction of a sovereign subject who knits together force and law (or, more properly, force and suspended law); this sovereign subject through his actions makes the spirit of the law live. Although these states would seem to be the opposite of codes and programs, I link them together—and to the experience of crises discussed earlier—through questions of agency or, more properly, as I explain later, authority.

Giorgio Agamben has most influentially theorized states of exception. He notes that one of the essential characteristics of the state of exception is "the provisional abolition of the distinction among legislative, executive, and judicial powers."[28] This provisional granting of "full powers" to the executive suspends a norm such as the constitution in order to better apply it. The state of exception is

> the opening of a space in which application and norm reveal their separation and a pure force-of-~~law~~ realizes (that is, applies by ceasing to apply . . .) a norm whose application has been suspended. In this way, the impossible task of welding norm and reality together, and thereby constituting the normal sphere, is carried out in the form of the exception, that is to say, by presupposing their nexus. This means that in order to apply a norm it is ultimately necessary to suspend its application, to produce an exception. In every case, the state of exception marks a threshold at which logic and praxis blur with each other and a pure violence without *logos* claims to realize an enunciation without any real reference.[29]

The state of exception thus reveals that norm and reality are usually separate—it responds to the moment of their greatest separation. In order to bring them together, force without law/*logos*—a living sovereign—authorizes a norm "without any reference to reality."[30] It is a moment of pure violence without *logos*. That is, if the relationship between law and justice—a judicial decision—usually refers to an actual case (it is an instance of *parole,* an actual speaking), a state of exception is *langue* in its pure state: language in the abstract and at its most mystical.

Given this, states of exception would seem the opposite of programming. Programs do not suspend anything, but rather ensure the banal running of something "in memory." Programs reduce the living world to dead writing; they condense everything to "source code" written in advance, hence the adjective *source.* This privileging of code is evident in common sense to theoretical understandings of programming, from claims made by free software advocates that free source code is freedom to those made by new media theorists that new media studies is, or should be, software studies. Programmers, computer scientists, and critical theorists have all reduced software—once evocatively described by historian Michael Mahoney as "elusively intangible, the behavior of the machines when running" and described by theorist Adrian Mackenzie as a "neighbourhood of relations"—to a recipe, a set of instructions, substituting space/text for time/process.[31]

Consider, for instance, the commonsense computer science definition of software as a "set of instructions that direct a computer to do a specific task" and the *OED* definition of software as "the programs and procedures required to enable a computer to perform a specific task, as opposed to the physical components of the system." Software, according to these definitions, drives computation. These definitions, which treat programs and procedures interchangeably, erase the difference between human readable code, its machine readable interpretation, and its execution. The implication is thus: execution does not matter—like in conceptual art, it is a perfunctory affair; what really matters is the source code.

Relatedly, several new media theorists have theorized code as essentially and rigorously "executable." Alexander Galloway, for instance, has argued powerfully that "code draws a line between what is material and what is active, in essence saying that writing (hardware) cannot *do* anything, but must be transformed into code (software) to be effective. . . . Code is a language, but a very special kind of language. *Code is the only language that is executable. . . .* Code is the first language that actually does what it says."[32] This view of software as "actually doing what it *says*" assumes no difference between source code and execution, instruction and result. Here the *says* is not accidental—although perhaps surprising coming from a theorist who argues in an article titled "Language Wants to Be Overlooked" that "to see code as subjectively performative or enunciative is to anthropomorphize it, to project it onto the rubric of psychology, rather than to understand it through its own logic of 'calculation' or 'command.'"[33] The statement "Code is the first language that does what it *says*" reveals that code has surprisingly— because of machinic, dead repetition—become *logos*. Like the king's speech in Plato's *Phaedrus*, it does not pronounce knowledge or demonstrate it—it transparently pronounces itself.[34] The hidden signified—meaning, the father's intentions—shines through and transforms itself into action. Like Faust's translation of *logos* with "deed"—*The spirit speaks! I see how it must read / And boldly write:*

"In the beginning was the Deed!"—software is word become action: a replacement of process with inscription that makes writing a live power by conflating force and law.

Not surprisingly, this notion of source code as source coincides with the introduction of alphanumeric languages. With them, human-written, nonexecutable code becomes source code, and the compiled code becomes the object code. Source code thus is arguably symptomatic of human language's tendency to attribute a sovereign source to an action, a subject to a verb. By converting action into language, source code emerges. Thus Galloway's statement, "To see code as subjectively performative or enunciative is to anthropomorphize it, to project it onto the rubric of psychology, rather than to understand it through its own logic of 'calculation' or 'command,'" overlooks the fact that to use higher-level alphanumeric languages is already to anthropomorphize the machine and to reduce all machinic actions to the commands that supposedly drive them. In other words, the fact that "code is law"—something Lawrence Lessig pronounces with great aplomb—is hardly profound.[35] Code, after all, is "a systematic collection or digest of the laws of a country, or of those relating to a particular subject."[36] What is surprising is the fact that software is code, that code is—has been made to be—executable, and that this executability makes code not law, but rather every lawyer's dream of what law should be: automatically enabling and disabling certain actions and functioning at the level of everyday practice. Code as law is code as police. Insightfully, Derrida argues that modern technologies push the "sphere of the police to absolute ubiquity." The police weld together norm with reality; they "are present or represented everywhere there is force of law. . . . They are present, sometimes invisible but always effective, wherever there is preservation of the social order."[37]

Code as law as police, like the state of exception, makes executive, legislative, and juridical powers coincide. Code as law as police erases the gap between force and writing, langue and parole, in a complementary fashion to the state of exception. It makes language abstract, erases the importance of enunciation, not by denying law, but rather by making *logos* everything. Code is executable because it embodies the power of the executive. More generally, the dream of executive power as source lies at the heart of Austinian-inspired understandings of performative utterances as simply doing what they say. As Judith Butler has argued in *Excitable Speech,* this theorization posits the speaker as "the judge or some other representative of the law."[38] It resuscitates fantasies of sovereign—again executive—structures of power. It embodies "a wish to return to a simpler and more reassuring map of power, one in which the assumption of sovereignty remains secure."[39] Not accidentally, programming in a higher-level language has been compared to entering a magical world—a world of *logos,* in which one's code faithfully represents one's intentions, albeit through its blind repetition rather than its "living" status.[40] As MIT professor Joseph Weizenbaum, creator of ELIZA and member of the famed MIT AI lab, has argued:

> The computer programmer . . . is a creator of universes for which he alone is the lawgiver. So, of course, is the designer of any game. But universes of virtually unlimited complexity can be created in the form of computer programs. Moreover, and this is a crucial point, systems so formulated and elaborated *act out* their programmed scripts. They compliantly obey their laws and vividly exhibit their obedient behavior. No playwright, no stage director, no emperor, however powerful, has ever exercised such absolute authority to arrange a stage or a field of battle and to command such unswervingly dutiful actors or troops.[41]

Weizenbaum's description underscores the mystical power at the base of programming: a power both to found and to enforce. Automatic compliance welds together script and force, again, code as law as police or as the end of democracy. As Derrida has underscored, the police is the name for

> the degeneration of democratic *power.* . . . Why? In absolute monarchy, legislative and executive powers are united. In it violence is therefore normal, conforming to its essence, its idea, its spirit. In democracy, on the contrary, violence is no longer accorded nor granted to the spirit of the police.

Because of the presumed separation of powers, it is exer-
cised illegitimately, especially when instead of enforcing the
law, it makes the law.[42]

Code as *logos* and states of exception both signify a decay of the
decay that is democracy.

Tellingly, this machinic execution of law is linked to the emergence of a sovereign user. Celebrations of an all-powerful user/
agent—"you" as the network, "you" as producer—counteract concerns over code as law as police by positing "you" as the sovereign
subject, "you" as the decider. An agent, however, is one who does
the actual labor, hence agent as one who acts on behalf of another.
On networks, the agent would seem to be technology, rather than
the users or programmers who authorize actions through their
commands and clicks. Programmers and users are not creators
of languages, nor the actual executors, but rather living sources
who take credit for the action. Similarly, states of exception rely
on *auctoritas.* The *auctor* is one who, like a father who "naturally"
embodies authority, authorizes a state of emergency.[43] An *auctor*
is "the person who augments, increases or perfects the act—or the
legal situation—of someone else."[44] The subject that arises, then,
is the opposite of the democratic agent, whose power stems from
protestas. Hence, the state of exception, Agamben argues, revives
the *auctoritas* as father, as living law:

> The state of exception . . . is founded on the essential fiction
> according to which anomie (in the form of *auctoritas,* living
> law, or the force of law) is still related to the juridical order
> and the power to suspend the norm as an immediate hold
> on life. As long as the two elements remain correlated yet
> conceptually, temporally, and subjectively distinct (as in
> republican Rome's contrast between the Senate and the
> people, or in medieval Europe's contrast between spiritual
> and temporal powers) their dialectic—though founded on
> a fiction—can nevertheless function in some way. But when
> they tend to coincide in a single person, when the state of
> exception, in which they are bound and blurred together,

becomes the rule, then the juridico-political system transforms itself into a killing machine.[45]

The reference here to killing machines is not accidental. States of
exception make possible a living authority based on an unliving
(or, as my spell-check keeps insisting, an unloving) execution. This
insistence on life also makes it clear why all those discussions of
code anthropomorphize it, using words such as *says* or *wants*. It is,
after all, as a living power that code can authorize. It is the father
behind *logos* that shines through the code.

  To summarize, we are witnessing an odd dovetailing of the
force of law without law with writing as *logos*, which perverts the
perversion that writing was supposed to be (writing as the bastard
"mere repetition" was defined in contrast to and as inherently en-
dangering *logos*). They are both language at its most abstract and
mystical, albeit for seemingly diametrically opposed reasons: one is
allegedly language without writing; the other writing without language. This convergence, which is really a complementary pairing,
because they come to the same point from different ends, puts in
place an originary sovereign subject. This originary sovereign subject, however, as much as he may seem to authorize and begin the
state of exception, is created belatedly by it. Derrida calls sovereign
violence the naming of oneself as sovereign—the sovereign "names
itself. Sovereign is the violent power of this originary appellation,"
an appellation that is also an iteration.[46] Judith Butler similarly
argues that through iterability the performative utterance creates
the person who speaks it. Further, the effect of this utterance does
not originate with the speaker, but rather with the community she
or he joins through speaking.[47] The programmer/user is produced
through the act of programming. Code as *logos* depends on many
circumstances, which also undermine the authority of those who
would write.

Sources, After the Fact

Source code as source—as *logos*—is a highly constructed and
rather dubious notion, not in the least because, as Friedrich Kittler

has most infamously argued, "there is no software," for everything, in the end, reduces to voltage differences.[48] Similarly (and earlier), physicist Rolf Landauer has argued, "There is really no software, in the strict sense of disembodied information, but only inactive and relatively static hardware. Thus, the handling of information is inevitably tied to the physical universe, its contest and its laws."[49] This construction of source code as *logos* depends on many historical and theoretical, as well as physical, erasures. Source code, after all, cannot be run unless it is compiled or interpreted, which is why early programmers called source code "pseudo-code."[50] Execution, that is, a whole series of executions, belatedly makes some piece of code a source. Source code only becomes a source after the fact. Source code is more accurately a re-source rather than a source. Source code becomes the source of an action only after it expands to include software libraries, after it merges with code burned into silicon chips, and after all these signals are carefully monitored, timed, and rectified. It becomes a source after it is rendered into an executable: source code becomes a source only through its destruction, through its simultaneous nonpresence and presence.[51] Even executable code is no simple source: it may be executable, but even when run, not all lines are executed, because commands are read in as necessary. The difference between executable and source code brings out the ways in which code does not simply do what it says—or more precisely, does so in a technical (crafty) manner.[52] Even Weizenbaum, as he posits the programmer as all-powerful, also describes him as ignorant because code as law as police is a fiction. The execution of a program more properly resembles a judicial process:

> A large program is, to use an analogy of which Minsky is
> also fond, an intricately connected network of courts of
> law, that is, of subroutines, to which evidence is transmit-
> ted by other subroutines. These courts weigh (evaluate)
> the data given to them and then transmit their judgments
> to still other courts. The verdicts rendered by these courts
> may, indeed, often do, involve decisions about what court
> has "jurisdiction" over the intermediate results then being

manipulated. The programmer thus cannot even know the path of decision-making within his own program, let alone what intermediate or final results it will produce. Program formulation is thus rather more like the creation of a bureaucracy than like the construction of a machine of the kind Lord Kelvin may have understood.[53]

This complex structure belies the conceit of source code as conflating word and action. The translation from source code to executable is arguably as involved as the execution of any command. Compilation carries with it the possibility of deviousness: our belief that compilers simply expand higher-level commands—rather than alter or insert other behaviors—is simply that, a belief, one of the many that sustain computing as such. It is also a belief challenged by the presence and actions of viruses, which—as Jussi Parikka has argued—challenge the presumed relationship between invisible code and visible actions and the sovereignty of the user.[54]

Source code as source is also the history of structured programming, which sought to reign in "go-to-crazy" programmers and self-modifying code. A response to the much-discussed "software crisis" of the late 1960s, its goal was to move programming from a craft to a standardized industrial practice by creating disciplined programmers who dealt with abstractions rather than numerical processes. This dealing with abstractions also meant increasingly separating the programmer from the machine. As Kittler has infamously argued, we no longer even write.[55] With "data-driven programming"—in which solutions are generated rather than produced in advance—it seems we even no longer program. Code as *logos* would seem language at its most abstract because, like the state of exception, it is language in pure state. It is language without *parole,* or, to be more precise, language that hides—that makes unknowable—*parole.*

To be clear, I am not valorizing hardware over software, as though hardware naturally escapes this drive to make space signify time. Hardware too is carefully disciplined and timed in order to operate "logically"—as *logos.* As Philip Agre has emphasized, the digital abstraction erases the fact that gates have "directionality in both space (listening to its inputs, driving its outputs) and in time (always moving toward a logically consistent relation between these inputs and outputs)."[56] This movement in time and space was highlighted nicely in early forms of "regenerative" memory, such as the Williams tube. The Williams tube used televisual CRT technology not for display, but for memory: when a beam of electrons hits the phosphor surface, it produces a charge that persists for .2 seconds before it leaks away. Therefore, if a charge can be regenerated at least five times per second, it can be detected by a parallel collector plate. Key here—and in current forms of volatile memory involved in execution—is erasability. Less immediately needed data do not need to regenerate, and John von Neumann intriguingly included within the rubric of "memory" almost all forms of data, referring to stored data and all forms of input and output as "dead" memory. Hence now in computer speak, one reverses common language and stores something in memory. This odd reversal and the conflation of memory and storage gloss over the impermanence and volatility of computer memory. Without this volatility, however, there would be no memory.[57]

This repetition of signals both within and outside the machine makes clear the necessity of responsibility—of continuous decisions—to something like safety (or saving), which is always precarious. It thus belies the overarching belief and desire in the digital as simply there—anything that is not regenerated will become unreadable—by also emphasizing the importance of human agency, a human act to continually save that is concert with technology. Saving is something that technology alone cannot do—the battle to save is a crisis in the strongest sense of the word. This necessary repetition makes us realize that this desire for safety as simple securing, as ensured by code, actually puts us at risk of losing what is valuable, from data stored on old floppy drives to CDs storing our digital images because, at a fundamental level, the digital is an event rather than a thing.[58] It also forces us to engage with the fact that if something stays in place, it is not because things are unchanging and unchangeable, but rather because they are continually implemented and enforced. From regenerative mercury-delay line tubes to the content of digital media, what remains is not what is static, but rather that which is continually repeated.

This movement does not mean that there are no things that can be later identified as sources, but rather than that constant motion and care recalls things in memory. Further, acknowledging this necessary repetition moves us away from wanting an end (because what ends will end) and toward actively engaging and taking responsibility for everything we want to endure. It underscores the importance of access, another reason for the valorization of digitization as a means of preservation. To access is to preserve.

By way of conclusion, I suggest that this notion of constant care can exhaust the kind of exhaustion encapsulated in "search overload syndrome." The experience of the undecidable—with both its reliance on and difference from rules—highlights the fact that any responsibility worthy of its name depends on a decision that must be made precisely when we know not what to do. As Thomas Keenan eloquently explains, "The only responsibility worthy of the name comes with the removal of grounds, the withdrawal of the rules or the knowledge on which we might rely to make our decisions for us. No grounds means no alibis, no elsewhere to which to refer the instance of our decision."[59] Derrida similarly argues, "A decision that would not go through the test and ordeal of the undecidable would not be a free decision; it would only be the programmable application or the continuous unfolding of a calculable process."[60] The undecidable is thus freedom in the more rigorous sense of the word—a freedom that comes not from safety but rather from risk. It is a moment of pause that interrupts our retroviral dissemination and induces the madness that, as Kierkegaard has argued, accompanies any moment of madness. The madness of a decision, though, differs from the madness described by Microsoft, which stems from the constant deferral of a decision. This deferral of decision stemming from a belief in information as decision catches us in a deluge of minor seeming decisions that defer our engagement with crisis—or rather renders everything and thus nothing a crisis. To exhaust exhaustion, we need to exhaust too the desire for an end, for a moment in which things can just stand still.

To exhaust exhaustion we must also deal with—and emphasize— the precariousness of programs and their predictions. That is, if they are to help us save the future—to help us fight the exhaustion of planetary reserves, and so on—they can do so only if we use the gap between their future predictions and the future not to dismiss them, but rather to frame their predictions as calls for responsibility. That is, "trusting" a program does not mean letting it decide the future or even framing its future predictions as simply true, but instead acknowledging the impossibility of knowing its truth in advance while nonetheless responding to it. This is perhaps made most clear through the example of global climate models, which attempt to convince people that something they can't yet experience, something simulated, is true. (This difficulty is amplified by the fact that we experience weather, not climate—like capital, climate, which is itself the product of modern computation, is hard to grasp.) Trusted models of global mean temperature by organizations such as Geophysical Fluid Dynamics Laboratory (GFDL) "chart" changes in mean temperature from 1970 to 2100.[61] Although the older temperatures are based on historical data, and thus verifiable, the future temperatures are not. This suturing of the difference between past and future is not, however, the oddest thing about these models and their relation to the future, although it is certainly the basis from which they are most often attacked. The weirdest and most important thing about their temporality is their hopefully effective deferral of the future: these predictive models are produced so that if they are persuasive and thus convince us to cut back on our carbon emissions, then what they predict will not come about. Their predictions will not be true or verifiable. This relationship is necessary because by the time we know whether their predictions are true or not, it will be too late. (This is perhaps why the George W. Bush administration supported global climate change research: by investigating the problem, building better models, they bought more time for polluters.) I stress this temporality not because I'm a climate change denier—the fact that carbon monoxide raises temperature has been known for more than a century—but because, by engaging this temporality in terms of responsibility, we can best respond to critics who focus on the fallibility of algorithms and data, as if the gap between the future and future predictions was reason for dismissal rather than hope.

This mode of deferring a future for another future is an engagement with the undead of information. The undead of information haunts the past and the future; it is itself a haunting. As Derrida explains, "The undecidable remains caught, lodged, as a ghost . . . in every decision, in every event of decision. Its ghostliness . . . deconstructs from within all assurance of presence, all certainty or all alleged criteriology assuring us of the justice of a decision, in truth of the very event of a decision."[62] This undeadness means that a decision is never decisive, that it can always be revisited and reworked. Repetition is not simply exhaustion, not simply repetition of the same that uses up its object or subject. What can emerge positively from the linking of crisis to networks—what must emerge from it if we are not to exhaust ourselves and our resources—are continual ethical encounters between self and other. These moments can call forth a new future, a way to exhaust exhaustion, even as they complicate the deconstructive promise of responsibility.

Notes

1. Adrian Mackenzie and Theo Vurdubakis, conference organizers, overview to *Codes and Conduct Workshop,* Institute for Advanced Studies, University of Lancaster, November 19–20, 2007, www.lancs.ac.uk/ias/annualprogramme/protection/workshop2/index.htm.

2. See Giorgio Agamben, *State of Exception,* trans. Kevin Attell (Chicago: University of Chicago Press, 2005).

3. As Barbara Johnson notes in her explanation of Jacques Derrida's critique of logocentrism, *logos* is the "image of perfectly self-present meaning . . . , the underlying ideal of Western culture. Derrida has termed this belief in the self-presentation of meaning, 'Logocentrism,' for the Greek word *Logos* (meaning speech, logic, reason, the Word of God)." Barbara Johnson, "Translator's Introduction," in *Dissemination,* trans. Barbara Johnson (Chicago: University of Chicago Press, 1981), ix.

4. *Oxford English Dictionary,* 2nd ed., s.v., "crisis."

5. Bill Gates, *The Road Ahead* (New York: Viking, 1995).

6. John Perry Barlow, "A Declaration of the Independence of Cyberspace," *Electronic Frontier Foundation (EFF),* February 9, 1996, http://w2.eff.org/.

7. See Wendy Hui Kyong Chun, *Control and Freedom: Power and Paranoia in the Age of Fiber Optics* (Cambridge, Mass.: MIT Press, 2006).

8. See Al Gore, "Forging the New Athenian Age of Democracy," *Intermedia* 22, no. 2 (1994): 14–16; and U.S. Supreme Court Decision, *Reno v. ACLU No. 96-511,* June 26, 1997, http://caselaw.lp.findlaw.com/.

9. For more on enlightenment as a stance of how not to be governed

like that, see Michel Foucault, "What Is Critique?" in *What Is Enlightenment?*, ed. James Schmidt (Berkeley: University of California Press, 1996), 382–98.

10. For examples, see George P. Landow, *Hypertext: The Convergence of Contemporary Critical Theory and Technology* (Baltimore, Md.: Johns Hopkins University Press, 1992); Sherry Turkle, *Life on the Screen: Identity in the Age of the Internet* (New York: Simon & Schuster, 1995), and *Women and Performance: A Journal of Feminist Theory* 17 (2007).

11. Senator Daniel R. Coats argued during congressional debate over the Communications Decency Act that "perfunctory onscreen warnings which inform minors they are on their honor not to look at this [are] like taking a porn shop and putting it in the bedroom of your children and then saying 'Do not look.'" Department of Justice Brief Filed with the Supreme Court 21 (1997) No. 96-511, http://groups.csail.mit.edu/mac/classes/6.805/articles/cda/reno-v-aclu-appeal.html.

12. "Godwin's Law," http://en.wikipedia.org/wiki/Godwin's_law.

13. For more on this, see Chun, *Control and Freedom.*

14. Kang Hyun-Kyong, "Cell Phones Create Youth Nationalism," *Korea Times Online,* May 12, 2008, http://koreatimes.co.kr/.

15. See McKenzie Wark, "The Weird Global Media Event and the Tactical Intellectual," in *New Media, Old Media: A History and Theory Reader,* ed. Wendy Hui Kyong Chun and Thomas Keenan (New York: Routledge, 2005), 265–76; and Geert Lovink, "Enemy of Nostalgia, Victim of the Present, Critic of the Future: Interview with Peter Lunenfeld," *Nettime Mailing List Archives,* July 31, 2000, www.nettime.org/Lists-Archives/. Lovink contends, "Because of the speed of events, there is a real danger that an online phenomenon will already have disappeared before a critical discourse reflecting on it has had the time to mature and establish itself as institutionally recognize knowledge." Geert Lovink, *My First Recession* (Rotterdam: V2/NAI, 2003), 12.

16. Wark, "Weird Global Media Event," 265.

17. Wendy Hui Kyong Chun, "The Enduring Ephemeral, or the Future Is a Memory," *Critical Inquiry* 35 (Autumn 2008): 148–71.

18. Ursula Frohne, "Screen Tests: Media, Narcicissm, Theatricality, and the Internalized Observer," *CTRL [SPACE]: Rhetorics of Surveillance from Bentham to Big Brother,* ed. Thomas Y. Levin et al. (Cambridge, Mass.: MIT, 2002), 252.

19. Jane Feuer, "The Concept of Live Television: Ontology as Ideology," *Regarding Television: Critical Approaches,* ed. E. Ann Kaplan (Frederick, Md.: University Publications of America, 1983), 12–22.

20. Mary Ann Doane, "Information, Crisis, Catastrophe," in *Logics of*

Television: Essays in Critical Criticism, ed. Patricia Mellencamp (Bloomington: Indiana University Press, 1990), 222.

21. Ibid., 238.

22. Thomas Y. Levin, "Rhetoric of the Temporal Index: Surveillant Narration and the Cinema of 'Real Time,'" *CTRL [SPACE],* 578–93.

23. See Tara McPherson, "Reload: Liveness, Mobility and the Web," in *The Visual Culture Reader,* 2nd ed., ed. Nicholas Mirzoeff (New York: Routledge, 2002), 458–70; and Alexander Galloway, ch. 2, *Protocol: How Control Exists after Decentralization* (Cambridge, Mass.: MIT Press, 2004).

24. See "Osama Bin Laden Virus Emails," *Hoax-Slayer,* last updated May 10, 2011, www.hoax-slayer.com/.

25. See D. Liben-Nowell and J. Kleinberg, "Tracing Information Flow on a Global Scale Using Internet Chain-Letter Data," *Proceedings of the National Academy of Sciences* 105, no. 12 (March 25, 2008): 4633–38.

26. Walter Benjamin, "The Story Teller," in *Illuminations* (New York: Harcourt Brace Jovanovich, 1969), 90.

27. Jacques Derrida, "Force of Law: The Mystical Foundation of Authority," *Acts of Religion,* ed. Gil Anidjar (New York: Routledge, 2002), 252.

28. Agamben, *State of Exception,* 7.

29. Ibid., 40.

30. Ibid., 36. According to Agamben, "The state of exception is an anomic space in which what is at stake is a force of law without law (which should therefore be written: force-of-~~law~~). Such a 'force-of-~~law~~,' in which potentiality and act are radically separated, is certainly something like a mystical element, or rather a *fictio* by means of which law seeks to annex anomie itself" (Ibid., 39).

31. See Michael Mahoney, "The History of Computing in the History of Technology," *Annals of the History of Computing* 10 (1988): 121; and Adrian Mackenzie, *Cutting Code: Software and Sociality* (New York: Peter Lang, 2006), 169.

32. Alexander Galloway, *Protocol: How Power Exists After Decentralization* (Cambridge, Mass.: MIT Press, 2004), 165–66. Emphasis in original. Given that the adjective *executable* applies to anything that "can be executed, performed, or carried out" (the first example of "executable" given by the *OED* is from 1796), this is a strange statement.

33. Alexander Galloway, "Language Wants to Be Overlooked: Software and Ideology," *Journal of Visual Culture* 5, no. 3 (2005): 321.

34. See Jacques Derrida's analysis of *The Phaedrus*: Jacques Derrida, "Plato's Pharmacy," in *Dissemination,* trans. Barbara Johnson (Chicago: University of Chicago Press, 1981), 134.

35. See Lawrence Lessig, *Code and Other Laws of Cyberspace* (New York: Basic Books, 1999).

36. *Oxford English Dictionary,* 2nd ed., s.v., "code."

37. Derrida, "Force of Law," 279, 278.

38. Judith Butler, *Excitable Speech: A Politics of the Performative* (New York: Routledge, 1997), 48.

39. Ibid., 78.

40. Fred Brooks, while responding to the disaster that was OS/360, also emphasized the magical powers of programming. Describing the joys of the craft, Brooks writes, "Why is programming fun? What delights may its practitioner expect as his reward? / First is the sheer joy of making things. . . . / Second is the pleasure of making things that are useful to other people. . . . / Third is the fascination of fashioning complex puzzle-like objects of interlocking moving parts and watching them work in subtle cycles, playing out the consequences of principles built in from the beginning. . . . / Fourth is the joy of always learning, which springs from the nonrepeating nature of the task. . . . / Finally there is the delight of working in such a tractable medium. The programmer, like the poet, works only slightly removed from thought-stuff. He builds his castles in the air, from air, creating by exertion of the imagination. . . . Yet the program construct, unlike the poet's words, is real in the sense that it moves and works, producing visible outputs separate from the construct itself. It prints results, draws pictures, produces sounds, moves arms. The magic of myth and legend has come true in our time. One types the correct incantation on a keyboard, and a display screen comes to life, showing things that never were nor could be." Fredrick P. Brooks, *The Mythical Man-Month: Essays on Software Engineering* (Reading, Mass.: Addison-Wesley Professional, 1995), 7–8.

41. Joseph Weizenbaum, *Computer Power and Human Reason: From Judgment to Calculation* (San Francisco: W. H. Freeman and Company, 1976), 115.

42. Derrida, "Force of Law," 281.

43. Agamben, *State of Exception,* 82.

44. Ibid., 76.

45. Ibid., 86.

46. Derrida, "Force of Law," 293.

47. Butler, *Excitable Speech,* 39.

48. Friedrich Kittler, "There Is No Software," *ctheory.net,* October 18, 1995, www.ctheory.net/.

49. Rolf Landauer, "Computation: A Fundamental Physical View," *Physica Scripta* 35, no. 1 (1987), 35.

50. For instance, *The A-2 Compiler System Operations Manual,* pre-

pared by Richard K. Ridgway and Margaret H. Harper under the direction of Grace M. Hopper (Philadelphia: Remington Rand, 1953), explains that a pseudo-code drives its compiler, just as "C-10 Code tells UNIVAC how to proceed. This pseudo-code is a new language which is much easier to learn and much shorter and quicker to write. Logical errors are more easily found in information than in UNIVAC coding because of the smaller volume" (1).

51. Jacques Derrida stresses the disappearance of the origin that writing represents: "To repeat: the disappearance of the good-father-capital-sun is thus the precondition of discourse, taken this time as a moment and not as a principle of *generalized* writing. . . . The disappearance of truth as presence, the withdrawal of the present origin of presence, is the condition of all (manifestation of) truth. Nontruth is the truth. Nonpresence is presence. Differance, the disappearance of any originary presence, is *at once* the condition of possibility *and* the condition of impossibility of truth. At once." Derrida, "Plato's Pharmacy," 168.

52. Compilation creates a logical—a crafty—relation rather than a numerical one—one that cannot be compared to the difference between decimal or binary numbers, or numerically equivalent equations, for it involves instruction explosion and the translation of symbolic into real addresses. For example, consider the instructions needed for adding two numbers in PowerPC assembly language:

```
li    r3,10    *load register 3 with the number 10
li    r4,20    *load register 4 with the number 20
add   r5,r4,r3    *add r3 to r4 and store the result in r5
stw   r5,sum(rtoc)    *store the contents of r5 (i.e. 30)
*into the memory location called "sum"
blr   *end of this piece of code
```

53. Joseph Weizenbaum, *Computer Power,* 234.

54. Jussi Parikka, *Digital Contagions: A Media Archaeology of Computer Viruses* (New York: Peter Lang, 2007).

55. Kittler, "There Is No Software."

56. Philip E. Agre, *Computation and Human Experience* (Cambridge: Cambridge University Press, 1997), 92. When a value suddenly changes, there is a brief period in which a gate will give a false value. In addition, because signals propagate in time over space, they produce a magnetic field that can corrupt other signals nearby ("crosstalk"). This schematic erases all these various time- and distance-based effects by rendering space blank, empty, and banal.

57. Memory is not static, but rather an active process. A memory must be held in order to keep it from moving or fading. Memory does not equal storage. Although one can conceivably store a memory, *storage* usually

refers to something material or substantial, as well as to its physical location: a store is both what and where it is stored. According to the *OED*, to store is "to furnish, to build stock." Storage or stocks always look toward the future. *Memory* stems from the same Sanskrit root for "martyr." Memory calls for an act of commemoration or renewal of what is stored. Memory is not a source, but an act, and by focusing on either memory or real time as sources, we miss the importance of this and other actions, such as the transformation of information into knowledge, of code into vision. Since the coded "source" of digital media can only operate by being constantly refreshed, degenerated, and regenerated, the critical difficulty of digital media thus stems less from its speed or source, but rather from the ways in which it runs.

58. Wolfgang Ernst thus argues that new media is a time-based medium. See Wolfgang Ernst, "Dis/continuities: Does the Archive Become Metaphorical in Multi-Media Space?," in *New Media, Old Media: A History and Theory Reader*, ed. Wendy Hui Kyong Chun and Thomas Keenan (New York: Routledge, 2006), 105–23.

59. Thomas Keenan, *Fables of Responsibility: Aberrations and Predicaments in Ethics and Politics* (Stanford, Calif.: Stanford University Press, 1997), 1.

60. Derrida, "Force of Law," 252.

61. Geophysical Fluid Dynamics Laboratory (GFDL), "NOAA GFDL CM2.1 Model," www.gfdl.noaa.gov/video/gfdlglobe_tref_d4h2x1_1970 _2100_30f_720x480.mov.

62. Derrida, "Force of Law," 253.

7

They Are Here

TIMOTHY MORTON

IN THIS CHAPTER, I analyze Toni Basil's video for the Talking Heads' song "Crosseyed and Painless" (1980). I strive to show that the way in which the video stages the proximity of poor African Americans to the broken tools of modernity, far from valorizing their immiseration, offers a way to think black environmental consciousness as symptomatic of and central to the emerging ecological age, the age of global warming.

I do this by thinking about nonhumans. Thinking antiracism has often proceeded by thinking within lines that preestablish thin and rigid boundaries between the human and nonhuman realms (subject and object, freedom and unfreedom, and so on). The task has quite rightly been to de-objectify, to de-commodify. Instead, this chapter proceeds by changing the sense of what is meant by the term *object*. I contend that this procedure provides a firmer logical structure for thinking race and antiracism. This is precisely because the lineage that brought us slavery and racism is also the lineage that brought us the anthropocentric boundary between human and nonhuman.[1] This boundary is predicated in part on another rigid distinction between *person* and *thing*.

Any attempt to make the human–nonhuman boundary a little less thin, a little less rigid, risks being seen as hostile to the lineage of antiracism. And any talk of objects risks raising the specter of objectification. Yet without this risk, a subtle anthropocentrism is reproduced, an anthropocentrism that is now under strain from science, from philosophy, and from the reality of a globally warming world.[2]

Is it possible to think antiracism without anthropocentrism?

This chapter is an incomplete, necessarily loose attempt at such a project.

Before she became famous with "Hey Mickey," before she was asked by an enthusiastic David Byrne to direct the memorable and often played video for Talking Heads' "Once in a Lifetime," Toni Basil directed the video for their song "Crosseyed and Painless."[3] This chapter shows how this video and the song are part of the anthem of global anxiety, the overwhelming sensation that underlies ecological thinking like a note that no one wants to hear, a certain high-frequency hum like the sound of a malfunctioning electric pylon. This is the sound of the end of the world, but also of the beginning of history. In so doing, the chapter considers the stone that the ecophilosophy builders cast away, the broken tool—the one golden key to the fact of coexistence with nonhumans. This consideration opens onto a deepened examination of the human attunement of anxiety, our home base, or rather, our contemporary "unhome," uncanny and strange. The chapter arrives there by using the insights of the emerging philosophy called object-oriented ontology (OOO).

The video narrates the story of a young man who is seduced into selling drugs by a street hustler, moving aside from the normal routine of work and play. He is threatened by a gangster. He finds a girlfriend and is disturbed by her sexual potency. Eventually they split up, and he is left to wander the streets again. Toni Basil employed the Electric Boogaloos, a stunning group of body poppers from Fresno and Long Beach. David Byrne paid between $10,000 and $15,000 out of pocket for the video. The Electric Boogaloos comprised Timothy "Popin' Pete" Solomon, Robot Dane, Skeeter Rabbit, McTwig (Twig Imai, the gentleman with the cigar), "Scarecrow Scally" Allen, and Ana Marie "Lollipop" Sanchez. They specialized in early hip-hop dance styles such as body popping and locking—people becoming robots becoming people. The first-ever moonwalk on video is by Skeeter Rabbit, not Michael Jackson at the MTV awards, as is often thought. Jackson learned it from Twig Imai and Skeeter.

The dance has to do with working with objects, working with tools: bouncing a basketball, tuning to the heft of the ball that asks to be bounced just that way (Figure 7.1). The larger frame is of

FIGURE 7.1. Lost My Shape—Trying to Act Casual. *In this opening scene from the Talking Heads' music video,* Crosseyed and Painless *(dir. Toni Basil), we witness a dance of the objects: Skeeter Rabbit (center) finds himself surrounded by a host of humans and nonhumans. Reproduced by permission of MSA Agency.*

humans tuning to industry, wearing masks, acting like machines. Still wider, the dance has do with African Americans trying to tune to the racist world: *trying to fit, trying to act casual, feeling like an accident,* as Byrne's lyrics put, moving to the rhythm of banking and high finance. Working in a factory. Making money, trying to love. Flooded with anxiety and fear. Objectified. They are bearing a message.

An overwhelming environmental threat hangs over these African Americans, what in Buddhism is called "all-pervasive pain." All-pervasive pain is not just the pain of being stabbed or of not getting that money you wanted by trying to sell those drugs, but what one teacher calls "an environmental creepiness."[4] Or as the song says, *Isn't it weird.* This is the pain of being in what Buddhism calls a "realm of existence"—being situated, phenomenologically, somewhere or other. *Environmental racism as the experience of environmentality as such*, of suffering as environmental. Not some blank "natural" environment (always a human product, a product of violence), but one that is charged with a certain irreducible appearance, a certain weirdness. At the back of one's mind there resides an overhanging sense of dread. This dread is what Emmanuel Levinas calls the *il y a*, the "there is," or what this song calls the "there was"—*There was a line / There was a formula*.[5] A story begins: Once upon a time, there was . . . But what? This is what narrative theory calls *aperture*, the feeling that something is beginning.

Aperture is precisely the feeling that we don't know yet; we can only work by hindsight. It seems to come from everywhere. The dancers are suspended in white space, as if nothing means enough, or anything, any more. Then all of a sudden they are in their world of cars and train tracks. Then back to white. The rugs keep being pulled out. Surrounded, they are, literally, by whiteness, a void that masks a deeper claustrophobia: a room that we discern in the tight shadows around the dancers, the square shape of the video frame. The video puts the characters in a claustrophobic space of whiteness, a waiting room with nothing in it, with no exit, nothing around it.

"Crosseyed and Painless" is a superb example of funk, a broken blues without a story, without that four-chord trick, that twelve-bar narrative, just popping in and out, locking into that first section, like a needle stuck in the groove of a broken record. Funk evokes the repetition compulsion, returning again and again to the same part of the city, like Freud in his essay on the uncanny, over and over again to the same strange part of town, the part that is your home, made stranger by the constant popping dislocation of the groove.[6] Funk burrows into that initial moment, the beginning of the blues sequence—the basic unhappiness that spawns the ironic enjoyment, the blue note. That chorus-like section that tries to fly from the sickening lurch of the verse, and seems for a few seconds to float above it, before descending back to uncanny home base, like a bird with a broken wing. No escape velocity can be achieved from the horrible gravity of the song, the centripetal torque emitted by the sharpened, shortened blues on heavy rotation.

Because this chapter makes frequent reference to David Byrne's lyrics for "Crosseyed and Painless," in a funk-like repetitive refrain, let us witness them here:

CROSSEYED AND PAINLESS

Lost my shape—Trying to act casual
Can't stop—I might end up in the hospital
I'm changing my shape—I feel like an accident
They're back!—To explain their experience

Isn't it weird/Looks too obscure to me
Wasting away/And that was their policy

I'm ready to leave—I push the facts in front of me
Facts lost—Facts are never what they seem to be
Nothing there!—No information left of any kind
Lifting my head—Looking for danger signs

There was a line/There was a formula
Sharp as a knife/Facts cut a hole in us
There was a line/There was a formula
Sharp as a knife/Facts cut a hole in us

I'm still waiting . . . I'm still waiting . . . I'm still waiting . . .
I'm still waiting . . . I'm still waiting . . . I'm still waiting . . .
I'm still waiting . . . I'm still waiting
The feeling returns/Whenever we close our eyes
Lifting my head/Looking around inside

The Island of Doubt—It's like the taste of medicine
Working by hindsight—Got the message from the oxygen
Making a list—Find the cost of opportunity
Doing it right—Facts are useless in emergencies

The feeling returns/Whenever we close our eyes
Lifting my head/Looking around inside

Facts are simple and facts are straight
Facts are lazy and facts are late
Facts all come with points of view
Facts don't do what I want them to
Facts just twist the truth around
Facts are living turned inside out
Facts are getting the best of them
Facts are nothing on the face of things
Facts don't stain the furniture
Facts go out and slam the door
Facts are written all over your face
Facts continue to change their shape

I'm still waiting . . . I'm still waiting . . . I'm still waiting . . .
I'm still waiting . . . I'm still waiting . . . I'm still waiting . . .
I'm still waiting . . . I'm still waiting.[7]

Working by hindsight, getting the message from the oxygen of a poisoned warming Earth, I argue that what seemed in 1980 like postmodern free play—*Facts all come with points of view*—turns out to be the disturbing truth of Lacan, that *there is no meta-language,* realized in the age of ecology.[8] Postmodernism was just the flashing neon sign on the tip of the iceberg. Irony becomes the food of phenomenological *sincerity,* the viscosity with which non-humans stick to us, live in our DNA, *are* our DNA. Because, as that other great '80s phenomenologist Buckaroo Banzai puts it, "Wherever you go, there you are."[9] Blues for a blue planet with no exit.

The lyrics are clownish, ironic, spiked with a faint message that becomes louder, like radio interference you keep hearing at the back of the station you are tuned to. *Lost my shape—Trying to act casual.* That's funny and ironic, but then: *Can't stop—I might end up in the hospital. I push the facts in front of me. Sharp as a knife. There was a formula.* The caesuras in each line allow for a twist of anxiety, uncertainty. They cause a kind of epistemological gap that might be hiding an ontological gap—is that a void or is it obscuring something? *The Island of Doubt—It's like the taste of medicine*: the unexpected twist in the second half of the line is as disturbing as it is funny. Moreover, the song seems to be talking about itself: talking about its use of caesura and ironic gaps—the knife, the device that makes the cut: *Facts cut a hole in us.* Analogous things happen in the video. Something keeps on coming, seeping through the gaps torn by the hood's knife. The world is torn open but there is no beyond, just another being, waiting with a knife, a sexy girl, a compelling memory, the promise of wealth, a lonely street, a suit, the smell of money, a dust mask, a briefcase, a rear windshield, an umbrella, a newspaper, a car.

The racist is the one who fills the gap between how a human appears and what a human is with some kind of metaphysical paste. It is strictly impossible, and thus ontological and political violence is what racism mimes in order to bomb thinking back to an age before there were uncertain facts (data) rather than absolute facts (metaphysics).

There is much to be said about that strange car at the close of Basil's video, so casually sitting in the driveway, covered with a sheet (Figure 7.2). The young man (played by Skeeter) does not notice it as he shuffles up the street. Does not notice as it glows through a range of electrical colors: iridescent blue, green, yellow, orange, red, magenta. The car is a device, a quotidian machine, a tool, waiting for its user. Yet it is also an entity in its own right, not waiting for anything. This occluded, hidden aspect of the car seems to become visible in the way it glows, a horrible rainbow that no one sees, a rainbow not as a sign of promise but of a threat, an existential threat: *Sharp as a knife. There was a formula.* Something is (already) here; *they are here.* The withdrawn thing power of the car, ontologically beneath what object-oriented philosopher Graham Harman would call its "tool-being," is unveiled for a second by the metaphorical fusion reaction of the video. Its hiddenness is on display, it hides in plain sight.[10]

The viewer wants to shout at Skeeter: "Look! For heaven's sake just look at the car!" But one is on the hither side of the screen, and he is on the yonder side. Yet, for a second, it is as if this dramatic aesthetic fourth wall dissolves, as we glimpse tools whose operation was withdrawn throughout the video—the chroma-keying (*color separation overlay* is the BBC term), the use of a broken video camera and an unusual color control, Brian Eno's fingers turning the knob so the car that is a not-car becomes the demonic rainbow

FIGURE 7.2. I'm Still Waiting. *In this still from the Talking Heads'* music video, Crosseyed and Painless *(dir.* Toni Basil)*, the car is glowing green, and will soon shift to blue tones. It is as if the car is alive, or sentient—it certainly seems to be half-communicating, just as humans blush. But we are left disturbingly unsure. Reproduced by permission of MSA Agency.*

in a sickening nowness of indeterminate dimension. The story is not over. The car glows knowingly, to no one, the fourth wall shattered, the video over. We have participated in a Dionysian ritual of coexistence, which is just what every tragedy really is. It's over for us. But not for that car, or that kid, or that street, or that song, that fades rather than ending. Aperture without closure.

Objects, objectification, and the status of tools are very much the issue of the video. Consider the fact that black people from the standpoint of racism, from the standpoint of environmental racism, are tools with souls (Aristotle's definition of a slave, *organon empsychon*), components of industry living next to the garbage, working under the overpass, the littered railway tracks, looking at normal life through the windshield of someone else's car.

Working-class black people are thrust up against the chatter of the foreign languages of nonhumans. They are in a disturbingly racialized position to experience "the mystery and melancholy of a street" (as Giorgio de Chirico put it), the melancholic uncanny of a world made of broken or uncared for objects: a parked car, perhaps abandoned, covered with cloth. From this vantage point, they experience the difficulty of doing anything, paralyzed by the inertia of things, unable to cut through it with the knife of big business, stuck in the garbage, trying to *push the facts in front of* one. Haunted by illusion, lies, anxiety, the black working class knows the secret life of things, the way they are in excess of their social role. Yet inner space does not provide a refuge from the outer world. There is no escape from this implicitly racist environmentality: *The feeling returns / Whenever we close our eyes.* Race, environment, nonhuman things are intertwined.

Again, this is by no means to glamorize racist poverty. It is instead to reveal a certain structure of feeling in which all humans are implicated—complicities with nonhuman beings, illuminating, disturbing, phantasmagorical. And it is to argue that the black working-class American experience is central to that structure of feeling.

What is happening? What is happening to the world? To ask Heidegger's founding question, perhaps at the right moment—How on Earth does it stand with Being?[11] What we are seeing, in that car shot, is the camera as its talks to the sky. This consists, more precisely, of an early 1980s conversation between broken tools, a burned-out tube in a Panasonic color video camera and a color control knob, a knob not present on contemporary video cameras at all. To accomplish this, we are also witness to the results of a car-shaped matte and a chroma-key setup via a vision mixer, probably the Grass Valley or CMX nonlinear video editor. Then the whole scene was filmed again to superimpose the shifting car-shaped color.

Chroma-keying exploits how an entity need not be present: it can be *zuhanden,* in Heidegger's terms, namely ready-to-hand, rather than *vorhanden,* present-at-hand, which is what happens when a tool ceases to function in a normal way—it suddenly springs to our attention. The car is replaced by a blue car-shaped matte that becomes transparent when fed through a vision mixer set up to key out that precise luminance of blue. In another shot, Skeeter wears a blue face mask that is similarly keyed out to allow the overlaying of the smoking factory. The blue screen (nowadays, because of digital sensors, the green screen) disappears. It is a beautiful example of a Heideggerian tool, because it is "before your very eyes," right in front of the camera. Yet it becomes transparent, allowing for different backgrounds to be placed behind the subject, in this case, the Electric Boogaloos and the car.

Transparent for whom? Here is the magical phenomenon that the video evokes. The tool is transparent not for a human but *for the camera itself,* the camera that is composing the video image out of Skeeter Rabbit popping and locking down the street, and the glowing colors that have been chroma-keyed into the outline of the car cover. With its blue color channel keyed out via a luminance key in the vision mixer that matches the brightness of the particular chosen shade of blue, one tool, the camera, makes another tool, the screen or matte, invisible. No wonder the video is so uncanny, such a perfect complement to the song. The equipment itself creates a complex dance between visibility and invisibility, presence and absence, transparency and opacity, surroundings as tools that glint into presence, like fish in a dark ocean, then vanish.

Sharp as a knife: a cut, a caesura, a break. A nonhuman has intruded from outside the narrative frame. This intrusion also possibly consists of another work of art altogether, a thin slice of something like Eno's 1981 video *Mistaken Memories of Mediaeval Manhattan.*[12] For it may well be Eno's broken camera that causes this astonishing smooth blend from blue to pink (Figure 7.3). Or at any rate, what we see in the video is Byrne's and Basil's homage to Eno's broken tool. (Eno was the producer of Talking Heads' *Remain in Light,* the album that contains "Crosseyed and Painless.")

As with his ambient music experiments, which emerged from a broken record player that wouldn't increase its volume, *Mistaken Memories* plays with a broken camera left on its side in floods of Manhattan light. Eno's video is a view of Manhattan sideways on, a broken, nonhuman Manhattan inhabited by light and camera tubes, phosphor screens, and building surfaces. This broken tool generated an anamorphic view of the same space, which lost its shape: *ana,* the Greek prefix, means "un-," while *morphic* means "pertaining to shape." The thing is un-shaping, contorting away

FIGURE 7.3. *Panasonic PK-600 video camera. Note the color controls, which gave Toni Basil and Brian Eno the ability to modulate color live. Photograph courtesy of Timothy Morton.*

from habitual human grasping and use. Harman has argued that the broken tool reveals something extraordinary about things—that they are never exhausted by their relation or by their use or by their proximity to other things, including humans. Broken tools force us to comprehend a nonhuman world in a physical, even nonconceptual way.

The molten car and the color-shifting dancers make a mockery of racist metaphysics, where appearance is inseparably glued to what a being is.

What we see in the iridescent car and in the chroma-keyed outlines of the color-shifting humans is a conversation between photons and the electron stream from the gun in the video camera tube, undoubtedly a Vidicon tube (Figure 7.4). The photoconducting surface at the front of the tube, probably made of selenium, is activated by photons incident upon it. This surface is then scanned by an electron gun. What happens when we view the picture is a conversation

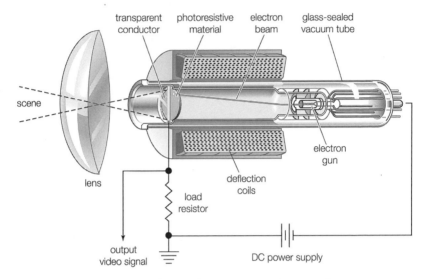

FIGURE 7.4. *Diagram of the Vidicon camera tube. A nonhuman drama of quantum events plays out in the tube. Photograph courtesy of* Encyclopaedia Britannica/UIG *via Getty Images. Reproduced by permission.*

between the classical physical level on which humans mechanically open access to the photoresistant surface behind the camera lens, and the quantum level that determines the picture. This quantum level involves the phosphor screen to which the camera is hooked up, and the television screen that displays the final video.

It is at this quantum level that we glimpse something decisively nonhuman. Moreover, since the classical level may be thought simply as an averaged-out, smoothed version of the quantum weirdness we shall explore soon, that level too is saturated, quite literally, with the nonhuman. Indeed, many contemporary younger quantum theorists are beginning to wonder aloud whether the classical level is drastically less real than the quantum, because larger and larger things (fullerenes [carbon molecules in a geodesic dome], a tiny tuning fork that is visible to the naked eye, diamonds), can be made to exhibit quantum behavior.[13]

Why is a brief survey of the quantum scale events incident in the shot significant for this essay? Because it shows the depth, complexity, and manifold nonhuman levels of the assemblage light–car–Skeeter Rabbit–street–lens–photoconducting screen–electron spray–electron gun–coaxial cable–electron gun–electron spray–phosphor screen–David Byrne–Brian Eno–Toni Basil–viewer. Weird distances and ambiguities are involved, strange accidents, and a history of nonhuman things that is wiped like a VHS tape when we only think, "It's a video of 'Crosseyed and Painless' with some special effects."

This history is not just for us, but rather for a shoal of sparkling sensual beings, the phenomenological fish that Edmund Husserl discovered, but which OOO applies to any interaction between any entities whatsoever. Husserl discovered that the vast ocean of reason that Immanuel Kant had opened up, the third dimension of thought that is the condition of possibility for thinking and understanding, was teeming with all kinds of phenomena: hoping, wishing, asserting, love, hate, judging.[14] These *intentional objects* are like fish swimming in the ocean, consisting of both a mind and its immanent object, locked together as if with a coaxial cable. In the same way we could see the chroma-keyed car cover and Skeeter with his factory-displaying mask on, and Ana Marie Sanchez lying sideways below Skeeter as he moonwalks across the museum steps, as phenomenological fish in the sensual interspace between video camera, vision mixer, and monitor. These entities are like in a kluge-like assemblage mind, not so different from the kluge that is the human brain, made of all kinds of primate, reptile, fish, and sponge components. These quasi-thoughts are what the song calls "facts." Somehow the video restores to the term *fact* the notion of making and crafting (Latin, *facere*). It does so by narrating the birth and death of shoals of fact fish.

In the cathode ray tube, the electron stream is made of quanta (literally "packets"), which is to say units of a certain kind that excite electrons in the phosphor, another kind of unit. To do this, they must deflect, smack into, penetrate. At this level, seeing and measuring are haptic. *To perceive* at this level means to hit with another quantum. Thus at this level there is no difference between

seeing a bemused philosopher seeing a billiard ball and that billiard ball smacking another one. This insight helps us to understand why OOO objects are quite similar to one another, insofar
as sentience is not that different from what we think of as physical,
nonsentient interaction.

In addition, at the quantum scale, it simply is not possible to
"see" before the smack. This gives rise to complementarity, the deep
reason for Heisenberg's uncertainty principle and the Schrödinger
equations.[15] To see is to change. The quantum is withdrawn "before" (but does it even make sense to speak of linear time here?)
it is measured: working by hindsight. The camera tube is already
damaged, before it is considered damaged by a human. A photon
hits the photoresistant screen. A jump in energy causes an electron
and its hole partner to be released into the conduction band. Many
times this happens, and the pattern is now detectable by the stream
from the electron gun. Watching the subsequent video image, we
are also watching a record of accidents. In a cathode ray tube, the
crystal lattices of the phosphor screen contain little impurities. It
is nothing other than the precipitate of abandoned object cathexes,
as Freud says of the human ego—in this case, the trace chemicals
or dopants that treated the lattice to make it nonhomogeneous and
thus to prolong the emission time (afterglow).[16]

The camera tube sees by being damaged. Each registration of
the electron from the gun is a little death, and the simultaneous
birth of something new—a fresh electron liberated from its place
in the crystal lattice. The liberation creates a little hole, which gives
rise to an electronic level in what is poetically called the "forbidden
gap." The electron and the hole—known collectively as an *exciton*—
floats about until it finds equilibrium again by slotting into an
impurity center. It gives up energy as luminescence, de-exciting
swiftly by scintillation, and de-exciting slowly by what is known,
also poetically, as the "forbidden mechanism." The mechanism is
forbidden because it's improbable that such scintillation could happen, except under excited conditions—and rarely even then. But
like the Forbidden City, forbidden colors still exist, demonstrating
how entities behave in ways that subvert the kinds of relations that
are expected of them. The fragile, "impossible," hallucinatory video
image is produced in part by fleeting and improbable forbidden

mechanisms. A fragile quantum magic could easily be fried away to classical nothing by too many electrons incident on the crystal lattice.

This is not a digital situation: it is analog. The forbidden gap and the forbidden mechanism are not totally out of bounds, just hard to access. This tells us that there are regions in objects such as crystal lattices that are opaque—they are obscure, not totally nonexistent. The gap is a symptom of a deeper entity withdrawn from access. Otherwise absolutely nothing could happen across it, because it is not even nothing—an *oukontic* nothing. The gap is a *meontic* nothing—a *nothingness*, a thingly nothing.[17] This idea of a nothing that is the mask of a something, not the total absence of anything at all, becomes very significant as we proceed.

We humans see a dot of color. In other words, we see a mistake, the memory of a mistake, the trace of scintillation, a mistaken memory. Memory in general is a kind mistake, a broken tool, the trace of accidents, anamorphosis, all the shocks that things are heir to.[18] Memory in this case just is inscribed in a crystal lattice that lost its shape, deformed into new form. We see the colorful display of an instability that has been canceled, working by hindsight. We see the past, the afterglow: *Working by hindsight.*

But at the quantum level what has taken place is a little drama of life and death, if for a moment I can indulge in what Jane Bennett has happily called a kind of "strategic anthropomorphism."[19] Or is it? Freud breaks the death drive down to a single-celled organism.[20] But why stop there? DNA is evidently an unstable molecule that is trying to get rid of itself, accidentally and ironically reproducing itself as soon as it unzips. And why even stop there? DNA needs ribosomes, which need DNA—so to break the vicious circle there must have been an RNA world of RNA replicants hitched onto nonorganic replicants, perhaps silicate crystals.[21] Are we at the level of life here or beyond it? Is life just a small, metaphysically dubious region of a much larger undead region neither living nor dead? And why stop at replicants such as RNA or those silicates? How can molecules replicate at all? Is there not some dance between stability and instability that is deeper still?

When too many photons hit the photoconducting surface in the tube—say when Eno had left his newly acquired tool lying on its side in a window in the full Manhattan sunshine—the tube "burns out." The death of a thing is its successful translation—success is never absolute, in this object-oriented world, but good enough to alter (that is, to damage) the thing in question. A photon or an electron shocks a crystal lattice into life—life, meaning inconsistency, namely the continual search for death, which in these terms would be consistency. The disequilibrium of a crystal lattice is such that it is flooded with its own excited electrons that flow about until they find their resting place: sparks of color as death. We see the story of a crystal lattice shocked into releasing photons of certain frequencies, defined packets, units, quanta: we see traces of the shock in the gorgeous disturbing color. We see the past.

Just as we cannot directly see death, only memories, pieces of paper in a wastebasket, some car keys, so the death happening in the tube cannot be seen directly.[22] The electron from the gun dies, liberating the electron from the lattice, a lattice of yttrium oxide sulfide (the red channel), zinc sulfide and copper (the green channel), and zinc sulfide with a few parts per million of silver (the blue channel), or rather a gigantic assemblage of lattices, gigantic at least from an electron's or photon's point of view.

Placing our eyes near the monitor, we humans see the trace of death in the video image. But there is also death at the quantum scale. Appearance is the trace of death, namely, the form of a thing, which just is the past: form is the past. The withdrawn essence of a thing on the other hand cannot be located in measurable ontically given space—not for us humans, not for the electron, not for the photon. This "before" of a photon is really a not-yet: the future that lies in wait inside the camera tube. The "essence" of the tube is the future, its appearance as burned-out electrons is the past. When too much past accumulates, the whole tube is burned out, which is to say that it crosses a certain threshold, but the threshold, like human death, is not thin or rigid. Still the tube records color, colors that are in fact quite lovely. It is truly a mistaken memory, as Eno's *Mistaken Memories* makes clear. The memory trace of electrons liberated from a crystal lattice by too many incident photons. The tube is ruined from a human point of view, and from the standpoint of commodity circulation—you cannot sell a broken camera. But the tube is still operational, still agential. From the human point of view it is a zombie, an undead being that scoffs at the rigid boundary between death and life.

The tube is thus an alien being from an alien world—an alien world just behind the video itself, just to the side of Skeeter Rabbit, just to the side of the street. This being is not located in some beyond, but right "here." I put *here* in quotation marks because the pastness of what the tube reveals undermines the temporal atomism that underwrites the metaphysics of presence, not by evaporating things into a flux, but by staging the intrusion of an alien being into a seemingly coherent world. It would be even better to say that this is evidence for the always-already, shifting and uneasy presence of an entity, a nonhuman, that car, that video tube, that Manhattan sky. Aliens in our midst. Or as Ian Bogost puts it, we are in *their* midst.[23] Whose midst is it anyway? This is not my beautiful car. *Lost my shape. I feel like an accident.* Racism is not simply politically violent—it is a ridiculous ontological violence, because appearance is profoundly severed from the being of a thing, yet a thing is not just nothing at all.

How something begins is precisely as an accident, as anamorphosis, as distortion.[24] An excitation appears in a crystal lattice. A cut is made by a knife, or a photon, producing a gap in the real that is then seen as a tear through which light comes. A blob that used to be a car begins to glow, a car that was always-already a blob of color, a distortion of metal, plastic, oil, and drivers. Oil is an anamorphic distortion of algae and dinosaur bones. We can only see things backward, *working by hindsight,* reading clues, getting the message from the oxygen.

As if we were able to think the conditions of the possibility of that video, working by hindsight—Kant's discovery of a vast hidden realm of transcendental space and time within, behind the back of, thought. There followed Husserl's discovery that this realm is not a cold empty realm of purity, but is teeming with phenomenological fish, which this chapter has equated with the phenomena seen not by humans but by the interobjective assemblage of video camera and vision mixer and monitor. Beneath this ocean of flashing fish moves the silent, horror-struck U-boat of Heideggerian Dasein through the cold darkness and opacity of Angst. And yet, in a further twist, it is as if traveling in a bathysphere released from the

U-boat, far beneath that gigantic ocean of a priori synthesis and intentional or sensual objects and (human) Dasein, we are invited by the video to detect an amazing coral reef of actually existing beings, already here, a Panasonic PK-600 video camera, Skeeter Rabbit, a burnt-out tube, the sky, David Byrne, someone's fingers on the color control, a CMX 600 nonlinear video editor, Twig Imai, video manually sliced by razor blades, SMPTE timecode, Toni Basil. *They're back!—To explain their experience.*

Video colors are facts about photons translating electrons. Traces of the past, stories are inscribed in phosphor. An illusion-like trail of facts scintillates, a trail that fades over time. Facts are the shadows of things, their echo, thrown into the past from an impossible futurality. *Facts are nothing on the face of things*: what a perfect OOO insight. Facts, the factical, facticity, are on the side of illusion and shadow play, precisely because there *are* real entities, real things that they don't touch. Underneath the Byrne and Eno postmodern frisson of unmeaning, there are entities: facts are precisely nothing on the face of them, distortions by their very nature.

And these facts are, as the song says, *useless in emergencies.* The current ecological emergency confronts us with the non-metaphysical intimacy of nonhuman beings. An emergency in which we grab for facts—but they might be broken, they might be lying. And furthermore, they are nothing on the face of things. They are a way not to see the face of things. They may be useful, but facts don't exhaust the emergency that just is the existence and coexistence of things. The line is sung with a half-knowingness, as if the narrator was double-, triple-checking his pocket for keys and wallet, obsessively, compulsively, to stave off anxiety, the sharp end of coexistence. The abyss of wishful thinking, a rope bridge suspended over the abyss of anxiety. A nonhuman panic sets in. *Lifting my head—Looking for the danger signs.*

Facts don't stain the furniture, yet *facts go out and slam the door,* and they lie. They *twist the truth around.* Or are they telling the truth? Between the flattened seventh and the tonic note of the funk sequence, there is nothing, not even nothing—an *oukontic* nothing, like the forbidden gap between electron levels, which an electron jumps across when excited by a photon in the crystal lattice on a phosphor screen. It is as if we are being shown two sides of the same thing, over and over, or are those the same side of two differ-ent things? *Isn't it weird / Looks too obscure to me.* Whose Möbius strip is this anyway? Why are we in this muddle? Because of things, because of nonhumans. Below the depths traversed by the Heideg-gerian U-boat, there is a gigantic coral reef of beings. Anxiety, Das-ein, Being, they all depend on the always-already of these sparkling beings, bouncing up and down like balls or David Byrne. Beneath facticity, that is, beneath the correlationist being-in-the-world that is the primordial facticity, there are things—facticity itself is noth-ing on the face of things.

I'm still waiting. The late eighteenth century was the age during which Western philosophy decided it could only talk about ac-cess to reality, not reality as such. It was also the beginning of the Anthropocene, the moment at which human history intersects with geological time, because since about 1780 humans begin to deposit a thin layer of carbon in Earth's crust, which can now be found in deep lakes and Arctic ice. In 1945 came the Great Ac-celeration, a vast increase in the magnitude of the Anthropocene, marked by the deposition of a thin layer of radioactive materials in Earth's crust courtesy of The Gadget, Little Boy, and Fat Man.

The basic attunement of the Anthropocene is *anxiety*, which is precisely the feeling of the loss of world—the end of the world, but not as we thought, a great bang or a void, but a prolongation of things in synchrony with the disappearance of meaningful backdrop—and thus the disappearance of the foreground as such. *The Island of Doubt—It's like the taste of medicine.* A totally white background, blank, white, a *meontic* nothing—nothing has enough meaning. The horrible familiarity and strangeness of anxiety, its uncanny creepiness that seems to lurk just off of the edge of our perception like a car in a driveway beside the street we're walking on, or a car approaching in your wing mirror. U.S. car wing mir-rors are object-oriented ontologists: they say, "Objects in mirror are closer than they appear." The trouble with ecology is that it brings everything too close. Things become vivid, yet unreal, at the very same time and for the very same reasons.

Underneath nihilism, not in spite of it but through it, down-ward, there are things. The postmodern hesitation and luxuriance in the slide of signification is a soothing elixir that blocks access to these beings that exist underneath nihilism. The postmodern island of doubt is a soothing oasis in the ocean of anxiety. Nihilism itself is a thicker version of this island of doubt, like a layer of seaweed that covers over the iridescent, painfully sharp beings that sparkle beneath the U-boat of Heidegger.

I'm still waiting. The feeling of beginning, what is called aperture, the sense of an opening. It is this sense of beginning, which just is the pure givenness that underscores the Kantian aesthetic dimension, which the Talking Heads' video exemplifies. The car winks at us, slightly provocatively—*it is the one that is still waiting,* not just human me, not just the narrator or Skeeter Rabbit. In order to have the attunement, the *Stimmung* of beauty, that perfect experience of one's unconditional abyss of reason, the frightening fact that we can indeed think beyond the human, beyond the light cone of Herman Minkowski, who geometrically proved the theory of relativity. Outside the light cone that propagates from events in the universe, objects cannot be specified as happening now, or then, or later, and we cannot be sure about where they are happening either.[25] Yet we can think them. We can think thirty million years ago, we can think the Oort cloud at the edge of the solar system, we can think events that cannot be located in space-time anywhere at all, events that actually exist. In order for all this, *there is already, always-already,* an entity, a being, an object. Not some vague whateverbeing, but a specific, unique being, as if the Levinasian *il y a* were an actual schizophrenic homeless guy sitting at the entrance to the church (the mise-en-scène of Coleridge's "The Rime of the Ancient Mariner").

The proximity of an alien presence underwrites the nihilistic abyss of reason that Kant plunges thinking, the third dimension of inner space that opens at the very beginning of the Anthropocene, the infinity within, because I can know infinity, because I know I cannot count to it, which is precisely what infinity is.[26] Just as kitsch, which is the aesthetic shit of the other, underwrites beauty, since in order to experience it, beauty must be, Kant argues, universalizable, that is, everyone should find this painting beautiful, but I shall not coerce you into finding it so. Thus someone else's beautiful thing might just be your shit, ugly and slimy and crappy, a shiny frosted Christmas ornament, a thing banished to the hinterlands of taste because it is precisely a thing. The unconditional, noncoercive givenness of beauty, which just is a projection of my reason, is predicated on a priori synthetic judgment, the third dimension beyond scholastic being that Kant opens up, that icy region of the mind's Antarctic analogous to the nihilistic probings of earthly space of the quasi-imperialist ancient mariner himself.

Yet this profoundly nonviolent being-with the beautiful thing is predicated on that thing's existence, which threatens me beneath the abyss of reason with a horrifying uncanny agency. The car winks at me knowingly. The aesthetic sheen, the German *Schein* of beauty, is undergirded by the glistening uncanny that opens up in the chameleon shifting of the car. It is like watching a shaft of sunlight from another world illuminate that car—another world just behind your head, just next to the apparatus that produces the video, the other world that is precisely Eno's camera gear, his broken tools sitting just to the left, just offscreen. This alien world is utterly intimate with this one, casting its strange light on it from a few inches away. Is this not more disturbing than the Kantian depths of inner space, more creepy even than the death of distant stars that we can detect if we push the radio telescope of speculative realism through the Kantian correlationist bubble?

Because this thing here, this television image, is winking at me, sending out a sonar pulse from underneath nihilism, not in spite of it, but through the abyss of reason, through the darkness, as if the silence and stillness of these infinite spaces that fills one with Pascalian dread exists only because that silence and stillness are the sound of someone breathing down one's neck two inches away from the back of the head:

> Like one, that on a lonesome road
> Doth walk in fear and dread,
> And having once turned round walks on,
> And turns no more his head;
> Because he knows, a frightful fiend
> Doth close behind him tread. (Coleridge, "The Rime of the
>   Ancient Mariner," part VI, lines 447–52)

Coleridge intuited it, at the very beginning of the Anthropocene. Poetry is sometimes a way to do philosophy when one lacks the thoughts. Inside the beauty is the a priori. Inside the a priori is the given. Inside the given is the thing, the object, this object, this actual cut-out piece of chroma-keyed video space, this space that is actually a substance, an oozing of photons and videotape.

Ecological awareness, then, far from being the glib world of "We are all earthlings," is the uncanny nightmare charnel ground realm.[27] Where nothing is exactly, ontically, precisely real, and all the more real for that. The demonic quality of art disturbs the philosopher, who rightly wards off the aesthetic dimension as a domain of "evil." It is evil to the extent that in order to be beautiful art, an object has already hypnotized us. We are always-already caught in the spooky agency, the shine of the headlights of the nonhuman has us under its spell. The very infinitude of reason's abyss, our capacity not simply to understand but to think, is suspended in the demonic interspace between things, a dreamtime that pulses with eerie light. Why "evil"? Because we cannot tell whether it is lying or not: "What constitutes pretense is that, in the end, you don't know whether it's pretense or not."[28]

Far from giving us a boring world of billiard balls that clunk in predictable, dull ways, OOO gives us a spooky world plagued with beings who may not be alive, who may not be intelligent—are we one of them? A kind of sort of world of good enough performativity, *precisely because objects are real,* not because they aren't. This OOO world is one of necessarily incomplete Turing test data, because each thing is hidden in a cosmological version of Turing's setup, behind the door of withdrawal, sending us sensual typescript about itself under the doorway. It is a claustrophobic world of illusion, precisely because there *are* real things.

Powerful art thus threatens us from this slightly evil place, and in so doing, it is fully and meaningfully ecological, whether or not its explicit content is ecological. This evil is the mask worn by trickster objects as they pull us down underneath modernity's nihilism into a "reanimist" universe of lies, traps, demons, and slapstick. We are pulled into this world not in spite of that nihilism, but underneath it, through it, out from under it like Danny in *The Shining.*

In the end, what is far more horrifying than absolutely nothing at all—the *oukontic* nothing—is the shifty, ghostly *meontic* nothing of nothingness, the pretense whose status as pretense one is unable to ascertain. When Skeeter empties his pockets in one of the video's final scenes, it is as if he is pulling out this nothingness—he wants it to be *oukontic*: "See, I got nothing, there is not even nothing here!" Yet instead his pockets rebel against his human intention, as Skeeter pulls out his basic anxiety, in the face of the cigar-chomping hustler with his tricksterish hand-jive, as if instead to say, "What do you want from me?" Skeeter's very pants subvert his wish to enter properly the human social symbolic order (Figure 7.5). As if the video were saying, "You are looking for aliens in the wrong place—they are in your pants pockets, they are under that car cover. They *are* that cover, hiding in plain sight. Right here, under your nose. Just behind you, a frightful fiend." In a dizzying perspective shift, it turns out that the abyss that we took to be an abyss of reason, or perhaps of swirling matter, behind things, is actually *in front of things*—and not only this, the abyss is emitted by things, like radio waves. It is the abyss of causality, otherwise known as the aesthetic dimension.

Givenness beyond the ontically given that I take to be real in a metaphysics-of-presence way. What is called Nature just is the reduction of things to their givenness for humans. This reduction must be policed, since it is inherently spurious and unstable. Instead we should look beyond nature, namely, beyond the beyond, to the things right in front of us, hiding in plain sight. They are here. Ecological awareness is always belated, finding oneself always already to have been inside something, inside a gigantic being called *biosphere,* a being that cannot be seen but can be inferred and computed with prosthetic cognizing devices. The affective equivalent of this gigantic being is the ocean of anxiety in which objects bob up and down in a menacing, Expressionist funk, halfway between clown and murderer. Acting evokes crime and art evokes evil: a magician with a cigar and a stash of money, a hip-hop dancer distorted by machines, a racist environment, a basketball, a car, a knife, exhaust from a factory smokestack. Facts lost, facts are never what they seem to be. I, an ocean of anxiety, dance around

FIGURE 7.5. *In this still from the Talking Heads' music video,* Cross-eyed and Painless *(dir. Toni Basil), Skeeter Rabbit (left) pulls nothingness out of his pockets. The video narrates his character's anxiety, a default condition of living in an ecological era. Reproduced by permission of MSA Agency.*

you, another ocean of anxiety. Since they are always displaced from their appearance, strung out in and as temporality just like humans, do knives and basketballs themselves experience anxiety, the one emotion that never lies? They distort, they are distortion, as we have seen in the case of the car—that car, a not-car, that ocean of color. They are here. The car is still, waiting.

Notes

1. Cary Wolfe is the architect of a de-anthropocentrism that grounds racism in speciesism. See Cary Wolfe, *Before the Law: Humans and Other Animals in a Biopolitical Frame* (Chicago: University of Chicago Press, 2012), and *Animal Rites: American Culture, the Discourse of Species, and*

Posthumanist Theory (Chicago: University of Chicago Press, 2003), 1–20, 21–43.

2. A precedent for this argument can be found in Monique Allewaert's account of "an emerging minoritarian colonial conception of agency" in *Ariel's Ecology: Plantations, Personhood, and Colonialism in the American Tropics* (Minneapolis: University of Minnesota Press, 2013), 1.

3. Talking Heads, "Crosseyed and Painless," *Remain in Light* (Sire, 1980).

4. Chögyam Trungpa, *Glimpses of Abidharma* (Boston: Shambhala, 2001), 74.

5. Emmanuel Levinas, *Existence and Existents,* trans. Alphonso Lingis, foreword by Robert Bernasconi (Pittsburgh, Penn.: Duquesne University Press, 1988), 45–60.

6. Sigmund Freud, "The Uncanny," *The Standard Edition of the Complete Psychological Works of Sigmund Freud,* ed. and trans. James Strachey, 24 vols. (London: Hogarth Press, 1953), 17:218–52.

7. David Byrne, Christopher Frantz, Tina (Martina) Weymouth, Jerry Harrison, and Brian Peter George Eno, "Crosseyed and Painless." Copyright 1980 WB Music Corp., Index Music, Inc., and E. G. Music, Ltd. All rights on Behalf of itself and Index Music, Inc. Administered by WB Music Corp. All Rights Reserved. Reprinted with permission.

8. Jacques Lacan, *Écrits: A Selection,* trans. Alan Sheridan (London: Tavistock, 1977), 311.

9. W. D. Richter, director, *The Adventures of Buckaroo Banzai across the Eighth Dimension* (20th Century Fox, 1984).

10. See for instance Graham Harman, *Tool-Being: Heidegger and the Metaphysics of Objects* (Peru, Ill.: Open Court Press, 2002).

11. Martin Heidegger, *Contributions to Philosophy (from Enowning),* trans. Parvis Emad and Kenneth Maly (Bloomington: Indiana University Press, 1999), 11.

12. Brian Eno, *Mistaken Memories of Mediaeval Manhattan* (Opal, 1981). I am grateful to Cary Wolfe for discussing this with me. See *What Is Posthumanism?* (Minneapolis: University of Minnesota Press, 2009), 290–93, 299.

13. See for instance A. D. O'Connell et al., "Quantum Ground State and Single Phonon Control of a Mechanical Ground Resonator," *Nature* 464 (April 1, 2010): 697–703.

14. Edmund Husserl, *Logical Investigations,* ed. Dermot Moran, trans. J. N. Findlay (London: Routledge, 2006), 95, 98–99, 100–104, 110–11.

15. David Bohm, *Quantum Theory* (New York: Dover, 1989), 99–115.

16. Sigmund Freud, *The Ego and the Id,* trans. Joan Riviere, rev. and ed. James Strachey, intro. Peter Gay (New York: Norton, 1989), 24.

17. Paul Tillich, *Systematic Theology 1* (Chicago: University of Chicago Press, 1951), 188.

18. Sigmund Freud, *The Ego and the Id*, trans. James Strachey Introduction by Peter Gay (New York: Norton, 1989), 24.

19. Jane Bennett, *Vibrant Matter: A Political Ecology of Things* (Durham, NC: Duke University Press, 2004), 119–20.

20. Sigmund Freud, *Beyond the Pleasure Principle,* trans. and ed. James Strachey (New York: Liveright, 1950), 32.

21. Richard Dawkins, *The Ancestor's Tale: A Pilgrimage to the Dawn of Life* (London: Phoenix, 2005), 582–94.

22. Jean-Paul Sartre, *Being and Nothingness: An Essay on Phenomenological Ontology,* trans. and ed. Hazel Barnes (New York: Philosophical Library, 1984), 41–42, 61–62.

23. Ian Bogost, *Alien Phenomenology or, What It's Like to Be a Thing* (Minneapolis: University of Minnesota Press, 2012).

24. Timothy Morton, *Realist Magic: Objects, Ontology, Causality* (Ann Arbor, Mich.: Open Humanities Press, 2013), 110–51.

25. David Bohm, *The Special Theory of Relativity* (London: Routledge, 2006), 189–90.

26. Immanuel Kant, *Critique of Judgment,* trans. Werner S. Pluhar (Indianapolis: Hackett, 1987), 519–25.

27. Sesame Street, "We Are All Earthlings," *Sesame Street Platinum All-Time Favorites* (Sony, 1995).

28. Jacques Lacan, *Le seminaire, Livre III: Les psychoses* (Paris: Editions de Seuil, 1981), 48.

8

Form / Matter / Chora

Object-Oriented Ontology and Feminist New Materialism

REBEKAH SHELDON

THE FIRST DECADES of the twenty-first century have seen a number of challenges to the centrality of epistemology in literary and cultural theory, from the rise of neuroaesthetics and machine reading to the return of phenomenology and affect theory. Despite their diversity, these new paradigms reflect an ambient dissatisfaction with the ascription of causality at the root of the theoretical enterprise by putting pressure on the equation between apt description and social change. In their own ways, each questions the importance of representation, often through an implicit argument that the distinction between reality and its mediation is out of sync with the direct intervention into material life characteristic of current practices in science and technology. Taken together, these schools of thought represent a newly emergent realism in the humanities.

Within this broad and interdisciplinary movement, two methods have attained particular visibility: speculative realism, especially object-oriented ontology (OOO), and new materialism, especially feminist new materialism. Indeed, their concurrent ascendency and their shared critique of representation have made it easy to understand them as versions of each other. As I endeavor to explain, however, this is a misapprehension. I look first at object-oriented ontology's famous rejection of "correlationism" before turning to the very different history that animates feminist new materialism.[1]

The term *correlationism* derives from Quentin Meillassoux's *After Finitude*, in which he defines it as "the idea according to which we only ever have access to the correlation between thinking and being, and never to either term considered apart from the other," a characterization that Meillassoux applies to all philosophical approaches since Kant.[2] For object-oriented ontologists, the effect of correlationism has been to dramatically limit the range of theoretical speculations to things that fall within human knowledge systems. As Ian Bogost explains in the introductory section of *Alien Phenomenology*:

> We've been living in a tiny prison of our own devising, one in which all that concerns us are the fleshy beings that are our kindred and the stuffs with which we stuff ourselves. Culture, cuisine, experience, expression, politics, polemic: all existence is drawn through the sieve of humanity, the rich world of things discarded like chaff so thoroughly, so immediately, so efficiently that we don't even notice.[3]

This critique of correlation—the "sieve of humanity" in Bogost's terms—gives object-oriented ontology its grounding; however, its most characteristic gesture is not Meillassoux's critique of correlation but Graham Harman's notion of object withdrawal. The two work hand in hand, for OOO does not just turn our attention toward the nonhuman, it does so in order to postulate an emphatically anti-relational ontology in which objects recline at a distance from each other and from the networks in which they are embedded, very much including but not limited to human cultural practices. Profoundly threshholded, Harman's objects stand at a remove even from themselves: internal organs are no less bounded objects than the bodies that house them, which are themselves distinct from what Timothy Morton calls "hyper-objects," like climate.[4] As Morton epigrammatically renders this point, it's objects all the way down.[5]

This antipathy to relations in favor of the things themselves makes object-oriented ontology difficult to square with existing critical orientations considered broadly, but its relationship with feminism has been particularly rancorous—a push-me-pull-you of accusation and desire for affiliation that has generated both a new subfield, object-oriented feminism, and numerous heated denunciations, including the injunction apocryphally attributed to Isabelle

Stenger's keynote speech at the 2010 Claremont Whitehead Conference, to stop talking about object-oriented ontology.[6]

The antagonism between these two fields is in some ways easily understood. After all, feminism is historically constituted around human subjectivity, sexed specificity, and the sculpting effects of culture. Add to that the origin of feminists' engagement with the sciences in a critique of scientific neutrality—a critique that argues quite precisely for the intercalation of culture between things and our experiences of them—and it becomes clear why the two fields have been wary of each other.

A glance at more recent scholarship, however, suggests that this agon reflects as much a set of overlaps as it does divergences. Feminist new materialism in particular has moved away from the critique of neutrality and toward the recognition of the wholly nondiscursive agency of other-than-human forces. As Myra Hird and Celia Roberts explain in "Feminism Theorises the Nonhuman," their introduction to their special issue of *Feminist Theory,* one important function of the "nonhuman" as an umbrella term to cover these new realisms is the way it calls attention to the myriad ecological, biological, and physical processes that have no truck with human epistemological categories whatsoever. "The majority of Earth's living inhabitants are nonhuman," they write, "and nonhuman characterises the deep nonliving recesses of the Earth, the biosphere and space's vast expanse." The world these nonhumans occupy "exists for itself, rather than for 'us.'"[7] For Hird and Roberts, this recognition prompts a critical modesty from out of which they seek to generate a realistic ethics attentive to the impact of human culture *and also* to the vivacity, vulnerability, and sometimes the surly intransigence of nature.

The distance between object-oriented ontology and feminist new materialism, therefore, is not a function of the ostensible anthropocentrism of a feminism grounded in identity politics, as it might initially appear. Rather, I argue that their differences result from the radically different ways in which these two fields treat human knowledge systems. For as much as they both contribute to the critique of epistemology, the *causal effects* assignable to knowledge-making practices continue to be prominent in their divergent understandings of the role and form of scholarship. For object-oriented ontology, epistemology is epiphenomenal, a second-order representation whose range of effects is limited to human knowers. For feminist new materialism, by contrast, epistemology is an agent with directly material consequences. This account of epistemology is captured by the consistent use of doubly articulated phrases in feminist theory, such as Donna Haraway's nature-cultures and Karen Barad's material-discursive intra-actions, phrases designed to collapse hierarchical dualisms and insist on the materializing force of broadly circulating ideas.[8] This perspective is emphatically *relational.* It begins from the assumption that ideas and things do not occupy separate ontological orders but instead are co-constituents in the production of the real.

It is possible, but mistaken, to read this conjunctive articulation as correlationist. Epistemology in these descriptions is not a sieve filtering out the material world and leaving only our relation to ourselves; rather, epistemology directly acts on material liveliness. For this reason, the term of art is *matter.* From Luciana Parisi's abstract matter to Jane Bennett's vibrant matter, feminist new materialism sees objects as a concrescence or intensive infolding of an extensive continuum. Matter draws together what appears separate and makes the totality subject to mutation and emergence.[9]

The ontological status of epistemology thus becomes legible as the result of the structuring privilege accorded to *form* in object-oriented ontology and *matter* in feminist new materialism. In this sense, the visibility and volubility of these two fields recapitulates the hoariest of philosophical binaries: the form/matter distinction. But this distinction is not only ancient. It is also central to philosophy's own sex/gender system, a system that feminist philosophy set out to reveal, disrupt, and overturn. In militating against the excesses of correlationism, object-oriented ontology and feminist new materialism restage an old antinomy—the being/becoming problem in Plato and Aristotle.

My aim for this chapter is to force a confrontation between these fields. More specifically, I use the challenge of object-oriented ontology and its privileging of form as an opportunity to reconsider the fidelity to matter in new materialism. If this is a confrontation, however, it is less to argue for one side over the other—though I suspect my leanings will be clear—than to wrest from their jagged edges and odd overlaps a concept both sides have neglected despite its centrality to the form/matter binary they both invoke. I mean the *chora*, that uneasy third term that Plato, in his cosmogony the *Timaeus*, can neither smoothly systematize nor quite go without.[10]

To get there, I first turn back to an earlier moment in feminism and its texturing of body, nature, and science in order to come forward again, and through this rehearsal to underscore and swerve a vector that cuts from feminist science to the contested status of matter and process in current thought.[11]

Feminist Epistemology

In "The Promise of Monsters," her contribution to the 1992 field-mapping anthology *Cultural Studies*, Donna Haraway proposes as the first principle of a feminist cultural study of science the mutual constitution and discursive construction of science, nature, and culture. "I take as self-evident," she writes, "the premise that 'science is culture.'" She continues, "Nature is . . . a tropos, a trope. It is a figure, construction, artifact, movement, displacement. Nature cannot pre-exist its construction. This construction is based on a particular kind of move—a tropos or 'turn.'"[12]

Nature cannot preexist its construction. This declaration might be taken as the motto for a particularly strong attractor in thought. As a method, its power comes from the way it affects an ontological-epistemological overturning. Where once we took nature as primary, the active partner whose inflexible laws order human social relations equally as much as they do the development of organs in a body or the rate of change of a falling object, now we reject this presupposition. We unmask it as performative ideology perpetuating what it claims merely to describe. We debunk it by finding contravening instances of internal differentiation. We neutralize it with historical variation. We trace it back to the archive and discover its ignominious origins. Against the racism, classism, sexism, and homophobia justified through recourse to an authorizing and law-giving nature, we do the good work of unveiling its construction. We learn to say "allegedly," as in: the *allegedly* biological pettiness of women, the *allegedly* contra-naturam of homosexuality, the *alleged* unfitness of those sterilized for being feeble minded or nymphomanical or born with a tendency toward criminality. Against all this we say, There is no law of nature. Nature is a construction.

Underlying this anti-natural, anti-biological orientation is a theory of representation, one that makes a particularly compelling sort of sense for professional readers of texts. Like the epistemology-ontology reversal that social construction effects, the characteristic gesture of this theory of representation is to invert common sense ideas about the operation of the senses. Thus Valerie Hartouni writes, "Seeing is a set of learned practices, a set of densely structured and structuring interpretive practices, that engages us in (re)producing the world we seem only to passively apprehend and, through such engagement, facilitates the automatic, *if incomplete,* operation of power."[13] In this passage, Hartouni urges us to complicate the naming theory of representation, that is, the notion that what representation represents precedes its representation, for which language merely provides a label. Or to put that more simply, she argues that what we think we know structures what we see, and not the reverse.

Samuel R. Delany makes a congruent point using Leonardo da Vinci's anatomical etchings of the child in womb. In "Rhetoric of Sex/Discourse of Desire," the first essay in his collection *Shorter Views,* Delany relates to the reader descriptions of three anatomical drawings from da Vinci's notebooks, one of a heart, one of the male urogenital system, and one of a fetus in a womb. Though these drawings have all of the characteristics of accuracy—"carefully observed, detailed, and rich in layerings" in Delany's words—what they depict does not correspond with contemporary anatomical understandings. Instead of mirroring the real, they import specific, culturally circulating ideas about how that anatomy should look. In the example of the womb, what we now see as shaped like an upside-down pear shows up in da Vinci's drawing as a sphere, corresponding to the "womb's presumed perfect, Renaissance sphericality."[14]

Delany takes this disparity as evidence of the distorting influence of culture, in terms highly reminiscent of the ones Hartouni uses in the passage above. Indeed, in the passage that closes this section of the essay, Delany makes clear that the purpose of this anecdote is to provide a definition of discourse: "It is the til-now-in-our-tale unnamed structuring and structurating force that can go by no better name than 'discourse,'" he writes, "and that force seems strong enough to contour what is apparent to the eye of some of the greatest direct observers of our world."[15] As this suggests, discourse isn't simply speech, but the syntax of assumptions that "contour" perception through their self-evidence—precisely for the way they appear identical to nature. For literary theorists, the resulting privilege was awarded less to knowledge-making practices per se— for it isn't really knowledge that causes us to see an apple-shaped womb where none exists—than it was to the sort of emotionally inflected, repetitive logic or structure generated by stories.

This kind of storytelling is not limited to fiction. One of the most important moves in feminist epistemology was the assertion made by feminist philosophers and scholars of science that notions of gender adhered in and were circulated by fields whose content was ostensibly distant from gender, or whose inclusion of gendered metaphors was merely coincidental or ornamental and therefore unnecessary to the substance or import of the theory. Thus in *Speculum of the Other Woman,* Luce Irigaray critically mimes—reveals through repetition and forced conjunction—the philosophical systems of Plato and Freud in an effort to show how central gender always already was to their allegedly neutral rational systems.[16] And not just the center but also the circumference, suspended in what Giorgio Agamben would later adumbrate as the constitutive exclusion, or what Irigaray diagnosis as the mute, passive substrate of a discourse that constitutes itself on women's exclusion.[17] It is no mistake, Irigaray contends, that women are caught up in relations of metaphor with the Earth, figured as the exploitable source of nurturance, with the womb as the origin from which manly activity proceeds, with nature as unruly, irrational primitive abundance, and with matter sculpted and stamped by transcendent form.[18] Far from accidental, these gendered topologies provide the coherence of these philosophical systems and coordinate a fungible chain of analogies and metonymies.

Thus the rhetoric of nature was held in suspicion not only for the way it was used to justify disenfranchisement and oppression. The dream of nature's unmediated transparency, itself a version of what Haraway calls the "paradise myth," was also the antagonist in the hard-won recognition that representations of ostensibly empirical phenomena tell us more about ourselves than they do about the things they putatively passively reflect. And it is here that the critical enterprise staked its ground in a refrain that is still prevalent amongst humanists and social scientists working today: change the story, change the reality—a task that begins with the drama of exposure.[19] In the wake of women's long reduction to earth, matter, nature, and origin, the foundational exposure was of culture behind the curtain of the concept of nature itself.

The Feminist Critique of Correlationism: Matter

Between these various examples, a problem develops. For it is one thing to say, as Hartouni does, that experience emerges out of structures of knowledge, or that ideation is founded on and perpetuates norms of sex and gender, as Irigaray does, and altogether another to say that the real is there under our distortions, waiting for the scales to fall from our eyes. Doing so pictures a Manichean split between an obscured real and a tendentious, deluded realm of human subjectivity. That we have no access to the real then forces us to confine our interventions to the level of culture and in so doing repeats the distinction between the activity of culture and the mute inscrutability of nature, a distinction whose consequences for women's lives feminist philosophers have made palpably apparent.

It is this version of cultural theory, often called *social construction,* that Meillassoux's "correlationist codicil" (*AF,* 13) accurately describes. As Meillassoux sees it, the problem with correlationism is that it can never affirm the independent existence of the real world. For the correlationist, no technology of empiricism—from logical argumentation to the techno-scientific apparatus—emerges without having the distorting influence of cultural assumptions built into its design. For this reason, the correlationist relates everything back to human knowledge systems. This is the famous "ancestrality" problem:

> Consider the following ancestral statement: "Event Y occurred x number of years before the emergence of humans."

The correlationist philosopher will in no way intervene in
the content of this statement. . . . She will simply add . . .
something like a simple codicil . . . : event Y occurred x
number of years before the emergence of humans—*for
humans* (or even, for *the human scientist*). . . . Accordingly,
when confronted with an ancestral statement, correlationism postulates that there are at least two levels of meaning
in such a statement: the immediate, or realist meaning; and
the more originary correlationist meaning, activated by the
codicil. (*AF,* 13–14)

As I have endeavored to demonstrate, this "shifting holistic world
of interrelated significances" is precisely the prophylactic that social construction set up against the imperialism of natural law.[20]

Working alongside the social constructionist understanding
of discourse as a veil obscuring the brute reality of material stuff,
however, is a different tradition. Karen Barad in her "Posthumanist
Performativity" starkly frames feminism's own internal critique:
"Language," she writes, "has been given too much power."[21] In its
bifurcation of a representational regime to which we have access
and a material reality that regime both reflects and occludes, lin-
guistically based approaches share a structure of belief with the
positivism they sought to overturn through the shared conviction
in the inherent properties possessed by the stuff of this world. Significantly, Barad's alternative is not to return to naïve realism but
rather to bring forward the crucial and hard-won link feminist science studies scholars forged between epistemology and materiality
by asking after the materializing effects of discourse. Barad aligns
what she calls "agential realism" with performativity. Using the
work of physicist Neils Bohr, she offers an account of performativity that highlights its material reality: "Apparatuses are not static
arrangements in the world that embody particular concepts to the
exclusion of others; rather, apparatuses are specific material practices through which local semantic and ontological determinacy
are intra-actively enacted."[22] For Barad, in other words, matters
and discourses are co-constituting, and so asking what knowledge
does is always a matter of asking after its ongoing entanglements.[23]
Indebted to Foucault's account of disciplinary apparatuses and

to Bruno Latour's actor-network theory as well as the physics on which she bases her analysis, agential realism insists that properties are the products of local intra-actions between actants of many kinds. Or, to put it epigrammatically, for Barad relations precede relata, which then alter relations. And properties, which we commonly understand as the possessions of individuals, are instead emergent features of entangled phenomena.

The point here is that intra-actions are live. Barad coins the term *intra-action* to undo the implicit understanding of interaction as the meeting of two already-formed objects. Rather, intra-actions instantiate boundaries anew. This has been a particularly productive approach for a feminist reading of science attentive to the fine-grained plasticity of bodies and the weird ontologies of physics. For example, in her *The Body Multiple,* Annamarie Mol urges us to move away from the question of how medicine knows the body to ask instead how medical practice *enacts* the body. She looks at the treatment of heart disease and the distance between a reductionist discourse of illness and the actual practice of stimulating, containing, molding, and redirecting entities: "Which entity? A slightly different one each time."[24] In *The Origins of Sociable Life,* Myra Hird gives this same interest in subindividual liveliness the name *microontologies* and uses it to examine the intra-active instantiations of bacteria, sex, and human sociality.[25] Stacy Alaimo's term is *transcorporeality,* a term that she uses in *Bodily Natures* to consider the constitutive openness that enables the systemic complexity of the environment to produce system-wide catastrophe.[26] That epistemology and ontology are linked—that what we know sculpts how we act—is our legacy from social construction. That matter also acts and in sometimes unexpected ways is the contribution of feminist new materialism and its difference from correlationism.

For feminist new materialism, the solution to the problem of women's historical assimilation with nature, matter, earth, and origin—the problem that led social constructionist feminism to culture—is to sidestep the essentially ideological use of these terms.[27] The world they find in its stead is rich, strange, and as transformative for our understandings of sex and gender as it is for our conception of time, space, matter, and individuality. It is perhaps tendentious but nonetheless true that these works were published—and certainly discussed and circulated—in the same period as, if not prior to, Meillassoux's *After Finitude,* Harman's *Tool-Being,* and the collectively edited *Speculative Turn* book in whose introduction Levi Bryant, Nick Srnicek, and Harman assimilate all contemporary thought as anti-realist: "In this respect," they write, "phenomenology, structuralism, post-structuralism, deconstruction, and postmodernism have all been perfect exemplars of the anti-realist trend in continental thought."[28] They continue:

> The first wave of twentieth century continental thought in the Anglophone world was dominated by phenomenology, with Martin Heidegger generally the most influential figure of the group. By the late 1970s, the influence of Jacques Derrida and Michel Foucault had started to gain the upper hand, reaching its zenith a decade or so later. It was towards the mid-1990s that Gilles Deleuze entered the ascendant, shortly before his death in 1995, and his star remains perfectly visible today. But since the beginning of the twenty-first century, a more chaotic and in some ways more promising situation has taken shape. While it is difficult to find a single adequate name to cover all of these trends, we propose "The Speculative Turn" as a deliberate counterpoint to the now tiresome "Linguistic Turn."[29]

The absence of women from this story of succession is remarkable both for its casual and apparently unwitting embrace of patrilineation, but also, and more incisively, for the distortions it relies on to produce such a clean line of descent.[30] For the production of a monolithic and homogeneous "linguistic turn" in the humanities is only possible through a constitutive misreading of Derrida, Foucault, and Deleuze and from the strategic exclusion of the work done in feminist science studies for the past two decades. As I hope to have demonstrated, it is in fact difficult to find a moment in feminist science studies when questions of embodiment, nature, science, realism, and referentiality were not explicitly at stake.

This then is the true intervention of object-oriented ontology: the way its forces new materialism together with social construction under the heading of correlationism. The assimilation of these fields—understood by their own practitioners as critical *antipodes*—has generated a sharp shock to criticism that has in turn allowed the middle ground and its array of objects to stand forth. And yet, against this critical tide, it is my contention that matter has not yet been given full rein to generate new methodologies for critical theory. The assimilation of feminist theories of matter with cultural construction elides the way that matter functioned as an *internal* critique of cultural construction, one that sought to retain the link between epistemology and materiality while also arguing for the autonomy and wayward agency of the extra-discursive world—or rather, their discontinuous co-modulations. Assimilating matter as the reverse side of cultural construction through the auspices of the correlationist's "co-" obscures the ways in which feminist new materialists have sought to inhabit the concept of matter as a site in which to build a materialist account of complex causality within open systems—one that adheres neither at the level of a closed totality nor from the perspective of the atomized individual but rather as a trans-individual assemblage whose motions are greater than the sum of its parts.

The Object-Oriented Critique of Correlationism: Form

It is no mistake, I am arguing, that the *Speculative Turn* volume in mapping the terrain from which object-oriented ontology emerged wrote out the history of feminist inquiry or that under the auspices of Mellaissoux's correlationism the critical antipodes of feminist new materialism on the one hand and social constructionism on the other, a particularly knotty and long-winded debate within feminism itself, get collapsed.[31] This collapse, I contend, is a way of confining the energy of those concerns, the propulsion that they produced for thinking the nonhuman, to a discredited discourse whose energy it can then usurp. OOO has been so provocative for feminist theorists because of its cannily unknowing usurpation of the energies of feminist thought and its relegation of that history to footnotes within its own autobiography.

This, however, would not rise much above the level of rhetoric were it not the case that the process of usurpation and confinement is also characteristic of OOO's objects, which gain their weird vitality by siphoning off and rendering sterile the plenum of non-object-bound energies. For as much as both fields have been hailed under the heading of materialism, OOO is as antimaterialist as it is anticorrelationist. In fact, Harman explicitly defines object-oriented ontology as "the first materialism in history to deny the existence of matter" (*TB*, 293), and its denigration of matter is foundational and pervasive. Tim Morton calls philosophies that favor concepts of flux, flow, process, pattern, and contingency over notions of stability, essence, solidity, interiority, and permanence "lava lamp materialism."[32] Bruno Latour, writing in his "Compositionist's Manifesto," cites Alfred North Whitehead's argument that matter is an Enlightenment idealization.[33]

The problem with matter for object-oriented ontology is that it allows us to skip over objects by seeing through them to the substratum that bears them, a process Harman calls "undermining" as opposed to what he calls the "overmining" of objects through historical contextualization or epistemological reading. The account of the object that animates object-oriented ontology sees the object as an eternal form, which can neither be sculpted by discourse nor obscured by representation because it is vacuum-sealed against these realms. What object-oriented ontology offers is the thing in itself—not the historical conditions of its emergence, not the meanings it circulates, but the object and its qualities in their tensile interrelations. But it is not a naïve object that they offer. For Harman, the object's resistance is a consequence of its general withdrawal from relations, including human perception. The object in OOO's sense is a "black box, black hole, or internal combustion engine releasing its power and exhaust fumes into the world."[34] Those fumes, or "plasma" as he refers to them in another instance, are the object's qualities, which are always limited, partial, multifarious, and brought into meaning-systems differently in different periods and cultures.[35] Despite this, the object retains its unity in the dignity of its seclusion. Its being does not bear on its meaning nor vice versa. "Objects," he writes, "are autonomous from all the features and relations that typify them, but on the other hand they are not completely autonomous."[36] He calls on us to give an account of this ambivalent, semi-detached object.

An example might help to clarify this matter-less ontology. In a thought experiment from his 2002 *Tool-Being*, Harman asks where we should look to find matter. He takes as his privileged instance a children's amusement park ride, the Ferris wheel. It is worth noting that this form of exemplification is typical of Harman's prose. He is less interested in the workings of a particular sphere—quantum physics in Barad's case, symbiogenesis in Hird's—than in using objects to adumbrate the workings of his philosophical system. The Ferris wheel, he argues, can be broken down into "numerous bolts, beams, and gears in its mechanism" (*TB*, 293). These pieces that *were* the Ferris wheel are now something different—bolts, beams, and gears. If they are recomposed in the production of a piece of public art, for example, they will once again be subsumed. But there is never a moment of indeterminacy between these positions when the bolts, beams, and gears return to a primordial state of undifferentiated matter. "Above all else," he concludes, "the 'parts' in question here are *form*, not matter. . . . What is real in the cosmos are forms wrapped inside of forms" (*TB*, 293). For Harman, even the relation between parts is a form, the pulley-and-lever system of the Ferris wheel forming a little machine whose functioning is separable from and in excess of the withdrawn objects (bolts, beams, and gears) that compose it. Because they are withdrawn, their potentiality is not exhausted. They can go on to take part in the machine of public art, or the assemblage called the dump. Wherever they wind up, they are still productive because they are still withdrawn. In contradistinction to materialism, he calls this "formalism" (*TB*, 293).

The Ferris wheel argument has the force of common sense. As Harman reminds us, we rarely think of the atoms of iron that compose an amusement park ride before we get on it, still less if our aim is to dismantle the ride and haul it off to the junkyard. Even if we were to get down to the infinitesimally small, however, we would still find forms that are separable from the totality that they compose, little machine atoms whose relations never exhaust the capacities of the individual entities that compose them to engender other relations. The torque on a bolt may distort its shape and strip its thread, weather may rust its metal—qualia, in other words, may change—but the bolt-qua-bolt remains unperturbed even when it is little more than a piece of broken, rusty metal. "If an entity always holds something in reserve," Harman writes, "and if this reserve also cannot be located in any of these relations, then it must exist somewhere else" (*TB,* 230). That somewhere else is in the unapproachable "molten core" at the center of the withdrawn object.[37]

For Steven Shaviro, the withdrawn quality of objects makes object-oriented ontology a version of substantialism, a claim that Levi Bryant embraces in his *Democracy of Objects*.[38] Drawing from Aristotle's account of substance, Bryant underscores Harman's essentially dualistic notion of the object as composed of virtual proper beings (or substance) and local manifestations separate from that substance.[39] Consolidated inside of the object, substance maintains its perforations whatever permutations its properties might exhibit; no cut or entanglement ever penetrates deeply enough. Rather than Aristotle's view of substance, then, I suggest that object-oriented ontology's split object recalls Plato's account of form and his foundational distinction between that which "always is and has no becoming" and that which "comes to be and never is" (*Timaeus,* 58C). For Plato of the *Timaeus* as for Harman, the substance of an object never changes, subsisting always in a self-same condition of being, while its accidental qualia and exogenous relations are alone capable of becoming and perishing away again.

And much as it did for Timaeus, this division between "that *in which* [a form] comes to be, and that *from which* what comes to be sprouts as something copied" (emphasis in original, 50D) requires a disruptive third term—the receptacle, chora, or womb, neither in the realm of being or becoming—whose evident deployment of sexed metaphors is very much to the point. Yet rather than retreat from the chora and its troubling sexual politics, I follow Judith Butler's lead in pushing the notion of the chora beyond the bounds of the systems that contains it. This potentiality, I argue, is generated from the stalled antinomy of object-oriented ontology and feminist new materialism—immanent in them both, but fully pursued by neither. The next section explores some of the limitations of matter in feminist new materialism.

The Persistence of Things

Harman's repudiation of matter reveals a surprisingly similar tendency in feminist new materialism. The examples we have reviewed of the performative co-constitution of bodies and discourses make rigorously concrete the way meaning matters. However, their very specificity privileges the demonstrable. As we saw in the Ferris wheel example, matter requires a willingness to entertain that which escapes the procedures of demonstration. For Harman, the very inability to put one's finger on matter proves its inexistence. But the recession of matter in demonstration afflicts feminist new materialism as well. I want to turn now to an example given to us by the political philosopher Jane Bennett in her *Vibrant Matter,* because in using matter to think about politics, Bennett's work exhibits its brilliance and also underscores its limitations.[40]

Bennett calls her approach a "vital materialism" and defines it as an attempt to "dissipate the onto-theological binaries of life/ matter, human/animal, will/determination and organic/inorganic" (*VM,* x) in order "to enhance receptivity to the impersonal life that surrounds us and infuses us" (*VM,* 4). To exhibit the value of this approach, she takes up the example of the 2003 North American Blackout. "To the vital materialist," she writes, "the electrical grid is better understood as a volatile mix of coal, sweat, electromagnetic fields, computer programs, electron streams, profit motives, heat, lifestyles, nuclear fuel, plastic, fantasies of mastery, static, legislation, water, economic theory, wire and wood" (*VM,* 25). Together, this assemblage of actants produces something else—literally volatility—through the mattering of power, or rather through the production of its failure. Irritable, jittery, tending toward change: this vision provides a clear and recognizable example of how fantasies of mastery solicit the excitability of electricity. Unlike social construction, the emphasis here is on the agency of power as it succumbs to and exceeds human management systems. No longer Delany's spherical womb and its emphasis on what the eye can see, it is because bodies are restive, not at all quiescent, that they can be bound and shaped to particular forms.

At the same time, however, Bennett's actants remain visually distinct on the page, both preceding and succeeding the relations that brought on the power failure, in a visual echo of the trademark listing style of OOO. These lists stand in metonymically for the randomness of the object world. Indeed, Bogost built his famous Latour Litanizer specifically to generate discontinuous sets of things.[41] Although Bennett's list is oriented toward relationality since her point is that each piece is entangled in an emergent phenomena with all the others, the list form itself highlights the separability of the objects it houses. What is missing from her list is the volatility as a quality of relations rather than of objects. Bennett wants to argue that the power failure, like Nietzsche's famous discussion of lightning in *On the Genealogy of Morals,* is not the product of the grid but instead one of its potential expressions. Yet it is exactly that emergent property that slips the noose of the list, operating in the gaps between its actants.

Bennett and Barad both insist that there is life in the interstices, an inorganic life that moves as vigorously through the biological as through the machinic and the ideational. My purpose in this very brief critique has been to show how easily the apprehension of that life recedes under the requirements of demonstration to be replaced by a network of discrete parts. Through the analytic of the network, Bennett can present the North American Blackout as a seamed whole rather than as a unified totality and thus avoid the pitfalls of essentialism. That very presentation, however, obscures what Hasana Sharp characterizes as the "supersaturation" of any system with "energetic force that is composing and recomposing in new forms, in response to new tensions, at all times."[42] More pointedly, the absence of a lexicon for apprehending that supersaturation then impoverishes our inquiry into its modes of composition and conceals the ways in which we enter into that composition.

The question, then, is not just of forms and matters, but of the space that holds them both. The persistence of things in feminist new materialism reveals the enduring difficulty of articulating a space or *plenum* that is also a *dunamis.* The more we see the former, the more obscured the latter becomes and vice versa. As Eugene Thacker writes, the contradiction between "an immanence that is placid, expansive, and silent, and a vitalism that is always folding, creating, and producing" appears irresolvable.[43] In rejecting materialism, what object-oriented ontology refuses is the possibility of a dynamized space between objects. By the same token, the persistence of things in feminist new materialism indicates a hesitancy to fully name and defend such a potentially irresolvable problematic. Yet this problem also reveals an enduring desire to collapse the distinction between plenum and dunamis.

Indeed, the language of spaces and forces evident in Sharp's "supersaturation" runs like a minor chord through the critical enterprise, subtending even apparently epistemological or linguistic accounts. It is evident, for example, in Foucault's discussion of his method in *History of Sexuality*, volume 1, where he writes:

> It seems to me that power must be understood in the first instance as the multiplicity of force relations immanent in the sphere in which they operate and which constitute their own organization; as the process which, through ceaseless struggles and confrontations, transforms, strengthens, or reverses them; as the support which these force relations find in one another, thus forming a chain or a system.[44]

Foucault's injunction can be and very often has been understood through the logic of the *dispositif*—the meeting of powers converging on each other via molar organizations, regulatory apparatuses, legal frameworks, discursive networks, and their various idioms and appurtenances—and for good reason.[45] Paying attention to the nodes that make up the "chain or system" operating within a sphere, as the *dispositif* model holds, however, has the effect of equating relations of force with exertions of power, collapsing effect into cause and writing out the concussive meetings between nodes. What it means for "a multiplicity of force relations" to "constitute their own organization," in other words, changes substantially if we take "force relations" on a physical rather than a sociological model.[46] In such a model, relations of force cannot be reduced to the actions of entities. In Manuel De Landa's account, the force relations of complex systems are the attractors and bifurcations that are both intrinsic features of dynamic systems and yet that "have no independent existence" and therefore cannot be understood as products of molar objects in any straightforward sense.[47] It is for this reason that Gilles Deleuze calls Foucault's thesis on power a "physics of action."[48] Yet even in De Landa's alternative conceptualization of a "single phylogenetic line cutting through all matter, 'living' or 'nonliving,'" the presence of terminology from evolution indicates the ease with which dunamis can become reconsolidated as a property of bodies that recline in the passive plenum of space.[49]

The Chora

I propose the chora as a way to grasp this dynamized space. The chora comes to us from Plato's *Timaeus,* which tells the story of how the temporal world arose from the eternal.[50] As this implies, much of the text concerns the split between the eternal world of forms—unchanging, apprehensible by the intellect but without sensuous equivalent—and the world to which we have access. Timaeus's account of the chora comes in the middle, breaking into the smooth flow of its narrative line. Timaeus finds that he can no longer make do with the two kinds—the realm of being and the realm of becoming—that have until this point satisfied. He runs into the necessity for that which should not be necessary, the product of "bastard reasoning . . . hardly to be trusted, the very thing we look to when we dream and affirm that it's necessary somehow for everything that *is*" (emphasis in the original, 52A).

The problem is this: To move into the temporal world of becoming, the transcendent form must have "birth and visibility" (50D). Eternal models must become imitations of themselves. If this is so, then the form must have something into which it descends, something separate from the copies that it will generate and that make up the temporal world. Since eternal forms cannot enter the realm of becoming, yet must put its impress into substance, then there must be a third realm. Form must be housed *somewhere* in *something* while it undergoes its transformation. To correct this difficulty, Timaeus conjures up a third kind, neither a model nor a copy, neither being nor becoming: the chora or the space of generation. Explicitly framed in hetero-reproductive terms, the chora is "mother," "womb," "wet-nurse," and "receptacle" (48C–50E) to the fathering form. The eternal form enters into the chora but takes nothing of her nature. She serves wholly as the space of transmission. Yet it is not for nothing that the chora is introduced late: it is both necessary and inassimilable, disrupting the distinction between being and becoming by taking part in both but being faithful to neither. Where, after all, did this third realm come from? Part of neither kingdom, the chora is the "wandering cause" (48C) that holds together and disrupts the movement from potentiality to actuality, swerves the smooth transition from model to copy and offers a notion of systemic agency that operates in the interstices between objects.

In her reading of these passages, Judith Butler highlights the passivity and shapelessness Plato assigns to the chora and that marks its difference from the active shaping of the "father" or the eternal form and the degraded, inauthentic activity of the copy in the world of becoming. As wandering cause, the chora holds the potential for uncontrolled generation, for dynamic change that is neither a product of the eternal form nor its diminution in the realm of becoming. While giving place to the spontaneous generation of new orders, the *Timaeus*'s family romance thus represents an attempt at domestication in what Butler calls a "topographic suppression": from matrix to place, from chora to plenum, from wandering cause to wet-nurse.[51] This topographic suppression is precisely Harman's move. He consolidates relationality and potentiality to the interior of the object. In so doing, he brings the chora into the object, providing each real sensible thing with its own internal generator, "the molten inner core of objects."[52] This, I suggest, represents a new kind of domesticization of the chora. No longer passive midwife of sensible form, dynamism is now locked in as the engine of form, vitalizing its limits and thresholds.

What would it look like to release the chora from this topographic suppression? At one point, Butler toys with the idea of what she calls an "irruptive chora" but ultimately rejects it as a false escape.[53] And yet this irruptive chora, it seems to me, is just what Plato's domestication sought to avoid and yet could not quite do without. As such, it offers an opportunity to imagine an autonomous, dynamic, temporalized space through which subindividual matters, vibratory intensities, and affects might cross and *be altered through that crossing.* This is the crucial point. The irruptive chora enables us to apprehend with what frequency the plenum or spatium is posed as passive, even in new materialist writing. My description of the chora, for example, is mostly consonant with Deleuze and Guattari's notion of the body without organs. In light of the irruptive chora, however, their description of "the unformed, unorganized, nonstratified or destratified body . . . [that] causes intensities to pass" seems strangely passive.[54] The contradiction between plenum and dunamis appears logical precisely because it begins from an originary cut between the given and the immutable and the contingent and mutational. A resurgent, vitalized under-standing of the "sphere," the "support," the "chain or . . . system," "the moving substrate" in Foucault; the "spatium" in Deleuze and Guatari; begins to suggest a way back to the chora in its activity, to inhuman reproductions, to an irruptive chora that exerts its own autonomous force.

What I am proposing bears resemblance to what Pheng Cheah, in a discussion of Deleuzian virtuality, introduces as a double artic-ulation between the virtual "speeds and intensities" that generate an actual object and the object itself. This causality goes in both directions: "On the one hand," Cheah writes, "the actual object is the accomplished absorption and destruction of the virtuals that surround it. On the other hand, the actual object also emits or cre-ates the virtual since the process of actualization brings the object back into relation with the field of differential relations in which it can always be dissolved and become actualized otherwise."[55] The dualism Cheah proposes between the actual object and its virtu-alities creates a separation between the background of speeds and intensities that get captured by the drag of organization and sedi-mented into an actual object whose constrained vibratory intensity then ripples back across the field of force relations.

Such an analytic could then ground a physics of force and a method that accounts for its operations. Taken in its most robust form, this revivified chora generates an ontology of material-affective circulation. As a *tertium quid,* the "third thing" that transmits and transforms dynamic form, the chora both enables and distorts the autopoiesis of apparently incorporeal matters like thought. As Brian Massumi writes, "No longer beholden to the empirical order of the senses, thought, at the limit, throws off the shackles of reenaction. It becomes directly *enactive*—of virtual events."[56] Thinking of rep-resentational media within the terms enabled by this analysis of the chora gives them autonomy from their human reception: they are autonomously mobile, subject to the same patterned movements as those that characterize physical and biological systems, and they are autonomously causal, interacting with each other to engender new vanishing points. In the final section I point to some ways of thinking the practice of choratic reading.

Practicing Choratic Reading

"Something's doing": the opening words of Massumi's *Semblance and Event* capture the premise of choratic reading and its point of intervention. Two decades of critical scholarship in feminist materialism and science studies have made it possible to say "There's happening doing" and to indicate by that phrase the agency of human and nonhuman bodies, organic and nonorganic vitalities, discourses and the specific material apparatuses those discourses are.[57] This critical posture has also begun to redound on the practice of scholarship itself. From Eve Kosofsky Sedgwick's largely conceptual call for a greater scholarly embrace of the sensual and reparative to object-oriented ontology's desire to "go outside and dig in the dirt," the questions of scholarship's own affective and material basis have started to receive serious treatment.[58] In *How We Think*, for example, N. Katherine Hayles argues for a "practice-based research" that would employ embodied interactions with other-than-verbal materials to generate unexpected kinesthetic and temporal experiences.[59] In similar fashion, Erin Manning and her collaborators run the SenseLab as a center for research creation by emphasizing what they call "the active passage between research and creation" in real-time and asynchronous collaborations.[60] Each of these examples widens and diversifies the modes in which scholarship gets made. By arguing that how we make things affects the things we make, Hayles, Manning, and Bogost demonstrate that the study of matter, affect, and embodiment need not and should not take place primarily through the study of texts but can instead be theorized through and as practice.

This laboratory model of criticism incisively shifts the scene of production. Operating on the other side of this relationship, scholars working in the digital humanities and in rhetoric have begun to develop alternatives to the linear essay. However, with notable exceptions, these emergent models—such as data visualization and other forms of machine reading—retain demonstrative argumentation as their primary goal.[61] Although machine reading allows us to find patterns at scales otherwise impossible, the questions and conclusions we bring to bear on these patterns have remained largely congruent with close reading's persuasive demonstration. By contrast, if choratic reading can be said to have an argument, it is that new concepts arise as much through affective engagement as through rational demonstration.

As one of the forces behind this shift, it would seem reasonable to assume that object-oriented ontology would proffer a new way to navigate the relations between cultural production, aesthetic form, and subject formation. Indeed, OOO has been called on to perform just such an analysis and Harman has duly responded. In his "Well-Wrought Broken Hammer" article published in *New Literary History*, Harman reviews examples of new criticism, new historicism, and deconstruction before positing his own "object-oriented method" (WWBH, 200). What he finds in his review is that each school of criticism fails in the same way that he understands pre-OOO philosophy to have failed. By "dissolving a text upward into its readings or downward into its cultural elements" (WWBH, 200) criticism never lands on the text itself.[62] Instead of these two procedures, Harman urges literary critics to work toward discovering qualities that make works of literature themselves. "Instead of just writing about *Moby Dick*," he writes, "why not try shortening it to various degrees in order to discover the point at which it ceases to sound like *Moby Dick*? Why not imagine it lengthened even further, or told by a third-person narrator rather than Ishmael, or involving a cruise in the opposite direction around the globe?" (WWBH, 202). The purpose of rendering such permutations is to discover what in the text is accidental—the qualia of the work—and what makes up its molten interior. As a method, then, its mode is primarily taxonomic, a categorizing enterprise with the added capacity to discriminate between the features of a work that allow it to "withstand the earthquakes of the centuries" (WWBH, 201) and those that prove irrelevant to its essential haecceity. Harman thinks of the new critics as having come closest to this goal in their focus on the individual work, and indeed such a method goes quite a ways toward weeding out of literary studies the very assertions that have made it a radical and generative field since the new critics: that texts speak more than they know, that the devil is in the weave of its details, that repetitions across texts are meaningful and therefore interpretable. None of this is really very surprising, of course.[63]

Yet several aspects of this method do surprise. It is first of all surprisingly epistemological. As we have seen, one of the defining features of object-oriented ontology's divided objects is their inaccessible interiors that repel "all forms of causal or cognitive mastery" (WWBH, 188). Starting from this definition, it is not at all clear that any amount of cutting or rearranging will bring the inner core of *Moby Dick* into relief. Nor is it clear what beside "causal or cognitive mastery" this act would contribute. Moreover, for a field that trumpets the democracy of objects, Harman's object-oriented method is singularly unimpressed by the force of criticism. Cutting into the text and recording the results frames the work of literature as primary and the work of criticism as merely adjunct reportage. Finally, and ironically, the examples Harman provides all focus on the text *as narrative plot.* The text's formal composition, its "structure of meanings" (WWBH, 190) is excluded from the outset as a clearly false prejudice of new criticism. With no relations inside or outside, object-oriented method reveals the immobility generated by interiorizing dunamism within a sterilized plenum. What object-oriented method cannot see is the material force of literature as it enters into composition with other vibrant matters.

Choratic reading, by contrast, begins from the assertion that acts of literature—very much including scholarly readings—are performed in material composition with the affordances of their media, the sensorium of their audiences, and the deformations of dissemination as they transduce across and are deformed by the irruptions of the choratic plane. In this sense, books and their readers form zones of intensity in composition with the interstitial field of already-circulating energies and the attractors and bifurcations of the choratic plane. The political purpose of interpretation informs the form of the reading as well as its content. Sedgwick has written at length about the unacknowledged affective register of hermeneutics. Rather than restricting the import of this affection to readers, choratic reading practices opens scholarly affect to flows of all kinds. By matching the affective milieu of its object, choratic scholarship can underscore, extend, thin out, modulate, or swerve its circulation.

Such a reading protocol transforms our angle of inquiry from the text as representational symptom to the dynamic form of the media object. To effect this transformation, I propose a lexicon of terms: *composition* highlights the interrelations between parts; *movement* refers to the characteristic circuiting of energy through that form; *sound* to the layers or tonal stacks striating it; *rhythm* to the vibratory milieu created by it; and, finally, *gesture* looks to the capacities for connection and the production of potentialities. Together, these properties illustrate the internal workings of a form and its relations to the aesthetico-political milieu. Employing this method of analysis allows us to pose questions about texts that concern their effects as form. In this context, we can ask what shape the text creates and how that shape circulates affective force, how it moves across time and how it forms relationships: from explosive forms meant to blast apart overly strong captures to shapes bristling with receptors or catalyzing shapes meant to actualize potentiality in encounters. Reading in this way emphasizes design and so alters the formal distinctions between creative and critical compositions.

"What does this have to do with science?," Elizabeth Grosz asks in the course of her little monograph *Chaos, Territory, Art.* As I hope I have demonstrated, feminist science studies has traced an arc through the question of representation, moving from the urgent and necessary epistemological task of untangling science's encoding of and complicity with sexed, gendered, raced, and anthropocentric assumptions through the hard-won and hard-maintained insistence on the ontological co-constitution of matters and discourses to the recognition of the wholly non-discursive agency of other than human forces. The question of representation, of the relations between things in the world and the stories we tell about those things, continues to animate feminist science studies. But we haven't yet asked what might happen to our sense of scholarship—of meaning, of concept, of learning—if we repose the question of representation, but this time to ourselves? What might we find if we begin from the premise that there is a material connection between the artifact of scholarship, its producers, and its audience? What might emerge if we invite our scholarship to inhabit other forms and allow those forms to emerge through the compositional process? What if we stop taking it for granted that we understand how ideas are transmitted? In answer to the question posed at the start of this paragraph, Grosz writes, "The material plane of forces, energies, and effects that art requires in order to create moments of sensation that are artworks are shared in common with science. Science, like art, plunges itself into the materiality of the universe."[64] Choratic reading is one attempt at the becoming-imperceptible of art, science, and criticism.

Notes

My thanks to Richard Grusin, Jamie Skye Bianco, Annie McClanahan, Karen Weingarten, Ted Martin, Julian Gill-Peterson, Joseph Varga, and an anonymous reviewer at the University of Minnesota Press for conversation, speculation, skepticism, camaraderie, and incisive commentary. Thanks also to the Center for 21st Century Studies at the University of Wisconsin-Milwaukee and the 2011–12 Center Fellows for the support needed to write this chapter.

1. Although this holds in general, it is worth noting that one of the key differences between speculative realism (SR) and object-oriented ontology concerns how they understand the consequences of correlationism. Graham Harman explains in "The Well-Wrought Broken Hammer: Object Oriented Literary Criticism," *New Literary History* 43, no. 2 (Spring 2012): 183–203, that where SR affirms the descriptive accuracy of mathematical statements about the world, OOO denies absolute knowledge. Hereafter, the article is abbreviated as WWBH in parenthetical citations in the text.

2. Quentin Meillassoux, *After Finitude: An Essay on the Necessity of Contingency* (London: Continuum, 2010), 5. Hereafter cited as *AF* in parenthetical citations within the text.

3. Ian Bogost, *Alien Phenomenology, or What It's Like to Be a Thing* (Minneapolis: University of Minnesota Press, 2012), 3.

4. Timothy Morton, "They Are Here: My Nonhuman Turn Talk," *Ecology without Nature* blog, May 4, 2012, http://ecologywithoutnature.blogspot.com/.

5. Timothy Morton, "Here Comes Everything: The Promise of Object-Oriented Ontology," *Qui Parle* 19, no. 2 (Spring/Summer 2011): 163–90.

6. I am aware of the irony involved here.

7. Myra Hird and Celia Roberts, "Feminism Theorises the Nonhuman," *Feminist Theory*, 12, no. 2 (August 2011): 111.

8. See Donna Haraway, *The Companion Species Manifesto: Dogs, People, and Significant Otherness* (Chicago: Prickly Paradigm Press, 2003); and Karen Barad, *Meeting the Universe Halfway: Quantum Physics and the Entanglement of Matter and Meaning* (Durham, N.C.: Duke University Press, 2007).

9. In this sense feminist new materialism brings together the emphasis on the productivity of discourse in Michel Foucault's account of power with Baruch Spinoza's cosmogony.

10. Plato, *Timaeus*, ed. Oskar Piest, trans. Francis Cornford (New York: Macmillan, 1959).

11. I am keenly aware of the problem with enacting lineages. My effort here is less to posit the differences between moments in feminist inquiry than to show their continuities. However, I do think that some delineation is required in the wake of OOO's collapse of distinction, as I explain following.

12. Donna Haraway, "The Promise of Monsters: A Regenerative Politics of Inappropriate/d Others," in *Cultural Studies*, ed. Lawrence Grossberg, Cary Nelson, and Paula A. Treichler (New York: Routledge, 1992), 296, 297.

13. Valerie Hartouni, *Cultural Conceptions: On Reproductive Technologies and the Remaking of Life* (Minneapolis: University of Minnesota Press, 1997), 8.

14. Samuel Delany, "Rhetoric of Sex/Discourse of Desire," in *Shorter Views: Queer Thoughts and the Politics of the Paraliterary* (Hanover, N.H.: Wesleyan University Press, 1999), 3, 4.

15. Ibid., 5.

16. Luce Irigaray, *Speculum of the Other Woman* (Ithaca, N.Y.: Cornell University Press, 1985).

17. See Giorgio Agamben, Homo Sacer: *Sovereign Power and Bare Life* (Stanford, Calif.: Stanford University Press, 1995).

18. This point is also made extensively by ecofeminists; see in particular Carolyn Merchant, *The Death of Nature: Women, Ecology, and the Scientific Revolution* (New York: Harper and Row, 1980).

19. On the "drama of exposure," see Eve Kosofsky Sedgwick's biting and bravura essay "Paranoid Reading, Reparative Reading, or You're So Paranoid You Probably Think This Essay Is about You," in *Touching Feeling: Affect, Pedagogy, Performativity* (Durham, N.C.: Duke University Press, 2003), 123–52.

20. Graham Harman, *Guerilla Metaphysics: Phenomenology and the Carpentry of Things* (Peru, Ill.: Open Court Press, 2005), 113.

21. Karen Barad, "Posthumanist Performativity: Toward an Under-standing of How Matter Comes to Matter," *Signs: Journal of Women in Culture and Society* 28, no.3 (2003): 801.

22. Ibid., 820.

23. For the physics behind this oversimplified summary, see Karen Barad, *Meeting the Universe Halfway: Quantum Physics and the Entan-glement of Matter and Meaning* (Durham, N.C.: Duke University Press, 2007), especially chapter 7.

24. Annamarie Mol, *The Body Multiple: Ontology in Medical Practice* (Durham, N.C.: Duke University Press, 2002), vii.

25. Myra Hird, *The Origins of Sociable Life: Evolution after Science Studies* (New York: Palgrave, 2009).

26. Stacy Alaimo, *Bodily Natures: Science, Environment, and the Ma-terial Self* (Bloomington: Indiana University Press, 2010).

27. In this sense, feminist new materialism picks up on Simone de Beauvoir's tact in *The Second Sex* of responding to the nature argument by looking directly at nature.

28. Graham Harman, *Tool-Being: Heidegger and the Metaphysics of Objects* (Peru, Ill.: Open Court Press, 2002), hereafter abbreviated as *TB* in parenthetical citations in the text. Levi Bryant, Graham Harman, and Nick Srnicek, eds., *The Speculative Turn: Continental Materialism and Realism* (Melbourne: re.press, 2011), 3.

29. Bryant et al., *Speculative Turn*, 1.

30. Blog commentary tends to point out that only one woman—Isabelle Stengers—was included in the collection. Though this is a relevant point, my argument is less concerned with inclusion per se than with the logic that drives the absence in the first place. For a good example, see "some background on Harman and Speculative Realism (and cool new book series)," *New APPS: Art, Politics, Philosophy, Science* blog, February 15, 2011, www.newappsblog.com/. It's worth noting that the commenter in question is Melinda Cooper whose work in *Life as Surplus: Biotechnology and Capitalism in the Neoliberal Era* (Seattle: University of Washington Press, 2008) well exemplifies feminist new materialist approaches.

31. This is less an interpretation than a restatement of Harman's own explicit position on the twin techniques of undermining and overmining in his "On the Undermining of Objects: Grant, Bruno, and Radical Phi-losophy," in Bryant et al., *The Speculative Turn*.

32. Timothy Morton, "Of Lava Lamps and Firehouses," *Ecology without Nature* blog, November 14, 2012, http://ecologywithoutnature.blogspot.com/.

33. Bruno Latour, "An Attempt at Writing a Compositionist's Mani-festo," *New Literary History* 41, no. 3 (Summer 2010): 471–90.

34. Harman, *Guerilla Metaphysics*, 95.

35. Ibid., 106.

36. Harman, "Undermining," 24.

37. Graham Harman, *Toward Speculative Realism* (New York: Zero Books, 2010), 133.

38. Levi Bryant, *Democracy of Objects* (Ann Arbor, Mich.: Open Humanities Press, 2011). Though I cannot fully discuss it here, staging Shaviro's chapter, "The Actual Volcano: Whitehead, Harman, and the Problem of Relations" in Bryant et al., *The Speculative Turn*, next to Eugene Thacker's *After Life* (Chicago: University of Chicago Press, 2010) and its rereading of Neoplatonism and scholasticism would be profitable.

39. Bryant is at pains to separate this notion of a substance that subtends qualities from the account of matter we have seen in feminist new materialism. His version, however, is also quite different than Harman's. For Bryant substance is "an absolutely individual system or organization of powers" (*Democracy*, 89) internal to the object. Referring to his blue mug, Bryant argues that this view of substance makes an object's qualities the effect or event of the object's own endo-relationships. For him "the mug blues" is a more accurate description of events. Though I don't have the space to elaborate on this point here, Bryant's notion of virtual proper being is far more relational than Harman's.

40. Jane Bennett, *Vibrant Matter: A Political Ecology of Things* (Durham, N.C.: Duke University Press, 2010); hereafter cited as *VM* in parenthetical citations within the text. I call on Bennett because her work, like Barad's, has been cited as "forerunner" to object-oriented ontology. This assimilation, I am arguing, reveals something about the persistence of things in feminist new materialism.

41. The Latour Litanizer uses Wikipedia to generate random lists. For a fuller explanation, see Bogost, *Alien Phenomenology*, esp. 95–96. The Litanizer is accessible from his website, www.bogost.com.

42. Hasana Sharp, *Spinoza and the Politics of Renaturalization* (Chicago: University of Chicago Press, 2011), 36.

43. Thacker, *After Life*, 208. Also see *After Life* for an elaboration of these terms.

44. Michel Foucault, *History of Sexuality*, vol. 1, trans. Robert Hurley (New York: Vintage Books, 1990), 92.

45. On the *dispositif*, see Michel Foucault, "The Confessions of the Flesh," in *Power/Knowledge: Selected Interviews and Other Writings, 1972–1977*, ed. Colin Gordon (New York: Vintage, 1980), especially pages 194–225. On molar versus molecular entities see, Gilles Deleuze and Félix Guattari, *A Thousand Plateaus: Capitalism and Schizophrenia*, trans. Brian Massumi (Minneapolis: University of Minnesota Press, 1987), esp. 31–36.

46. Foucault, *History of Sexuality 1*, 92.

47. Manuel De Landa, "Nonorganic Life," in *Incorporations*, ed. Jonathan Crary and Sanford Kwinter (New York: Zone Books, 1992), 138.

48. Gilles Deleuze, *Foucault*, trans. Seán Hand (London: Continuum Books, 1999), 60.

49. De Landa, "Nonorganic," 138.

50. For a related account of the chora and feminist theory, see Emanuela Bianchi, "The Interruptive Feminine: Aleatory Time and Feminist Politics," in *Undutiful Daughters: New Directions in Feminist Thought and Practice*, eds. Henriette Gunkle, Chrysanthi Nigianni, and Fanny Soderback (New York: Palgrave Macmillan, 2012).

51. Judith Butler, *Bodies That Matter: On the Discursive Limits of "Sex"* (New York: Routledge, 1993), 42.

52. Harman, *Toward Speculative Realism*, 133.

53. Butler, *Bodies That Matter*, 48.

54. Deleuze and Guattari, *A Thousand Plateaus*, 43.

55. Pheng Cheah, "Non-Dialectical Materialisms," in *New Materialism: Ontology, Agency, and Politics*, eds. Diana Coole and Samantha Frost (Durham, N.C.: Duke University Press, 2010), 86.

56. Brian Massumi, *Semblance and Event: Activist Philosophy and the Occurrent Arts* (Cambridge, Mass.: MIT Press, 2011), 122.

57. Ibid., 1.

58. Bogost, *Alien Phenomenology*, 133.

59. N. Katherine Hayles, *How We Think: Digital Media and Contemporary Technogenesis* (Chicago: University of Chicago Press, 2012).

60. "About" page, *Senselab*, www.senselab.ca/wp2/about/.

61. For distance and machine reading, see Franco Moretti's Literary Lab at Stanford University. For a compelling alternative, see the University of Victoria's Maker Lab and its Kits for Culture project.

62. It is worth noting that this parallel between philosophy and literary criticism suggests that the same episteme subtends them both, contrary to Harman's assertion at the start of the essay that "the various districts of human knowledge have relative disciplinary autonomy" (WWBH, 183).

63. For a far more interesting version of speculative reading see Eileen A. Joy, "Weird Reading," *Speculations: A Journal of Speculative Realism* 4 (2013): 28–34.

64. Elizabeth Grosz, *Chaos, Territory, Art: Deleuze and the Framing of the Earth* (New York: Columbia University Press, 2008), 61.

9

Systems and Things

On Vital Materialism and Object-Oriented Philosophy

JANE BENNETT

THE RECENT TURN TOWARD NONHUMANS in the humanities and social sciences takes place within a complex swarm of other intellectual, affective, scientific, and political-economic trends.[1] I think that two such trends are especially relevant. The first is a growing awareness of the accelerating concentration of wealth within neoliberal economies, as expressed by the Occupy movement and by the renewed vitality of Marx-inspired political analyses.[2] Marxisms speak powerfully to the desire for a radical, forceful counterresponse to the injustices of global capitalism. But "historical materialisms" are not perceived as offering an equally satisfying response to a second set of trends, those described roughly as ecological: the growing awareness of climate change and the possibility that the Earth may have entered the geo-political epoch of the Anthropocene.[3] Here, various vital materialisms arise to supplement and complement historical materialisms. They are inspired by twentieth-century feminisms of the body, as in the work of Simone de Beauvoir, Luce Irigaray, and Judith Butler; the phenomenology of Iris Young; the Spinozism of Moira Gatens; and the creative Darwin of Elizabeth Grosz. They also draw sustenance from a longer tradition of philosophical materialism in the West, where fleshy, vegetal, mineral materials are encountered not as passive stuff awaiting animation by human or divine power, but as lively forces at work around and within us.

Ancient atomism is influential here, especially Lucretius's *clinamen* or swerving *primordia*. This image will go on to inspire other theorists, less "atomistic" than Lucretius, to defend other versions of a sensate, ever-evolving universe. The Romantic poet Erasmus Darwin, for example, writes in his 1803 *Temple of Nature* that "the wrecks of Death are but a change of forms; / Emerging matter from the grave returns, / Feels new desires, with new sensation burns."[4] And in the twentieth century, Michel Serres will spin Lucretian physics into an ontology of *noise* or the "percolating" vibrancy within all (only apparently stable) things.[5]

Other notables in this tradition include, as already noted, Baruch Spinoza, for whom every body (person, fly, stone) comes with a *conatus* or impetus to seek alliances that enhance its vitality; Henry Thoreau, the American naturalist who detects the presence of an effusive, unruly Wildness inside rocks, plants, animals, and locomotives; and Walt Whitman, who "aches with love" for matter because, after all, "Does not all matter, / aching, attract all matter?"[6] These and other evocations of *lively* materiality downplay the differences between organic and inorganic, and they persist despite Immanuel Kant's 1790 pronouncement that the very idea of lively matter "involves a contradiction, since the essential character of matter is lifelessness, *inertia*."[7]

The nonhuman turn, then, can be understood as a continuation of earlier attempts to depict a world populated not by active subjects and passive objects but by lively and essentially interactive materials, by bodies human and nonhuman. Some of the impetus to reinhabit the tradition also comes from the voluminous mountains of "things" that today surround those of us living in corporate-capitalist, neoliberal, shopping-as-religion cultures. Novelty items, prepackaged edibles, disposable objects, past and future landfill residents, buildings, weeds, books, devices, websites, and so on, and so on—all these materialities make "calls" upon us, demand attention. It's getting harder not to notice their powers of enabling and refusing us, of enhancing and destroying what we want (to have, to do, to be and become). Theorists of the nonhuman want to see what would happen—to perception and judgment, to sympathies and antipathies, to physical and intellectual postures, to writing styles and research designs, to practices of consumption and production, and to our very notions of self and the human, if what Graham Harman has termed the "allure" of objects were to have more pride of place in our thinking. It no longer seems satisfactory to write off this allure as wholly a function of the pathetic fallacy or the projection of voice onto some inanimate stuff.[8]

Perhaps the big project of the nonhuman turn is to find new techniques, in speech and art and mood, to disclose the participation of nonhumans in "our" world. This would require the invention and deployment of a grammar that was less organized around subjects and objects and more capable of avowing the presence of what Bruno Latour called "actants." It would also require closer attention to the work of those in physical and natural sciences who also recognize the power of materials to shape, induce, even hail other bodies.[9]

The focus of this chapter, however, is less broad. Its goal is to explore some of the internal philosophical differences within the nonhuman turn, in particular those between object-oriented philosophy and the various vital materialisms currently emerging.[10]

Withdrawal and Vitality

One such difference stems from a tendency for the former to follow Heidegger on the question of "things" and the latter to follow Deleuze and Guattari's notion of a quite active and expressive "matter-movement" or "matter-energy" that "enters assemblages and leaves them."[11] Heidegger considered the uncanny agency of things in several of his late essays, where the incalculability of the Thing and its persistent withdrawal are emphasized, whereas Deleuze and Guattari highlighted the positive or productive power of things to draw other bodies near and conjoin powers. A key inspiration here is the "Nomadology" section of *A Thousand Plateaus*, in which Deleuze and Guattari mark the way metal does not just resist human endeavors but has "traits of expression" of its own that push and pull upon the endeavoring body of the metallurgist. "In short, what metal and metallurgy bring to light is a life proper to matter, a vital state of matter as such, a material Vitalism":

> Let us return to the example of the saber, or rather of
> crucible steel. It implies the . . . the melting of the iron at
> high temperature [and] . . . the successive decarbonations;
> [but] corresponding to these singularities are traits of

expression—not only the hardness, sharpness, and finish, but also the undulations or designs traced by the crystallization and resulting from the internal structure of the cast steel.... Each phylum has its own singularities and operations, its own qualities and traits, which determine the relation of desire to the technical element (the affects the saber "has" are not the same as those of the sword).... At the limit, there is ... a single machinic phylum, ideally continuous: the flow of matter-movement, the flow of matter in continuous variation, conveying singularities and traits of expression....[12]

If for Heidegger things expose the limits of human knowing, for Deleuze and Guattari people, places, and things forge heterogeneous connections and form something like a compound, extended mind: "Metallurgy is the consciousness or thought of the matter-flow, and metal the correlate of this consciousness."[13] As the Deleuzean Bernd Herzogenrath puts it, matter is "equipped with the capacity for self-organization—matter is thus *alive, informed* rather than *informe* ('formless'): 'matter ... is not dead, brute, homogeneous matter, but a matter-movement bearing singularities ... , qualities and even operations.'"[14]

Object-oriented ontologists or speculative realists, and I will be using Graham Harman and Tim Morton as my examples, are instead attracted to Heidegger's focus on the object's negative power, its persistent *withdrawal* from any attempt to engage, use, or know it. Indeed, "objects" could not hope for more staunch defenders than Harman and Morton, who include in the category objects pretty much everything: human individuals, literary texts, alcohol, spoons, plants. An object is, says Morton, a "weird entity withdrawn from access, yet somehow manifest."[15] Withdrawn *and* manifest. *Withdrawn:* even as a rat or a plastic bottle cap is producing an arresting effect on me and captures my attention, the speculative realist (who eschews the label "materialist") insists that *none* of the bodies at the scene were wholly present to each other. Objects exist, says Harman, as "entities ... quite apart from any relations with or effects upon other entities in the world."[16] *Manifest:* despite this apartness, objects are *coy*, always leaving hints of a secret otherworld, "alluding" to an "inscrutable" reality "behind the accessible theoretical, practical, or perceptual qualities." Objects are expert players of the game of hide-and-seek. It is thus important not to overstate the contrast between the Harman and Morton on the one hand and a vital materialist position on the other. The status of the object's Heideggerian withdrawal is not quite that of a human postulate: insofar as it is something that we *sense,* it is something that comes from the outside. The thing's act of seeking cover is, says Heidegger, a "draft" from the "Open," a beckoning *call* of sorts.[17]

In what follows, I consider the way such a figure of the object and its powers is positioned by Morton and Harman as a repudiation of "holism." They include in that category assemblage-theories of various sorts, in which circulate bits and pieces of Deleuze, Latour, Manning, De Landa, Massumi, Haraway, Shaviro, Whitehead, Spinoza, Foucault, Romantic poets. I also try to make explicit just what turns—politically, ethically—on the object-philosophers' strong claims about the apartness of objects. What difference would it make if I came to experience myself more explicitly as one essentially *elusive* object among others? What is at stake for political and ethical life (in North America?) in the fight against systems- or process-theories, especially since all the parties share a critique of linguistic and social constructivism? Since, that is, all parties see the nonhuman turn as a response to an overconfidence about human power that was embedded in the postmodernism of the 1980s and 1990s?

Relationality

At the heart of object-oriented ontology, says Harman, is a "deeply non-relational conception of the reality of things."[18] But why such a "deep" animosity toward relational ontologies? One minor motive may be the pleasure of iconoclasm: for Harman and Morton "networks, negotiations, relations, interactions, and dynamic fluctuations" are golden calves—and they enjoy smashing idols. (Who doesn't?) System-oriented theory has, they say, already had its day and no longer yields philosophically interesting problems: the "programmatic movement toward holistic interaction is an idea once but no longer liberating," and "the real discoveries now lie on the other side of the yard."[19]

But the stakes are higher, too. In "Aesthetics as First Philosophy," Harman implies that there are ethico-political as well as philosophical liabilities to a relational or network or open-system or *umwelt* approach: a "vision of holistic interactions in a reciprocal web . . . this blurring of boundaries between one thing and another, has held the moral high ground in philosophy for too long. . . . The political reflexes associated with terms such as essence ('bad') and reciprocal interplay ('good") must be recalibrated. . . ."[20] Elsewhere, Harman goes so far as to call it a "prejudice" to approach the world in terms of "complex feedback networks rather than integers."[21] But what is the alternative to "prejudice" here? It could be something like reasoned judgment, in which case the claim would be that object-oriented philosophy is more rationally defensible, a newbie perspective less encrusted with unthinking habit, mainstream culture, or normal subjectivity than relation-oriented theory. Or it may be that Harman would acknowledge that object-oriented philosophy itself includes a prejudice in favor of (a theoretical privileging of or conceptual honing in on) the mysterious object. But what *this* would then call for is an explicit account of the *virtues* or *stakes* of favoring mysterious objects over complex systems of relations, virtual and actual.

But maybe there is no need to choose between objects or their relations. Since everyday, earthly experience routinely identifies some effects as coming from individual objects and some from larger systems (or, better put, from individuations within material configurations and from the complex assemblages in which they participate), why not aim for a theory that toggles between both kinds or magnitudes of "unit"? One would then understand "objects" to be those swirls of matter, energy, and incipience that can hold themselves together long enough to vie with the strivings of other objects, including the indeterminate momentum of the throbbing whole. The project, then, would be to make both "objects" and "relations" the periodic focus of theoretical attention, even if it remained impossible to articulate fully the "vague" or "vagabond" essence of "thing" or any "system."[22] Even if, that is, one could not give equal attention to both at once.

This is just what those passé philosophers Deleuze and Guattari do in *A Thousand Plateaus*. One of their figures for (what I am calling) the system dimension is "assemblage," another is "plane of consistency." The latter is characterized by Deleuze and Guattari as "in no way an undifferentiated aggregate of unformed matter."[23] (Neither assemblage nor plane of consistency qualifies as what Harman describes as a "relational wildfire in which all individual elements are consumed."[24]) My point, in short, is that despite their robust attempts to conceptualize groupings, Deleuze and Guattari also manage to attend carefully to many specific entities—to horses, shoes, orchids, packs of wolves, wasps, priests, metals, and so on. Indeed, I find nothing in their approach inconsistent with the object-oriented philosopher's claim that things harbor a *differential* between their inside and outside or an irreducible moment of (withdrawn-from-view) interiority.

The example of *A Thousand Plateaus* also highlights the obvious point that not all theories of relationality, even if monistic, are holistic on the model of a smoothly functioning organism. There are harmonious holisms but also fractious models of systematicity, which allow for heterogeneity within and even emergent novelty, onto-pictures that are formally monistic but substantively plural.[25] The whole can be imaged as a self-diversifying process of territorializations and deterritorializations (Deleuze and Guattari) or as creative process (Bergson, Whitehead), or as some combination therein (the various new materialisms).[26] Or take the model of relationality that William Connolly, following William James, calls "protean connectionism": in contrast to both methodological individualism and organic holism, connectionism figures relations as "typically loose, incomplete, and themselves susceptible to potential change.... The connections are punctuated by 'litter' circulating in, between, and around them. Viewed temporally . . . connectionism presents a world in the making in an evolving universe that is open to an uncertain degree."[27] It makes sense to try to do justice *both* to systems and things—to acknowledge the stubborn reality of individuation *and* the essentially distributive quality of their affectivity.

Harman rejects the very framing of the issue as things-operating-in-systems in favor of an object-oriented picture in which aloof objects are positioned as the sole locus of activity. On occasion, however, even Harman finds himself theorizing a kind of relation—he calls it "communication"—between objects. He does try to insulate this object-to-object encounter from depictions that *also* locate activity in the relationships themselves or at the systemic level of operation, but I do not think that this parsing attempt succeeds. Neither do I quite see why it is worth the trouble, though it does bespeak of the purity of Harman's commitment to the aloof object: "The real problem is not how beings interact in a system: instead, the problem is how they withdraw from that system as independent realities while somehow communicating through the proximity, the touching without touching, that has been termed allusion or allure. . . ."[28] I concur that some dimensions of bodies are withdrawn from presence but see this as partly due to the role they play in this or that relatively open system.

In the text just quoted, Harman goes on to defend the view that communication via proximity is not limited to that between *human* bodies. The materialist would agree. Morton makes a similar, anti-anthropocentric point when he says that "what spoons do when they scoop up soup is not very different from what I do when I talk about spoons. . . . Not because the spoon is alive or intelligent (panpsychism), but because intelligence and being alive are aesthetic appearances—for some other phenomenon, including the object in question."[29] By engaging in what Bruno Latour might call a "horizontalizing" of the ontological plane, Morton and Harman allow their *ecological* sympathies to come to the fore, sympathies that, in Harman's case, might not be so apparent given his philosopher's insistence that *objects of thought* are objects, too. In the following quotation, however, Harman concerns himself with ordinary (non-ideational) objects:

> If it is true that other humans signal to me without being fully present, and equally true that I never exhaust the depths of non-sentient beings such as apples and sandpaper, this is not some special pathos of human finitude. . . . When avalanches slam into abandoned cars, or snowflakes rustle the needles of the quivering pine, even these objects cannot touch the full reality of one another. Yet they affect one another nonetheless.[30]

Hyperobjects

Morton also agrees that process or assemblage are undesirable conceptualizations ("Objects are [ontologically] prior to relations"), and he shares the judgment that attempts to juggle both system and thing are ultimately "reductionist."[31] The reduction consists in the fact that for Deleuze et al., "some things are more real than others: flowing liquids become templates for everything else" and thus there is a failure to "explain the givenness of the ontic phenomenon."[32] Morton here helpfully points out the way in which ontologies of becoming tend to be biased toward the specific rhythms and scales of the human body.

Morton also exposes the human body–centric nature of the figure of a "flowing liquids" ontology: "I marvel at the way . . . syrup lugubriously slimes its way out of a bottle. . . . But to a hypothetical four-dimensional sentient being, such an event would be an unremarkable static object, while to a neutrino the slow gobs of syrup are of no consequence whatsoever. There is no reason to elevate the lava lamp fluidity . . . into the archetypical thing."[33] Perhaps there is no reason to do so—*if*, that is, we are in fact capable of transcending the provincial pro-human-conatus perspective from which we apprehend the world. If we are not, then a good tack might be to stretch and strain those modes to make room for the outlooks, rhythms, and trajectories of a greater number of actants, to, that is, get a better sense of the "operating system" upon which we humans rely.

Morton also offers a pragmatic, political rationale for his devotion to the coy object: no model of the whole (flowing or otherwise) can today help us cope with what he elsewhere calls "hyperobjects."[34] And this is the part of his position that raises the strongest objection to even a fractious-assemblage model.

"Hyperobjects are phenomena such as radioactive materials and global warming." They are "mind-blowing" entities, because their ahuman time scales and the extremely large or vastly diffused quality of their occupation of space unravels the very notion of "entity." It also becomes hard to see how it is possible to think hyperobjects by placing them within a larger "whole" within which we humans are a meaningful part, because hyperobjects render us kind of moot. For Morton, "this means that we need some other basis for making decisions about a future to which we have no real sense of connection." Evidence of the unthinkability of the hyperobject "climate change" is the fact that conversations about it often devolve into the more conceptualizable and manageable topic of weather. Weather, even with its large theater of operation, remains susceptible to probabilistic analysis, and it can still be associated with the idea of a (highly complex) natural order. Weather, in short, is still an "object." But with "climate change," it's much harder, impossible, really, says Morton, to sustain a sense of the existence of "a neutral background against which human events can become meaningful. . . . Climate change represents the possibility that the cycles and repetitions we come to depend on for our sense of stability and place in the world may be the harbingers of cataclysmic change."[35]

Modesty

In recent essays, Morton and Harman focus their objection to relationism around the claim that " 'everything is connected' is one of those methods that has long since entered its decadence, and must be abandoned."[36] Here again we see that one of the reasons for their rejection of "relationism" is that it distracts attention from the "non-connections" between objects (their withdrawn nature). But what, precisely, are the ill effects they fear? Harman and Morton don't say it outright, but it seems clear that one of their targets is human hubris. Their claim about the withdrawal of the object functions as a litany, a rhetorical tic that suggests something about the ethical impetus behind their position: object-orientedness is (what Foucault would call) a technique of self that seeks to counter the conceit of human reason and to chastise (what Nietzsche called) the "will to truth."

The desire to cultivate theoretical modesty is indeed noble. But object-oriented philosophy has no monopoly on the means to this end. Contemporary materialisms (inspired by Deleuze, Thoreau, Spinoza, Latour, neuroscience, or other sources) that affirm a vitality or creative power of bodies and forces at all ranges or scales also cut against the hubris of human exceptionalism. Morton's wholesale rejection of materiality as a term of art is perplexing; he seems to recognize no version except that associated with matter as a flat, fixed, or law-like substrate. What is more, does not a focus on the sensuous stuff of bodies save relationism from the "hologram" version that Harman rightly criticizes?[37]

I find myself living in a world populated by materially diverse, lively bodies. In this materialism, things—what is special about them given their sensuous specificity, their particular material configuration, and their distinctive, idiosyncratic history—matter a lot. But so do the eccentric assemblages that they form. Earthy bodies, of various but always finite durations, affect and are affected by one another. And *they form noisy systems or temporary working assemblages* that are, as much as any individuated thing, loci of effectivity and allure. These (sometimes stubborn and voracious but never closed or sovereign) systems enact real change. They give rise to new configurations, individuations, patterns of affection. Networks of things display differential degrees of creativity, for good or for ill from the human point of view.[38] There may be creative evolution at the system level, if Bergson and contemporary complexity theorists are on the right track.[39]

I say this because Harman argues that a philosophy such as mine, which connects hiding-and-seeking objects to assemblages, can have no account of change. This is because, the argument continues, there must be an unactualized surplus for something to happen differently. But systems as well as things can house an underdetermined surplus, and assemblage-theories can offer an account of the emergence of novelty without also rendering the trajectory, impetus, drive, or energetic push of any existing body epiphenomenal to its relations.

Objects / Things / Bodies

Harman says that the distinction between "objects" and "things" is irrelevant for his purposes, perhaps because he does not want to restrict himself unduly to the (weird) *physicality* of objects or to the power that they exhibit in (relatively) direct, *bodily* encounters with us. I am more focused on this "naturalist" or Romantic realm, and here I find the term *thing* or *body* better as a marker of individuation, better at highlighting the way certain edges within an assemblage tend to stand out to certain classes of bodies. (The smell and movement of the mammal to the tick, to invoke Jakob von Uexküll's famous example.[40]) "Thing" or "body" has advantages over "object," I think, if one's task is to disrupt the political parsing that yields only active (manly, American) subjects and passive objects. Why try to disrupt this parsing? Because we are daily confronted with evidence of nonhuman vitalities actively at work around and within us. I also do so because the frame of subjects-and-objects is unfriendly to the intensified ecological awareness that we need if we are to respond intelligently to signs of the breakdown of the Earth's carrying capacity for human life.

Texts as Special Bodies

I close by turning briefly to things that are literary: the essay and the poem. Like all bodies, these literary objects are affected by other bodies, or, as Morton puts it, "A poem is not simply a representation, but rather a nonhuman agent."[41] I also proclaim that the effectivity of a text-body, including its ability to gesture toward a something more, is a function of a *distributive network* of bodies: words on the page, words in the reader's imagination, sounds of words, sounds and smells in the reading room, and so on, and so on—all these bodies co-acting are what do the job.

There are also, it seems, some features of the text-body that are not shared or shared differentially by bodies that rely more heavily on smell and touch, and less heavily on the conveyances that are words. I'm not qualified to say too much about the affectivity of a text as a material body, and I can only gesture in the direction that Walt Whitman takes when he says that poetry, if enmeshed in a fortuitous assemblage of other (especially nontext) bodies, can have material effects as real as any. If you read *Leaves of Grass* in conjunction with "the open air every season of every year of your life," and also bound in affection to "the earth and sun and the animals," while also going "freely with powerful uneducated persons and with the young and with the mothers of families," then "your very flesh shall be a great poem and have the richest fluency not only in its words but in the silent lines of its lips and face and between the lashes of your eyes and in every motion and joint of your body."⁴²

Texts are bodies that can light up, by rendering human perception more acute, those bodies whose favored vehicle of affectivity is less wordy: plants, animals, blades of grass, household objects, trash. Another example is this passage from *Finnegans Wake*, where Joyce describes Shem the Hoarder's living space:

> The warped flooring of the lair and soundconducting walls thereof, to say nothing of the uprights and imposts, were persianly literatured with burst loveletters, telltale stories, stickyback snaps, doubtful eggshells, bouchers, flints, borers, puffers, amygdaloid almonds, rindless raisins, alphybettyformed verbage, vivlical viasses, ompiter dictas, visus umbique, ahems and ahahs, imeffible tries at speech unasyllabled, you owe mes, eyoldhyms, fluefoul smut, fallen lucifers, vestas which had served, showered ornaments, borrowed brogues, reversible jackets, blackeye lenses, family jars, falsehair shirts, Godforsaken scapulars, neverworn breeches, cutthroat ties, counterfeit franks, best intentions, curried notes, upset latten tintacks, unused mill and stumpling stones, twisted quills, painful digests, magnifying wineglasses, solid objects cast at goblins, once current puns, quashed quotatoes, messes of mottage.⁴³

Perhaps the most important stake for me of the nonhuman turn is how it might help us live more sustainably, with less violence toward a variety of bodies. Poetry can help us feel more of the liveliness hidden in such things and reveal more of the threads of connection binding our fate to theirs.

Notes

1. To cite just some examples: Michelle Bastian, "Inventing Nature: Re-writing Time and Agency in a More-Than-Human-World," *Australian Humanities Reviews* 47 (2010): 99–116; Nicky Gregson, H. Watkins, and M. Calestant, "Inextinguishable Fibres: Demolition and the

Vital Materialisms of Asbestos," *Environment and Planning A* 42, no. 5 (2010): 1065–83; Steven Shaviro, "The Universe of Things," www.shaviro.com/Othertexts/Things.pdf; Graham Harman, "The Assemblage Theory of Society," in *Towards Speculative Realism* (Winchester, U.K.: Zero Books, 2010); Aaron Goodfellow, "Pharmaceutical Intimacy: Sex, Death, and Methamphetamine," *Home Cultures* 5, no. 3 (2008): 271–300; Anand Pandian, "Landscapes of Expression: Affective Encounters in South Indian Cinema," *Cinema Journal* 51, no. 1 (Fall 2011): 50–74; Eileen A. Joy and Craig Dionne, eds., *"When* Did We Become Post/Human?," special issue, *Postmedieval: A Journal of Medieval Cultural Studies* 1, no. 1/2 (Spring/Summer 2010); Jussi Parikka, *Insect Media: An Archaeology of Animals and Technology* (Minneapolis: University of Minnesota Press, 2010); Bruce Braun and Sarah Whatmore, "The Stuff of Politics: An Introduction," in *Political Matter: Technoscience, Democracy, and Public Life* (Minneapolis: University of Minnesota Press, 2010); Stefanie Fishel, "New Metaphors for Global Living," PhD diss., Johns Hopkins University, 2011; and Jane Bennett, *Vibrant Matter* (Durham, N.C.: Duke University Press, 2010).

2. Jodi Dean articulates clearly this desire: "Instead of a politics thought primarily in terms of resistance, playful and momentary aesthetic disruptions, the immediate specificity of local projects, and struggles for hegemony within a capitalist, parliamentary, setting, the communist horizon impresses on us the necessity of the abolition of capitalism and the creation of global practices and institutions of egalitarian cooperation." Jodi Dean, "The Communist Horizon," *Kasama Project,* August 30, 2012, http://kasamaproject.org/. See also Jodi Dean, *The Communist Horizon* (London: Verso, 2012).

3. Ian Baucom's 2013 seminar for the School for Criticism and Theory at Cornell University describes the issue thus: "Human history, human culture, human society have now come to possess a truly geological force, a capacity not only to shape the local environments of forests, river-systems, and desert terrain, but to effect, catastrophically, the core future of the planet as we enter into the long era of what the atmospheric chemist Paul Crutzen and other climate researchers have called the 'Anthropocene.'" http://english.duke.edu/uploads/media_items/spring-2013 -course-descriptions-graduate-only-rev5.original.pdf.

4. Erasmus Darwin, *Temple of Nature; or, The Origin of Society: A Poem, with Philosophical Notes* (London: J. Johnson, 1803), canto 4, lines 398–400; electronic ed., ed. Martin Priestman, www.rc.umd.edu/editions/ darwin_temple/toc.html.

5. See Michel Serres, *Genesis,* trans. Geneviève James and James

Nielson (Ann Arbor: University of Michigan Press, 1995), and *The Birth of Physics*, trans. Jack Hawkes (Manchester, U.K.: Clinamen Press, 2000).

6. Walt Whitman, "I Am He Who Aches with Love," book 4, Children of Adam, *Leaves of Grass.*

7. "The concept of it [lively matter] involves a contradiction, since the essential character of matter is lifelessness, *inertia*" (emphasis in original). Immanuel Kant, *Critique of Judgment* (1790), sec. 73, #394. Given Kant's own flirtation with Johann Blumenbach's notion of *Bildungstrieb*, I can't help but hear the definitiveness of his claim here as an attempt to ward off a vitalism gestating inside his own thinking.

8. I think that the notions of "pathetic fallacy" and "prosopopoeia," even if stretched creatively, are not right for my project. Satoshi Nishimura defines the former as the "ascription of human characteristic to inanimate objects, which takes place when reason comes under the influence of intense emotion." Satoshi Nishimura, "Thomas Hardy and the Language of the Inanimate," *Studies in English Literature: 1500–1900* 43, no. 4 (Autumn 2003): 897. The notion of a pathetic fallacy, like that of prosopopoeia, assumes and insinuates that only humans (or God) can indeed engage in transmissions across bodies. The pathetic fallacy and prosopopoeia remain closely aligned with Kant's categorical distinction between life and matter.

9. My *Vibrant Matter* was in part a response to a call from some lively matter: some items of trash on the street on a sunny day called me over to them and for a few hyper-real moments I saw from the inside out (so to speak) how I too was an element in an assemblage that included these other things. My attempt to give an account of this encounter confounded and was confounded by the grammar of subjects and objects.

10. These latter are sometimes called "new" materialism, but that is unfortunate, for the label both imposes an impossible burden of creation (ex nihilo!) on the "new" materialisms and disrespects the ongoing vitality and political importance of the "old," historical materialisms.

11. Gilles Deleuze and Félix Guattari, *A Thousand Plateaus*, trans. Brian Massumi (Minneapolis: University of Minnesota Press, 1986; Continuum Books, 2004), 449. Citations refer to the Continuum edition.

12. Ibid., 448.

13. Ibid., 454.

14. Bernd Herzogenrath, "Nature/Geophilosophy/Machinics/Ecosophy," in *Deleuze/Guattari & Ecology*, ed. Bernd Herzogenrath (New York: Palgrave, 2009), 6.

15. Timothy Morton, "An Object-Oriented Defense of Poetry," *New Literary History* 43, no. 2 (Spring 2012): 208.

16. Graham Harman, "The Well-Wrought Broken Hammer," *New Literary History* 43, no. 2 (Spring 2012): 187.

17. See Martin Heidegger, "The Age of the World Picture," in *The Question Concerning Technology, and Other Essays,* trans. William Lovitt (New York: Harper, 1982). "Everyday opinion sees in the shadow only the lack of light, if not light's complete denial. In truth, however, the shadow is a manifest, though impenetrable, testimony to the concealed emitting of light. In keeping with this concept of shadow, we experience the incalculable as that which, withdrawn from representation, is nevertheless manifest in whatever is, pointing to Being, which remains concealed" (appendix 13, p. 154). Related is Graham Harman's notion of the "allure" of the object's mysterious withdrawal from the realm of our knowing. Graham Harman, *Guerrilla Metaphysics: Phenomenology and the Carpentry of Things* (Chicago: Open Court Press, 2005).

18. Harman, "Well-Wrought Broken Hammer," 187.

19. Ibid., 187–88.

20. Graham Harman, "Aesthetics as First Philosophy: Levinas and the Non-Human," *Naked Punch* 9 (Summer/Fall 2007): 21–30.

21. Harman, "Well-Wrought Broken Hammer,"188.

22. The terms are those of Deleuze and Guattari in *A Thousand Plateaus*: "It seems to us that Husserl brought thought to the decisive step forward when he discovered a region of *vague and material* essences (in other words, essences that are vagabond, inexact and yet rigorous), distinguishing them from fixed, metric and formal essence. . . . They constitute fuzzy aggregates. They relate to a *corporeality* (materiality) that is not to be confused either with an intelligible, formal essentiality or a sensible, formed and perceived thinghood" (emphases in original, 449–50).

23. Deleuze and Guattari, *A Thousand Plateaus,* 78.

24. Harman, "Well-Wrought Broken Hammer," 191.

25. My thanks to Alex Livingston for this formulation.

26. As Katrin Pahl shows in *Tropes of Transport: Hegel and Emotions* (Evanston, Ill.: Northwestern University Press, 2012), Hegel too offers a holism or relationism at odds with the organic model.

27. William Connolly, *A World of Becoming* (Durham, N.C.: Duke University Press, 2011), 35.

28. Harman, "Aesthetics as First Philosophy," 25.

29. Morton, "An Object-Oriented Defense," 215.

30. Harman, "Aesthetics as First Philosophy," 30.

31. Morton, "An Object-Oriented Defense," 217.

32. Ibid., 208.

33. Ibid.

34. And in defining the stakes *ecologically,* I reveal the presence in me of a bias toward *human* bodies (even as I share Harman's and Morton's desire to become more alert to the power, beauty, and danger of the non-humans around and within a human body).

35. Timothy Morton, "Hyperobjects and the End of Common Sense," *The Contemporary Condition* blog, March 10, 2010, http://contemporary condition.blogspot.com/.

36. Harman, "The Well-Wrought Broken Hammer," 201.

37. Harman is right, I think, to note that "both philosophical and political problems arise when individual selves and texts are described as holograms, as the relational effects of hostile others and disciplinary power" ("The Well-Wrought Broken Hammer," 193). But I do not think that there are many theorists in the humanities who still today would endorse such a strong version of constructivism.

38. A political example of this creative power is William Connolly's account of how the "evangelical-capitalist resonance machine" induced from out of the (human and nonhuman) bodies of American culture a new set of actants: Christian-fundamentalist-free marketeers. William Connolly, "The Evangelical-Capitalist Resonance Machine," *Political Theory* 33, no. 6 (December 2005): 869–86.

39. See, for example, Stuart A. Kauffman, *Reinventing the Sacred: A New View of Science, Reason and Religion* (New York: Basic Books, 2008), and Terence Deacon, *Incomplete Nature: How Mind Emerged from Matter* (New York: Norton, 2012).

40. Jakob von Uexküll, *A Foray into the Worlds of Animals and Humans: with, A Theory of Meaning,* trans. Joseph D. O'Neil (Minneapolis: University of Minnesota Press, 2011; originally published by Verlag von Julius Springer, 1934).

41. Morton, "An Object-Oriented Defense," 215.

42. Walt Whitman, "Preface 1855," in *Leaves of Grass and Other Writings,* ed. Michael Moon (New York: Norton, 2002), 622.

43. James Joyce, *Finnegans Wake* (Oxford: Oxford University Press, 2012), 183.

Acknowledgments

THIS BOOK ORIGINATED in a conference, The Nonhuman Turn in 21st Century Studies, which was hosted at the Center for 21st Century Studies (C21), University of Wisconsin–Milwaukee, on May 3–5, 2012. I first thank the conference organizing committee: Mary Mullen, C21 deputy director; John Blum, C21 associate director; and Rebekah Sheldon, the 2011–12 C21 Provost Postdoctoral Fellow. Together the committee proved essential to the success of the conference in so many ways: the development of the initial call for papers; the assembly of a list of extraordinary plenary speakers; the selection of papers and the formation of panels for the conferences breakout sessions; and the overall organization and administration of the conference. I also thank Mike Darnell and Stephanie Willingham, who worked as successive business managers for the Center, for their good work, as well as the two C21 graduate project assistants, Selene Jaouadi-Escalera and Kendrick Gardner, for their hard work in making the conference a success. Finally I thank Johannes Britz, provost and vice chancellor for Academic Affairs; Rodney Swain, dean of the College of Letters and Sciences; and Jennifer Watson, associate dean of the College of Letters and Science, for their support.

The editing and production of this book could not have happened without the exceptional work of John Blum, who serves as the Center's editor. John is a careful and tireless manuscript editor who brings a wealth of experience to the task of manuscript preparation. I also thank Doug Armato, director of University of Minnesota Press, for his role in bringing the Center's book series to Minnesota. The Nonhuman Turn is the first publication in what promises to be an extended run. I thank Erin Warholm-Wohlenhaus and Alicia Gomez for helping bring the book into print. Finally, I express my thanks to current C21 deputy director Emily Clark for her unparalleled leadership and to the book's contributors, without whom this book would not exist.

Contributors

Jane Bennett is professor of political science at Johns Hopkins University. She is editor of the journal *Political Theory* and author of *Vibrant Matter: A Political Ecology of Things.*

Ian Bogost is the Ivan Allen College Distinguished Chair in media studies and professor of interactive computing at the Georgia Institute of Technology, where he also holds an appointment in the Scheller College of Business. He is founding partner at Persuasive Games LLC, an independent game studio, and contributing editor to the *Atlantic*. He is the author of *Alien Phenomenology, or What It's Like to Be a Thing* (Minnesota, 2012) and *How to Do Things with Videogames* (Minnesota, 2011).

Wendy Hui Kyong Chun is professor of modern culture and media at Brown University. She is the author of *Programmed Visions: Software and Memory* and *Control and Freedom: Power and Paranoia in the Age of Fiber Optics.*

Richard Grusin is director of the Center for 21st Century Studies and professor of English at the University of Wisconsin–Milwaukee. He is the author of *Premediation: Affect and Mediality after 9/11*; *Culture, Technology, and the Creation of America's National Parks*; and (with Jay David Bolter) *Remediation: Understanding New Media.*

Mark B. N. Hansen is professor of literature, and media arts and sciences, at Duke University. He is the author of *Feed-Forward: On the Future of Twenty-First-Century Media*; *Bodies in Code: Interfaces with New Media*; and *New Philosophy for New Media.*

Erin Manning holds a university research chair in relational art and philosophy at Concordia University (Montreal, Canada), where she is director of the SenseLab (www.senselab.ca). She is coauthor (with Brian Massumi) of *Thought in the Act: Passages in the Ecology of Experience* (Minnesota, 2014) and author of *Always More Than One: Individuation's Dance* and *Relationscapes: Movement, Art, Philosophy.*

Brian Massumi is professor of communication at the University of Montreal. He is coauthor (with Erin Manning) of *Thought in the Act: Passages in the Ecology of Experience* (Minnesota, 2014), author of *Semblance and Event: Activist Philosophy and the Occurrent Arts,* and translator of Gilles Deleuze and Félix Guattari's *A Thousand Plateaus.*

Timothy Morton is Rita Shea Guffey Chair of English at Rice University. He is the author of *Hyperobjects: Philosophy and Ecology after the End of the World* (Minnesota, 2013); *Realist Magic: Objects, Ontology, Causality*; *The Ecological Thought*; and *Ecology without Nature.*

Steven Shaviro is the DeRoy Professor of English at Wayne State University. He is the author of *The Universe of Things: On Speculative Realism* (Minnesota, 2014); *Post Cinematic Affect; Without Criteria: Kant, Whitehead, Deleuze, and Aesthetics*; and *Connected, or, What It Means to Live in the Network Society* (Minnesota, 2003).

Rebekah Sheldon is assistant professor of English at Indiana University. She has received postdoctoral fellowships in the School of Literature, Media, and Communication at Georgia Tech and at the Center for 21st Century Studies at the University of Wisconsin–Milwaukee.

Index

abstraction, 2, 14, 60, 62, 91;
and computer programming,
157–58; language as, 150, 152,
155, 157; and Whitehead, 31,
46–47, 49, 73–74, 132
actor-network theory, viii, xv–xvi,
202. *See also* Latour, Bruno
affect: of fear, 105; as human and
nonhuman, xvii–xviii; scholarly, 216; turn to, xvii
affect theory, viii, xv–xviii, 193;
and trauma theory, xviii
affectivity, xix, xxiv, 111, 112, 229;
of a text, 234, 235; and Whitehead, xvi–xvii
After Finitude (Meillassoux),
193–94, 200–201, 203
Agamben, Giorgio, 149, 154,
163n30, 199. *See also* state of
exception
agency: of epistemology, 196; of
the future, 108, 113, 123; and
Heidegger, 225; human, xx,
xxv, 129, 139–40, 148–49, 154,
158; human and nonhuman,
xv, xxvi, 214; on a network,
154; new media, 144; non-
human, viii, xi–xii, xvi, xvii,
187–88, 195, 217; and performativity, 201–2; of power, 208;
and the subject, 122; systemic,
212; technical, 129; and tendency, 118; of a video camera,
182

agent. *See* agency
agential realism, 201–2
Agre, Philip, 157–58
Alaimo, Stacy, 202
Alien Phenomenology (Bogost), 25,
85, 88, 99, 183, 194
animality: and artfulness, 2, 10,
75; and humanity, xxii, 10,
13–14; and sympathy, 11, 14.
See also animals; instinct;
sympathy
animals: and adaptation, 7; and
affectivity, xvii; artfulness of,
75; experience of, 4, 7; as nonhuman, vii, x, xix, xxi–xxii,
21, 24, 208; as thinking and
feeling, 21, 29–30; for Thoreau,
224; for Whitman, 234–35.
See also animality; instinct;
sympathy
Anthropocene, vii, 185–86, 188,
223, 236n3
anthropocentrism, 20, 24, 167, 195,
217; anti-, 230
anthropomorphism, 24–25,
151–52, 155, 181
anxiety, 169, 172, 175, 184–86,
189–90; and Anthropocene,
185; global, 168; low-level, 112
aperture, 170, 174, 186
Aristotle, 174, 196, 207
assemblage: material as, 233; mind
as, 179; nonhuman turn as, x;
nonhumans as, 179; objects as,